Karate Masters

Jose M. Fraguas

ℓℓ𝗣 UNIQUE PUBLICATIONS
Burbank, California

Disclaimer

Please note that the author and publisher of this book are NOT RESPONSI-BLE in any manner whatsoever for any injury that may result from practicing the techniques and/or following the instructions given within. Since the physical activities described herein may be too strenuous in nature for some readers to engage in safely, it is essential that a physician be consulted prior to training.

First published in 2001 by Unique Publications.

Library of Congress Catalog Number: 2001 131954
ISBN: 0-86568-188-0

Unique Publications
4201 Vanowen Place
Burbank, CA 91505
(800) 332–3330

Second edition
05 04 03 02 3 5 7 9 10 8 6 4 2

Printed in the United States of America.

Editor: Todd Hester
Design: Patrick Gross
Cover Design: George Chen

Here I want to see those men of hard voice.
Those that break horses and dominate rivers;
those men of sonorous skeleton who sing
with a mouth full of sun and flint.

Here I want to see them. Before the stone.
Before this body with broken reins.
I want to know from them the way out
for this captain stripped down by death.

—Federico García Lorca (1898–1936)
    Spanish poet and dramatist.

Dedication

First and foremost I wish to dedicate this book to my parents, who brought me into this world and gave me love and support. I would also like to dedicate it to all the teachers who took the time to make the martial arts part of my life and helped me to grow mental and spiritually.

When a book project crosses the finish line it's all too easy to forget how it all began and I can't let that happen. This book is also dedicated the memory of Jose Vicente Ruano, a great human being and karateka, who in 1981 gave me the idea of saving my interviews, and then later filled the project with fire and energy once he learned I was finally working on it. His friendship and tutelage were true blessings for which I shall be forever grateful. Rest in peace, my brother.

Acknowledgments

I would like to thank all my instructors, past and present, for giving me the understanding and knowledge to undertake all the martial arts projects I've done during my life. I would also like to thank all my friends whose constant encouragement motivated me to keep going and keep growing.

Many people were responsible for making this book possible, some more directly than others. I want to extend my gratitude to all who so generously contributed their time and experience to the preparation of this work. Special thanks go to Todd Hester (editor of the work); Germany's Norbert Schiffer (director of *Satori-Verlag* and *Budo* magazine); David Chambers (founder and editor of *Dragon Times*); John Cheetham (editor of *Shotokan Karate* magazine); France's Thierry Plée (President of *Budo Editions);* Don Warrener (director of Rising Sun Productions); Okinawan karate great and master calligrapher Tetsuhiro Hokama; photographers Ed Ikuta (Los Angeles, CA) and Arthur Tansley (Tokyo, Japan); *Gekkan Karate Do* magazine (Fukushodo, Ltd., Japan); Isaac Florentine (film director and passionate karateka); James Tawatao (Chief Instructor at Ozawa Sensei Dojo in Las Vegas); Terry O'Neill (editor of England's *Fighting Arts International);* and finally to Curtis F. Wong, who made everything possible.

I would foremost like to give my most heartfelt gratitude to all the masters appearing in this book. Not only did they so generously give me an enormous amount of personal time for the long interviews, but they also provided me with great pictures to illustrate the work as well.

You all have my enduring thanks,
—Jose M. Fraguas

About the Author

Born and raised in Madrid, Spain, Jose "Chema" Fraguas began his martial arts studies with judo, in grade school, at age 9. From there he moved to taekwondo and then to kenpo karate, earning a black belt in both styles. During this same period he also studied shito-ryu karate under Japanese masters Masahiro Okada and Yashunari Ishimi, eventually receiving a fifth-degree black belt. He began his career as a writer at age 16 by serving as a regular contributor to martial arts magazines in Great Britain, France, Spain, Italy, Germany, Portugal, Holland, and Australia. Having a black belt in three different styles allows him to better reflect the physical side of the martial arts in his writing: "Feeling before writing," Fraguas says.

In 1980, he moved to Los Angeles , California. His open-minded mentality helped him to develop a realistic approach to the martial arts. Seeking to supplement his previous training, he researched other disciplines such as jiu-jitsu and muay Thai.

In 1986, Fraguas founded his own book and magazine company in Europe, authoring dozens of books and distributing his magazines to 35 countries in three different languages. His reputation and credibility as a martial artist and publisher became well known to the top masters around the world. Considering himself a martial artist first and a writer and publisher second, Fraguas feels fortunate to have had the opportunity to interview many legendary martial arts teachers. He recognizes that much of the information given in the interviews helped him to discover new dimensions in the martial arts. "I was constantly absorbing knowledge from the great masters," he recalls. "I only trained with a few of them, but intellectually and spiritually all of them have made very important contributions to my growth as a complete martial artist."

Steeped in tradition yet looking to the future, Fraguas understands and appreciates martial arts history and philosophy and feels this rich heritage is a necessary stepping stone to personal growth and spiritual evolution. His desire to promote both ancient philosophy and modern thinking provided the motivation for writing this book. "If the motivation is just money, a book cannot be of good quality," Fraguas says. 'If the book is written to just make people happy, it cannot be deep. I want to write books so I can learn as well as share."

The author currently lives in Los Angeles, California, where he is the General Manager of CFW Enterprises, the world's leading martial arts publishing company.

Introduction

I've been both lucky and fortunate. Some of my best days were spent interviewing and meeting the masters appearing in this book. There is little I enjoy more than "gnawing" on a great interview while time slows and sometimes even seems to stop. Having the opportunity to meet and interview the most relevant and prestigious martial artists of the past four decades is something that every martial artist doesn't have the chance to do. Hopefully, in some small way, this will help make up for that.

Meeting the masters and having long conversations with them that were published in magazines around the world allowed me to do more than simply "scratch the surface" of the technical aspects of their respective styles, but to also research and analyze the human beings behind the teachers. Some of the dialogues and interviews began by simply commenting about the superficial techniques of fighting, and ended up turning into a very uncommon spiritual conversation about the philosophical aspects of the martial arts.

Although they are all very different, considering their respective styles and backgrounds, they all share a common thread of the traditional values such as discipline, respect, positive attitude, dedication, and etiquette.

For more than 25 years I've faced the long odds of interviewing these fighters and martial arts masters, one-on-one, face-to-face, and with no place to run if I asked a stupid question. Many times, it was a real challenge to not just make contact with them, but also how to make the interview interesting enough to bring out the knowledge that resided inside them. In every interview I tried to absorb as much knowledge as I could, ranging from their training methods, to their fighting methods, and to their philosophies about life itself.

Their different origins and cultural backgrounds heavily influenced them but never prevented them from analyzing, researching, or modifying anything that they considered appropriate. They always kept an open mind to improving both their arts and themselves. From a formal philosophical point of view many of them follow the wisdom of Zen and Taoism—others just use common sense.

They devoted themselves to their arts, often in solitude, sometimes to the exclusion of other pursuits most of us take for granted. They worked themselves into extraordinary physical condition and stayed there. They ignored distractions and diversions and brought to their training a great deal of concentration. The best of them got as good as they could possibly get at performing and teaching their chosen art, and the rest of us watched them and, leading our "balanced lives," wondered how good we might have gotten at something had we devoted ourselves to whatever we did as ferociously as these masters embraced their arts. In that respect they bear our dreams.

It would be wonderful to find a single martial artist who combined all the great qualities of these fighters—but that's impossible. That, however, was one of the things that inspired me to write this book. I wanted to preserve some things that were said a long time ago, of which not many people today are aware.

If you read carefully between the lines, you'll see that none of these men were trying to become a "fighting machine" or training in order to create the most devastating martial arts system known to man. They focused, rather, on how to use the martial arts to become a better person. There are many links that once discovered open a wide spectrum of possibilities, not only to martial arts, but to a better existence as individuals.

The interviews often lasted as long as three or four hours of non-stop talking. I would begin at their school and finish the conversation at a restaurant or coffee shop. A lot of information in these interviews had been never published before and some had to be trimmed either at the master's request or edited to avoid creating senseless misunderstandings later on. It is not the questions that make an interview. An interview is either good or bad depending on the answers given. Considering the masters in this book, I had an easy job. My goal was to make these masters comfortable talking about their life and training—especially those who trained under the founders of original systems. In modern time, there are not many who have had the privilege of living and learning under the legendary founders.

"The masters are gone," many like to say. But as long as we keep their teachings in our heart, they will live for ever. To understand the martial arts properly it is necessary to take into account the philosophical and psychological methods as well as the physical techniques. There is a deep distinction between a fighting system and a martial art, and a general feeling in the martial arts community is that the roots of the martial arts have been de-emphasized, neglected, or totally abandoned. Martial arts are not a sport—they are very different. Someone who chooses to devote themselves to a sport such as basketball, tennis, soccer, or football, which is based on youth, strength, and speed chooses to die twice. When you can no longer do a certain sport, due to the lack of any one of those attributes, waking up in the morning without the activity and purpose that has been the center of your day for twenty-five years is spooky. Martial arts can and should be practiced for life. They are not sports, they are a "way of life."

A true martial arts practitioner—like an artist of any other kind—be this a musician, a painter, a writer or an actor, is expressing and leaving part of himself in every piece of his craft. The need for self-inspection and self-realization of "who" he is becomes the reason for a journey in search of that perfect technique, that great melody, that inspiring poetry, that amazing painting or that Academy Award performance. It is this motivation to reach that "impossible dream," that allows a simple individual to become an exceptional "artist" and "master" of his craft.

Many of the greatest teachers of the fighting arts share a commonly misunderstood teaching methodology. They know the words that could be used to pass their personal experience to their students have little or no meaning. They know that to try "self-discovery" in quantitative or empirical terms is a useless task. A great deal of knowledge and wisdom (the ability to use knowledge in a proper and correct way) comes from what is called the "oral traditions," which martial arts, like every other cultural aspect, has. These oral traditions have been always reserved for a certain kind of student and have been considered "secrets." I believe these secrets are such because only few very special students, perspicacious and with a keen sense of introspection, have the minds to attain them. As Alexandra David-Neel wrote: "It is not on the master that the secret depends but on the hearer. Truth learned from others is of no value, the only truth which is effective and of value is self-discovered...the teacher can only guide to the point of discovery." In the end "The only secret is that there is no secret," or as Kato Tokuro, probably the greatest potter of the last century, a great art scholar, and the teacher of Spanish painter and sculptor Pablo Picasso (1881–1973) said: "The sole cause of secrets in craftsmanship is the student's inability to learn!"

As human beings, we are always tempted to follow straight-line logic towards ultimate self-improvement - but the truth is that there are no absolute truths that apply to all. You have to find your own way in life whether it be in the martial arts, in business, or in cherry picking. Whatever path you pursue, you have to distill your personal truths to what is right for you, according to your own life. The quest for perfection is actually quite imperfect and is not in tune with either human nature or human experience. To have any hope of attaining even a single perfection, you have to concentrate on a single pursuit and direct all your energies towards it. In this sense, perfection comes from appreciating your endeavors for their own sake - not to impress anyone - but for your own inner satisfaction and sense of accomplishment.

Martial arts are a large part of my life and I draw inspiration from them, both spiritually and philosophically. I really don't know the "how" or the "why" of their affect on me, but I feel their influence in even my most mundane activities. It's not a complex thing where I have to look deep into myself to find their influence. All human beings have sources or principles that keep them grounded, and martial arts is mine. I believe that is when the term "way of life" becomes real. In bushido, the self-discipline required to pursue mastery is more important than mastery itself - the struggle is more important than the reward. A common thread throughout the lives of all the masters is their constant struggle towards self-mastery. They realized that life is an ongoing process, and once you achieve all your goals you are as good as dead. But this process is not all driven by action. Often the greatest action is inaction, and the hardest voice to hear is the sound of your inner voice. You need to sit alone and collect your thoughts, free from all forms of technology and distraction, and just think. It is perhaps the only way to achieve mental and spiritual clarity.

I don't believe that great books are meant to be read fast. I've always thought that really good writing is timeless, and that time spent reading doesn't detract anything from your life, but rather adds to it. So take your time. Approach the reading of this book with either the Zen "beginner's mind" or "empty cup" mentality and let the words of these great teachers help you to grow not only as a martial artist but as a human being as well. O

Contents

空手道

Harry Cook

He Conquers, Who Conquers Himself

*HARRY COOK IS A RARITY IN THE WORLD OF KARATE—WHILE YOU DON'T HEAR NEGA-
TIVES ABOUT HIM, HE IS A CONTROVERSIAL FIGURE WITH VERY OUTSPOKEN VIEWPOINTS.
BUT THOSE VIEWPOINTS ARE CENTERED IN HIS LOVE OF "REAL" KARATE, AND HIS FEAR
THAT IT MIGHT SOMEDAY DISAPPEAR. WHEN YOU ASK HARRY COOK A QUESTION HE'LL
GIVE YOU AN ANSWER WITHOUT WORRYING ABOUT THE FALLOUT. THIS BRITISH
KARATEKA AND MARTIAL ARTS HISTORIAN HAS A KNOWLEDGE SECOND TO NONE AND
DARES TO SPEAK HIS MIND. RESEARCH AND DEVELOPMENT ARE HIS SPECIALTIES, AND HE
IS PERHAPS BEST KNOWN AS AN AUTHOR AND CONTRIBUTOR TO MANY MARTIAL ARTS
MAGAZINES AROUND THE WORLD. AS A TEACHER, HARRY COOK IS SUPERB. HEAD
INSTRUCTOR OF THE SEIJINKAI KARATE DO ASSOCIATION, HE INSTRUCTS IN ENGLAND,
WHERE HE RESIDES. HIS DECADES OF USEFUL EXPERIENCE AND KNOWLEDGE ARE A GREAT
SOURCE OF INSPIRATION TO ALL WHO FOLLOW THE TRUE ART OF KARATE-DO.*

Q: How long have you been practicing martial arts?
A: I began training in karate in September or October 1966. A couple of
school friends showed me a few techniques and we trained together somewhat informally in the school gym. I had dabbled with a little bit of judo
before that but nothing serious. I joined my first dojo in January 1967 and
started training properly.

Q: How many styles have you trained in?
A: I began training in wado-ryu and then switched to shotokan once the
wado-ryu dojo effectively ceased to operate after the instructors, both green
belts, left. In 1970 I went to Durham University to study Chinese and I met
Miss Rose Li and trained in tai chi chuan. I also established the Durham
University karate dojo which was quite successful in the British University
championships. Later I went to Japan and trained in Okinawan goju-ryu
with Morio Higaonna at the Yoyogi Shurenkai dojo. I have also trained a little in uechi-ryu, shito-ryu, aikido, jiu-jitsu and wing chun. I was fortunate to
meet Master Gato about ten years ago and was able to learn some Brazilian
capoeira of the Group Senzala. In weapons I have some experience in iaido

"In the mid-1960s we had a very hazy idea of the details of karate technique."

and jodo, and for the past twelve years or so I have trained in Okinawan weapons of the Motokatsu Inoue line under my good friend Julian Mead. From Julian I have also had the opportunity to see the Yuishinkai way of performing kata and bunkai, which I have found very useful and interesting. I also have an instructors certificate in muay Thai from the Phraya Pichai camp, and although I don't teach that art I have great respect for the tough training methods used by practitioners of Thai boxing; in many ways their approach reinforces my perception of the values of traditional karate. The syllabus of our group, the Seijinkai Karate-Do Association, makes use of techniques and kata drawn from both shotokan and goju-ryu, and training methods derived from a wide range of systems. This reflects both my background and the experience of a number of our senior members who have experience in the Filipino martial arts and various other systems.

Q: Who were your first teachers?
A: The first two people to teach me anything about karate were my school friends George Hay and Maurice Rutherford; they held the advanced grade of 8th kyu! Actually my first real instructor was Mr. Ken Smith, who was the senior instructor in the Sunderland Martial Arts Academy, the shotokan dojo I joined in early 1968. That dojo was affiliated to the Karate Union of Great Britain, a JKA affiliate, and so when Enoeda sensei, Asano sensei, or any of the senior instructors came to instruct, I trained in the class with everybody else.

Q: Could you tell us some interesting stories of your early days in karate training?
A: You must understand that in the northeast of England in the mid-1960s we had a very hazy idea of the details of karate technique, and accordingly some of our training was a little rough and clumsy at times, both physically and technically. When I entered my first competition, for example, I man-

aged to knock out my opponent with a back elbow to the solar plexus. I was really proud and I couldn't understand why I was disqualified. No one had ever told me to pull or mute the strikes in sparring, and to be honest I didn't know what I was doing. Another memory which springs to mind is of a demonstration we were asked to do for a local college. One of the members of the dojo decided to break a wooden board with a *mawashi-geri* (roundhouse kick). Nothing special, you might think, but he had never done it before or had seen it done. Now the board was, in fact, a wooden plank, and in wado-ryu, as far as we knew at the time, mawashi-geri was performed with the instep of the foot. So he kicked the plank and broke it, much to our amazement; unfortunately he also broke his foot!

Q: How do Westerners respond to traditional Japanese training?
A: This all depends on what you mean by "traditional." If you mean marching up and down the dojo in straight lines performing basic techniques, bellowing "oous" at every comment from the instructor and performing thousands of push-ups and sit-ups for every minute error in a technique, then I would say this is not "traditional" in the real sense of the word, but is simply a version of Japanese military discipline of the 1930s which filtered through Japanese university karate clubs and was later spread to the West by those instructors who knew no other approach. Having said that, of course, there are many Westerners who enjoy the paramilitary approach because it provides a form of emotional security. I think it is all a bit adolescent actually, and when you grow up you really shouldn't need that kind of thing as much. That kind of strict training is certainly of benefit to low belt grades, it certainly was to me, but it can become too restrictive for seniors and can actually inhibit real progress. The real traditions of the Japanese martial arts are best seen in the classical sword and related systems, and I certainly think that Westerners respond very well to the "real" traditional approach.

Q: Were you a natural at karate?
A: No, I was hopeless. I was a fairly natural athlete before I did karate—a good sprinter and I played on the school rugby team and so on—but performing the basic techniques of karate was a real challenge. I think that was part of the reason I became so fascinated by karate and the other martial arts: the challenge to actually achieve any kind of ability was continuous, and in fact still is. Probably that is why I still really enjoy training.

"I also became very aware of the importance of conditioning and developing the ability to hit hard with single punches and kicks."

Q: How has your personal karate changed or developed over the years?
A: When I was a university student I really enjoyed fighting in the university league and the championships, but to be honest I wasn't too keen on kata. Now obviously in shotokan the instructors insist that you learn and train in kata and so I dutifully practiced kata, but I really didn't appreciate them at all. I had a reasonable kata style, but it was superficial—OK for tournaments or passing gradings but there was no real depth of understanding of the intent behind the moves. This changed when I went to Japan and began training with Higaonna sensei and one of his students at the dojo, Steve Bellamy. Once I began to develop some understanding of the applications of the goju kata, the shotokan kata began to make more sense, and I could see some practical or realistic ways to apply the techniques. I don't mean the silly kind of applications you usually see in demonstrations where people jump over bo attacks or perform choreographed defenses to preset karate-style attacks. I mean functional defenses to the kinds of attacks used in the street, i.e. swinging punches, head butts, grabs, that kind of thing.

I also became very aware of the importance of conditioning and developing the ability to hit hard with single punches and kicks. This in turn led me to training with equipment. I have said many times that it is fundamentally more efficient, and better for the body, to train your striking techniques by hitting a target such as a kick bag, makiwara, focus pads, et cetera, rather than performing endless repetitions into thin air, which in the long run is damaging to the joints. My good friend Graham Noble introduced me to the pleasures of training on the air bag and focus mitts, and since then I have developed a number of approaches to training which suit the members of the Seijinkai. In my experience, many high grade karateka who don't train on bags, overestimate their striking power. When I am training by myself I rarely perform techniques in the air, except of course when I practice kata. I would much rather hit something, even if it is just a piece of plastic foam hanging on a string. You can correct your technique because of the feedback from the target, whereas kicking or punching thin air can become simply a stamina exercise, or at best become a matter of concentrating only on the outer form or body feeling. I often train by trying to punch a tennis ball tied to my head with a length of elastic! I was shown this somewhat odd method by a professional boxer, and while many of my friends think I am strange, they stop laughing when they try to do it. It is not easy, but with continued practice your speed, timing, distance appreciation, et cetera, all improve. Again, in principle it is not so different from a number of famous Japanese swordsmen who would hone their skills by trying to cut raindrops or birds in flight. It is just a modern adaptation of that idea. I also train quite extensively with weights to develop strength and stamina, As far as I am concerned weight training of some kind is absolutely necessary if you want to improve your power levels. Power is a combination of speed and strength. Correct technique will give you the required speed, and when you add muscular strength the result is power. I have seen many modern karateka with excellent form but poor power levels—as far as I am concerned their training methodology is lacking something vital.

Q: With all the technical changes during the last 30 years, do you think there is still "pure" shotokan, shito-ryu, et cetera?

A: Actually I don't think there ever was any pure karate systems in the sense that they were passed on unchanged. The shotokan that Gichin Funakoshi brought to Japan in 1922 was basically his version of the Itosu line of shorin-ryu which Itosu had modified from the karate he learned from Matsumura. This, in turn, changed and adapted to the new demands created by the young Japanese university students who began training in the 1930s and '40s. After Funakoshi's death the development of tournament karate created another kind of shotokan, and bringing shotokan to the West introduced other factors. Shito-ryu went through a similar kind of development. For example Chojiro Tani and his followers created shukokai, which is a form of shito-ryu. expressly developed for tournaments. Of course, other branches or approaches to shito-ryu survived and prospered. Goju-ryu shows a similar line of development, with quite a wide variation of technique within Okinawa and Japan. Of course, each line of development of any style's claims to be the one and only pure line, but actually that is simply for business or prestige reasons. Actually I think there is only one style of karate: the two arms, two legs and one head style. Most systems make use of very similar techniques based on hard and soft movements, and utilize straight and circular techniques to a greater or lesser extent. Where there are differences of approach in applying techniques, the critical factors tend to be the weight, size, speed and power of the practitioner rather than the style he practices. Lightweights of all styles tend to fight in similar ways, as do heavyweights. Miyamoto Musashi said it well in his *Gorin no Sho* when he pointed out that in reality there are only a few practical ways to cut the enemy down with a sword, and when many variations of these basic methods are taught, especially with exotic or "secret" movements, it is simply for commercial reasons. As many Buddhist and Taoist teachers have pointed out, change is the natural order of the universe; this being the case a "pure" system is impossible as new factors constantly spring up to introduce changes to all systems. The open availability of martial arts magazines, books, videos, et cetera, means that practitioners of all styles routinely have access to information which people such as Gichin Funakoshi and Chojun Miyagi could only dream about. That, in itself, is a process of introducing changes in technique, training methods, and strategies to all systems. I think this has always happened, but the speed of change is now much more rapid.

Q: So is it beneficial to mix styles such as shotokan and goju-ryu together?
A: I have been criticized for teaching shotokan and goju-ryu together, by both shotokan and goju-ryu instructors, although none of the critics have actually had any experience training in my classes; but as a far as I am concerned, styles are temporary emanations of a more profound reality. Gichin Funakoshi said that he made use of kata from the shorei and shorin traditions; Chojun Miyagi based goju-ryu on Fukien White Crane and other systems; Kenwa Mabuni developed shito-ryu by combining the methods of his teachers Kanryo Higaonna and Yasutstune Itosu; wado-ryu was created by Hironori Ohtsuka by mixing the karate of Gichin Funakoshi and Choki Motobu with the jiu-jitsu of the Shinto Yoshin Ryu and ideas taken from ken-jitsu; kyokushinkai was initially based on shotokan and goju-ryu and then absorbed ideas from muay Thai, and uechi-ryu was a development of Fukien Tiger boxing. All of these methods were created by modifying, adapting and changing older models. This is the real tradition of karate's evolution, and different styles or *"ryu"* are only important in the sense that a ryu reflects one instructor's approach, or possibly a group of instructors. You should not expect any ryu to be passed on unchanged. Change is necessary

if the vitality of the system is to be maintained. If you try to pass on something without improvement it will inevitably stagnate and die. Gichin Funakoshi said in his biography that in time the student well may surpass his teacher—to achieve that, the student may need to introduce new ideas into the system. What is wrong with that?

Q: What is your opinion of full contact karate and kickboxing?
A: I think that the emergence of kickboxing systems within the karate world was inevitable, once the development of those skills needed for non-contact karate tournaments became the dominant aspect of karate training. There was a need to know if the techniques worked in a less controlled environment, but of course there is the prob-

"Change is necessary if the vitality of the system is to be maintained."

lem. By wearing boxing gloves or pads on your hands and feet, you can land the blows, but the effects of the blows are muted and so you eventually end up doing a kind of boxing in long trousers, where you need to throw combinations to finish the opponent. Now proponents of this approach say that it is more realistic, but in the street you would not have time to put on your boxing gloves, and as far as I know attacks to the joints, groin, et cetera are forbidden in full contact, so it has its own restrictions. When boxers have got involved in street scuffles they have damaged their hands, this is what happened to Mike Tyson and Mitch Green, so throwing those kinds of techniques in a real fight might not be the solution. All forms of gloved fighting has rules, and as Higaonna sensei said to us, "Sparring has rules, real fighting does not." Actually if you look at the history and techniques of the old prize ring you will see that it shared many of the approaches found in the older karate systems, including hand conditioning, body conditioning, use of throwing techniques, et cetera. Full contact fighters should be thanked for pointing out the importance of correct conditioning and the ability to hit hard and take a hit, because some Western karate teachers seem to have forgotten this.

Events such as the UFC are also of great interest because they brought the need for effective grappling skills to the attention of the martial arts world. It should be pointed out that according to many of the older karate teachers half or more of the applications of the kata involve painful throws and locks which take the opponent to the ground before he is punched or kicked. The fact that kata has been judged primarily in a visual way, especially in Japanese and Korean systems, has obscured the older approach and that is why the UFC should be of interest to traditional karateka. However I think a word of caution should be noted. Throwing an opponent does not mean going to the ground with him. Fighting on the ground only makes sense when you are facing an opponent in a match. In the real world it is foolish: you may dominate the attacker, obtain the top position or "mount" and go in for the strangle or whatever and while you are doing that the friends of your opponent will kick your head in and wrap a bottle around your face. Actually this is the reason why W.E. Fairbairn excluded fighting on the ground in his training methods for commandos and other special forces during WWII. He said that dealing easily with someone on the ground took years of training and in time of war it is not unlikely that you would be attacked by two or more opponents. "Fair" fighting, which pits one against one, only happens in organized events, and if an attacker pulls a knife the whole scenario changes. Azato told Gichin Funakoshi to regard his limbs as swords. We could update that advice and remember that knives are easy to buy and conceal. The aim should be to finish the opponent off as quickly as possible—as Jack Dempsey pointed out you should always try to knock your opponent out in a street fight. That is why I still like the idea of training to finish the opponent off with a single technique even though that might be difficult to do. My good friend Graham Noble once interviewed unlicensed boxer and all-round hard man Roy Shaw. Mr. Shaw was asked how many people he had faced in the street at one time, and he said "four." When asked what he did he said that he had hit each one of them once, that is four punches and dropped each one with a single punch. He observed that you have to get into a solid stance and blast the punch in as hard as you can before quickly moving onto the next target. Well to me this sounds very like traditional karate teachings and resembles the four-punch sequence seen in "unsu" kata. Obviously in the basic practice of the kata it is a fixed sequence with set directions, et cetera, but in application, or bunkai, this sequence would resemble the scenario mentioned by Mr. Shaw. Of course, you then have to train to develop a very effective punch, good timing, et cetera.

Actually, I have just finished reading Ken Shamrock's book *Inside the Lion's Den* which is about his life and the UFC. As far as I could see, the values he expresses and the emphasis on tough practical training reflects the traditional ideas of many Oriental martial arts. If you ignore the journalistic hype which surrounds the UFC you can see, as Mr. Shamrock points out, that UFC fighting is actually safer than boxing. As for people being knocked out or damaged in UFC events I can remember seeing competitors being "sparked" in the early karate competitions in Britain, a time that many senior British karateka now regard as the "good old days." I think that the UFC is OK, and that

"I think that the UFC is OK, and that many of the criticisms stem from the fact that it makes the critics feel uncomfortable because it highlights deficiencies in their own training methodology."

many of the criticisms stem from the fact that it makes the critics feel uncomfortable because it highlights deficiencies in their own training methodology.

Q: Do you think that karate in the West has caught up with Japanese karate?

A: Actually, I think that in some ways it is better. This should not be a surprise. Karate came to Japan in the 1920s. Within 30 years or so the Japanese had established their own systems and had created their own approach to karate. In the 1950s the obvious direction that the main groups were taking was towards the development of a tournament format, especially among the younger generation. So in a little over 30 years the JKA and others had their own approach well established. But WWII caused severe disruption to the development and spread of karate, so in real terms we are talking about 20

"In terms of depth of understanding I think that there are many Westerners who now understand the kata at least as well as many Oriental teachers."

years or so of development. Karate came to the West in the late 1950s, so we have had over forty years to acquire the skills. And bear in mind the information explosion, continuous peace, improved nutrition and training methods, so it is not a surprise that Western karate should produce some outstanding performers. In the area of kata performance and competition the West may lag behind to a small degree, but this is just looking at the surface performance. In terms of depth of understanding I think there are many Westerners who now understand the kata at least as well as many Oriental teachers and in some cases a little better. I have trained with many Oriental instructors over the years and while I have been impressed at the quality of their basic techniques, I have been somewhat less than impressed by their understanding of concepts such as *"riai,"* the correct understanding of the martial considerations when they try to explain the application of those techniques. Kanazawa sensei pointed out that if a *bo* instructor saw some of the defenses taught by shotokan teachers to attacks from the bo he would laugh. Therefore it is important to train with weapons in order to understand the way the weapon is used. I think that some Westerners have gone further down this path than many Japanese, because of the nature of Western education which encourages the development of an inquiring mind. Actually, I cover this area quite extensively in my book *History of Shotokan,* which, of course, everybody should buy!

*"Actually the heavier, stronger bodies and longer limbs
of Westerners are an advantage, as long as speed
and flexibility are developed and maintained."*

Q: You mentioned the bo. Do you think it helps your karate to train with weapons?

A: If you are primarily interested in karate as a competitive sport then no, weapons have no place in the training format. However, if you are interested in the wider, more traditional approach, then yes, you must train with weapons, especially if you really want to understand the applications of kata such as *"jitte," "bassai sho,"* et cetera. I once spent a few pleasant hours talking to Shirai sensei during a course in Scotland and he told me that Shinken Taira was invited to teach weapons for the JKA Instructor's Course. Shirai continued to practice his weapons but the others did not, which is why, Shirai said, some quite senior JKA teachers really do not understand how to defend against a real weapons attack.

From a self-defense point of view I think you need to train against knives, chains, and bottles. Of course, in training you need to use blunted or mock weapons at first. One useful approach is to use a marker pen as a substitute for a knife. The slash marks left by the ink show where the weapon could have gotten through if it had been for real. There was a book, *Bloody Iron,* published by Paladin Press some years ago by Jenks and Brown, which showed a kind of sparring method using the sharpened tip of a pair of fingernail clippers. I tried that once or twice and while you get some quite nasty scratches, you also gain some understanding of the realities of knife fighting. I think that all instructors who claim to teach defenses against a knife should adopt something of this approach. You can use a rolled-up belt to simulate the attack of a chain or bottle.

Q: Do you feel there are any fundamental differences between karateka from different countries?
A: Yes, there are differences; Japanese karateka will often work very hard to perfect their basic techniques without asking why the training is necessary, and will take quite a long term view of their training. They do not expect results in the short term. In general, Japanese karateka seem to be more flexible in the ankles and hips than Europeans or Americans, and the ratio of ankle to knee, and knee to hip seems to different in Japanese and Western physiques. However, I don't think these differences matter too much, and Westerners can achieve the same standards as the Japanese. Actually the heavier, stronger bodies and longer limbs of Westerners are an advantage, as long as speed and flexibility are developed and maintained.

Q: Karate is now often referred to as a sport. Do you agree with this definition?
A: If sport is a form of amusement, a diversion, a plaything, as in the Oxford Dictionary definition, then karate is not a sport, but if we use the classical Greek idea of sport then karate could be considered a sport. To the Greeks of the 7th and 6th centuries BC, the point of practicing sports was the development of a balanced human personality—this ideal was known as *"kalokagathia."* This ideal was also enshrined in the growth of amateur sport in Europe and America in Victorian times. It was the American poet Grantland Rice who wrote in the 1920s,

> *"For when the One Great Scorer comes; To write against your name; He marks—not that you won or lost—But how you played the game."*

As far as I can see, the values expressed in these older ideas of sport seem to be the same as Gichin Funakoshi's famous dictum that the ultimate aim of karate lies in the perfection of the practitioner's character, which of course is a fundamental belief of all Budo. Of course, much of modern karate is taught only as a sport, and it is noticeable that most of the larger karate associations choose their grading examiners from those who do well in competitions and award high grades to successful competitors, so the sporting values become more entrenched in the infrastructure of karate. That is OK for those who want to pursue that line, but those who find this approach limiting or boring simply leave and follow a different path. The tribalism, sometimes moronic behavior, cheating, drugs, and crass commercialism associated with much of modern sport has little appeal to intelligent adults. The sporting approach appeals mainly to young men and women, but eventually you grow up and need something a little deeper.

"It is important to train with weapons in order to understand the way the weapon is used."

Q: Do you feel that you still have further to go in your studies?

A: Of course! Higaonna sensei once said that he challenged himself everyday through the practice of karate, and that pretty much sums it up for me. If you are interested in the ideals of Budo as well as practical self-defense, and by the way I don't see why they should be mutually exclusive, then the greatest enemy you face is your own over-inflated ego. You need to train in order to hold the ego in check so, in effect, training never comes to an end. In terms of training with other systems I would like to investigate Fukien White Crane as I think it is the system that most influenced the early development of goju-ryu, and as I am fascinated with the history of the martial arts this would help to satisfy my curiosity to some extent.

Q: What's your opinion about makiwara training?

A: If you want to learn to hit hard then you need to train on the makiwara or some substitute such as a punch bag or focus pads. It has been said that without *"kime"* or focus there is no karate, and without hitting something you cannot develop kime. I know that it has been claimed that makiwara training is bad for the hands, but I would like to see the published research to prove this assertion. The *British Journal of Sports Medicine* pointed out in 1985 that there was no evidence that traditional karate training led to arthritis or tendonitis of the hands—at least there was no evidence of damage in the hands of the people in the study. Mas Oyama, the founder of kyokushinkai karate was a staunch believer in makiwara training. He had his hands x-rayed in 1955 and in 1970 and no evidence of any kind of degenerative disease was found, and the density and size of his bones and joints were normal.

The boxer "Two Ton" Tony Galento toughened his fists by bashing a brick wall. His hands became so hard that he could punch his way through a solid door without damage to himself. I am not suggesting that everybody start punching brick walls, but it shows that many of the scare stories are just that—stories not evidence. Some instructors of Chinese boxing and Indian Kalari claim that training methods which involve striking a hard target are dangerous, as the heart may be damaged. They believe that the shock produced when the fist hits the target travels up the arm and damages the heart. If this theory fields any validity we would expect to find a high level of heart disease among blacksmiths and those who regularly use rivet guns or road drills. As far as I know no one has ever made this connection, and these warnings have no basis is any scientific understanding of the human body.

Q: Do you think the practitioner's personal training should be different that his teachings?
A: This depends on the individual, but my own training does not necessarily reflect what I will be teaching at that time. For example, if I intend to introduce a new kata to my dan grades then I will practice that kata myself for a month or so before I teach it to them. This is to make sure that I am doing it correctly and to allow myself time to formulate the best way to explain the applications, derived techniques, et cetera. Of course, some things like impact training—the basic body mechanics of technique—are so fundamental that you will inevitably practice what you'll teach. It is important that an instructor work on the things he cannot do well or finds very difficult. This keeps him in touch with the difficulties often faced by his own students and should help him to be a better instructor. I once watched a big, fat, so-called shotokan "high grade" berating some brown belts because their kata was poor, They were exhausted after performing the kata numerous times at his direction. I remember thinking that he should not be telling them what to do, he should show them. The problem was, of course, that if he tried to perform

the kata correctly he would probably have had a heart attack or burst! He was an instructor in name only, and his high grade was meaningless.

Q: When teaching the art of karate what is the most important element, self-defense or tradition?

A: Well, as far as I am concerned, learning effective methods of self-defense is the tradition which defines the physical practice of the art. Sport training can be fun, but it is essentially unreal in that it has to work within a set of rules designed with aesthetics, safety, and audience appeal in mind. If the concept of self-defense is absent then you are not doing karate: you are simply performing some kind of military aerobics designed to instill obedience

"Sport training can be fun, but it is essentially unreal in that it has to work within a set of rules designed with aesthetics, safety, and audience appeal in mind."

and group solidarity and get you fit, or you are practicing a combat sport, or a performance art intended to be seen by spectators, something like a dance. The fundamental *"raison d'etre"* of the traditional teachings of karate is the development of effective fighting or self-defense skills. Ideas such as *"zanshin,"* fighting spirit, tolerance to pain and minor injuries, et cetera are there to enhance your physical skills of kicking, punching, blocking, striking, throwing, and locking. Without such ideas there is no karate.

Q: What's the proper ratio training ration of kata and kumite?

A: This question implies that these aspects of karate are somehow fundamentally different and separate. Kata teaches you the movements and body mechanics; kumite allows you to practice those movements with a partner, either in a pre-arranged way or in a free situation. This essentially is what bunkai is. If you assume that kumite simply means the development of competition fighting skills performed according to the rules, then why bother with the kata? On the other hand if you are interested in the more traditional

"When you perform your kata alone, your knowledge of the applications brings the kata to life."

approach then first learn the kata and then practice all the different ways you can apply the techniques. For seniors, simply going through the movements of the kata in thin air, polishing the outer form of the techniques, might have some kind of aerobic value; but I feel it is more productive to actually practice the applications of the techniques in a variety of situations. Obviously, lower grades need to practice the form of the kata more to improve the quality of their movements, but there comes a point when this approach becomes subject to the law of diminishing returns and further real progress is difficult if not impossible. It has been pointed out that we learn techniques in relatively unchanging circumstances i.e. kata, where the sequence is fixed; but we develop skill by adapting to changing conditions, i.e. the faster we can adapt to the reality of the situation the higher the level of skill. To create changing circumstances we need a training partner; this is kumite. As far as I am concerned you cannot really say you can do a kata properly until you can make use of the techniques and principles of that kata against a determined, uncooperative opponent. In the same way that punching a makiwara is fundamentally a more efficient way of developing your striking power, training with an opponent is fundamentally a more efficient way of understanding and hence improving your kata. When you perform your kata alone, your knowledge of the applications brings the kata to life; without this interplay between kata and kumite the kata have no meaning except as exercise. Part of the problem with modern karate is that this essential unity has been fractured, and so kata and kumite are now viewed as separate entities. This, in my view, is an error which needs correcting—but the artificial demands imposed on kata by tournament values makes it very difficult to put things right.

Q: So do you think it is necessary to engage in free-fighting to achieve good fighting skills in the street?

A: Yes. You need to experience the random nature of free-fighting, but the sparring should not always resemble that seen in tournaments. Sometimes competition free-fighting is over-refined from a self-defense point of view—that kind of sparring is a highly specialized skill used in a very artificial environment. I think that engaging in what we used to call *"randori,"* kumite, or dojo fighting is of greater benefit. I think the goju people now call it *"iri-kumi."* You also need to spar in body armor to allow heavier blows to be applied, including hook punches and to spar against someone wielding padded weapons of varying lengths. Simply sparring against one opponent is not enough; you need to face two or three opponents at once to get a realistic understanding of the chaos of fighting, and within the need for safety there should be minimum restrictions of allowable versus illegal attacks and techniques.

Q: Some people think going to Japan to train is highly necessary. Do you share this point of view?

A: Again it depends on the individual and where he trains. Certainly, I bene-fited greatly from my time in Japan, but I was very lucky and found an excellent dojo and teachers. I visited some dojo in Tokyo and Kyoto which I thought were poor, so simply being in Japan does not guarantee good karate. I think that it is now possible to find skilled teachers in the West in most styles. You should also remember that many of the best Japanese and Okinawan karateka now live in Europe and America, or regularly teach in those areas, so high-quality instruction is available outside Japan. I have trained with Westerners who have recently returned from Japan, or have had them in my class, and to be honest in some cases I was less than impressed by their karate.

Q: What do you consider to be the major changes in the art since you began your training?

A: In some ways it has become less physical, and health and safety are now considered to be of more importance than they were in the past. When I began training in karate there were very few women in the dojo and no children. The influx of large numbers of women and children has tended to lessen the levels of contact which were once considered normal. For exam-ple, when I was a beginner we were taught to block with full power, and arm and leg conditioning was quite normal. Of course, the women trained the same way and conditioned their arms in the same way; they put up with the bruises and pain, but of course some left, as did some men. As instructors became more professional and making money became important, especially after the Bruce Lee boom in the '70s, this kind of training became less common, as the instructors did not want to lose members to other dojo where the pain levels were not so high. Karate became part of the fitness boom, and so was viewed as a kind of Oriental aerobics which would also teach you self-defense. The kind of person who joined a karate dojo in the '60s and '70s now does muay Thai or similar systems because Thai boxing has retained its martial tradition and image. Karate has in many ways lost the martial aspect, which I think is a mistake. Of course, people might say that I am simply looking backwards to a golden age that never really existed, but I was talking recently to one of my seniors who has returned to karate after a twenty-year-plus layoff. His daughter wanted to learn karate so they both joined a local shotokan dojo. After a few weeks the girl gave up, but he continued to train. Of course, he wore a while belt when he began to train again, and although his techniques were very rusty he took into the training the same attitudes he had developed in the 1960s and '70s. After a few weeks he was asked to leave the dojo by the senior instructor, as the members were watching him rather than the instructor! His martial spirit and attitude did not fit into what was essentially an exercise session pretending to be a karate class.

A number of senior Japanese instructors have said that the spirit of karate has declined. For example, Shiro Asano, the senior Shotokan Karate International teacher in Great Britain observed in an interview that because of the influence of competitions, karateka no longer need to make a strong properly-focused technique. The idea of the single killing blow has been replaced by what he called "the small punch." He said that there aren't many people doing real karate. Well, he may be tight but if he is who is to blame? It is the fault of the senior Japanese teachers who promoted karate in that way. It is the fault of those teachers who failed to give the correct lead to their students. It is certainly not the fault of the Western students who trained and performed as they were taught. Many JKA and SKI shotokan, wado-ryu, shito-ryu and goju-ryu instructors used tournaments as a vehicle to promote their systems, and directed their most skilled students into tournaments to represent their styles or associations. Then they turn around and say that Westerners do not understand the true spirit of karate and are obsessed with sport! Hypocrites!

Q: Who would you like to have trained with that you have not—dead or alive?

A: The two most obvious teachers are Gichin Funakoshi and Chojun Miyagi. There are those I could possibly have trained with and didn't such as Motokatsu Inoue, Shigeru Kimura, and Donn Draeger. But the Elizabethan swordmaster George Silver would have to be high on my list, too. I could go on and on—there are too many to list.

Q: What would you say to someone who is interested in starting to learn karate-do?

A: Fill this form in, pay your fees and join the class! Just kidding. Seriously, he or she should be as clear as they can about their reasons for learning karate. Read some books and magazines to get a clear idea of what karate actually is and then visit all the dojo in the area, watch the classes, talk to the instructors and dojo members, and select the dojo which they find most appealing—

"Always judge an instructor by his students, not by what he says he has or is."

style, system, and political affiliation are of little importance. What is critical is the personalities and skills of the instructors and the quality of the students they produce. Always judge an instructor by his students, not by what he says he is.

Q: What keeps you motivated after all these years?

A: Karate is a challenge. Like sanchin kata, it challenges you on the physical, intellectual, spiritual, and psychological level. I suppose I am basically an addict, but I find there is always some new area to explore—a new challenge to face.

Q: Do you have a particularly memorable karate experience which has remained with you?

A: Yes, it happened dining the final match of the British Universities Karate Federation Championships held in Hull in 1974. My team, Durham, was the defending champions and we met the home team, Hull, in the finals. After five fights the result was a draw and so both teams selected one person to fight for the decision. As captain of the Durham team I stood up to face the captain of the Hull team, a taekwondo black belt who had already beaten me in the past. 1974 was my last year at university and so I felt tremendous pressure to win. I knew I wouldn't fight again in this event and all the Durham team were tired and injured after a long day of competition. As I faced my opponent across the area I was determined to beat him, and I could see by the look on his face that he felt the same. The crowd was yelling and shouting advice and the match started. We fought for a couple of minutes, both very witty, and ended up with a half point each. We were given a minute extension, but neither of us scored. Then we were told that we would get one more minute and if there was no result the referee and judges would decide the winner. As we faced each other across the area I felt something in myself change; the noise of the crowd faded away and I felt calm and very relaxed, no tension anywhere and no worries. The match started again and as I moved towards my opponent, somehow I knew what he was going to do. As he began his roundhouse kick I stepped in and swept him with my right foot, hitting him with a *mawashi-geri* as a follow-up when he was off-balance and in the air. His techniques appeared unbelievably slow to me and I felt as if no effort was required. In fact, I didn't do anything, it all seemed to happen of its own accord, and had nothing really to do with me. I didn't feel particularly elated at winning, and when the teams got together afterwards my opponent congratulated me and said that it didn't really matter who had won, as the fight had been a good one for both of us. I understood exactly what he meant and I felt the same way. Friends who saw me said that my speed, timing, et cetera, had radically improved, but I really didn't know what they were talking about—it all seemed so slow and obvious at the time.

Of course, it didn't last, and the next time I fought I was back to my usual standard, but I've never forgotten the odd combination of intensity and relaxation I felt at the time. I take no credit for it, but one of the reasons I continue to train is the chance that it might happen again. Later when I read Maslov's work on peak experiences I understood what had happened, but I don't know how to make it happen, or if, indeed, such a thing is possible again.

Q: How do you think a practitioner can increase their understanding of the spiritual aspect of karate?

A: If by "spiritual" you mean the effect that training has on the character of the student, rather than some kind of religious experience, then the karateka needs to study and understand the philosophies that influenced the development of Oriental societies. It is necessary to look at Buddhist, Taoist and Confucian works to understand the thought processes which underpin the physical practice of the martial arts. More specifically, looking at the various codes written by Matsumura, Itosu and Funakoshi will indicate the points that need work and study by the karateka.

Q: How much training should a senior karateka be doing to improve at the art?

A: Again this depends to a large degree on the individual. I think it is not necessarily the amount of training that is important, but the type and quality of the training which is critical. Trying to perform techniques at the age of 60, as

"It is necessary to look at Buddhist, Taoist and Confucian works to understand the thought processes which underpin the physical practice of the martial arts."

if you were 20 years old, is foolish. You need to find a more economical way of moving and a way to make each technique more efficient. Senior karateka need to take more time with flexibility training and train with weights to maintain strength and muscle. I think if you have the time you could train every day, as long as the training is varied and not excessively strenuous. One useful approach is to use a pulse rate monitor to control the intensity of your training, which should ensure that you gain the maximum benefit from the workout. Seniors need to have very clear idea of which areas they want or need to improve, and they should have specific training methods which help them achieve their goals. Of course, the goals need to be realistic and based on their past experience, current physical condition, and so on. I have had the good fortune to train with a number of instructors who were both

"Without any doubt the single most important characteristic of a successful karateka is his or her ability to accept hard training and never give up."

senior in age and experience, and the intensity of their training was impressive. Actually last summer a group of Seijinkai members came with me to California and we were lucky enough to train with Shinyu Gushi sensei, who is a senior karataka in all ways. As far as I could see he seemed to train all the time, either physically or mentally. Higaonna sensei is the same, as is Hiroshi Fujimoto sensei.

Q: What do you consider to be the most important qualifies of a successful karateka?
A: Of course this depends what you mean by "successful." A person could become a world champion or a fifth dan or higher grade, but if he or she has a really poor character, then as far as I am concerned they are still not a success as a practitioner of the way of karate. They might be a good technician, but if we are talking in more general terms, then without any doubt the single most important characteristic of a successful karateka is his or her ability to accept hard training and never give up. Mark Saltzman said that his instructor, Pan Ching Fu, offered to teach him real kung-fu, but only if he could *"chi ku"* or "eat bitter," and many other instructors have expected the same from their students. In fact, it was usually the ability to endure, coupled with the desire to learn, which was the deciding factor when a teacher accepted a student. I also think that a good sense of humor is important to balance the ego as well. My first instructor, Ken Smith, used to tell us that to get better we needed "karate oil" or "sweat." I think that through hard work and an honest appreciation of your own strengths and weaknesses, progress is always possible. Laziness and the ego, however, can prevent progress, so it is necessary to always try and keep what is known in Zen and Budo as *"shoshin,"* the beginner's mind, always open to learning. This applies to

both beginners and instructors. Even if you are an instructor you should not be afraid to become a student again.

Q: What advice would you give to students on supplementary training?
A: Well, as you probably know, goju-ryu makes extensive use of a system of supplementary training known as *"hojo undo,"* as did most forms of karate in the past. In the Seijinkai we make extensive use of both traditional and modern training tools to improve the karateka's strength, power, speed, stamina and flexibility. In a way we are returning to the question you asked about makiwara training, which is, of course, the classic form of supplementary training. Without supplementary training your karate is not complete. E. J. Harrison translated two Japanese texts which were published as *The Manual of Karate* in 1959. This was the first karate book in English, I think, or certainly the most available to karateka in Great Britain in the early days. There is a really interesting chapter on training equipment which points out that if you don't train on the equipment then the power and efficacy of your karate will be reduced by 50 percent. From my experience in Britain and Japan I think that this is correct.

Q: Why is it, in your opinion, that a lot of students start falling away after two or three years of training?
A: I think you would need a book to answer this question because there are so many reasons. The fundamental reasons are connected both with the nature of karate training and with the character or personality of the student. First of all, many people come to karate with unreasonable expectations; they might want to become the "world's deadliest fighter" in six months or whatever, but don't really want to put up with the hard work and the pain that goes with acquiring real fighting skills. Of course, some of the training is repetitive hard work, and some people cannot take it. During a class I was teaching in The Republic of Ireland a young female 1st kyu, about 17 or 18, stood out by the lack of effort she was putting into her blocking during some kumite drills. She complained loudly to her opponent, telling her to go softer and slower (her training partner was a younger lower-graded girl by the way) and then she complained to me that she was getting hit by her partner's punches. When I told her to block harder and move out of the way faster, she said that she hadn't come to get bruises on her arms. I asked her what she had come for, and she said that her father had promised her a sports car if she managed to gain a black belt in karate. I then told her to stop training with me because she wouldn't get her sports car. She took my advice, trained elsewhere and is now the proud owner of both a nice shiny sports car and a nice shiny new

"Many people come to karate with unreasonable expectations; they might want to become the "world's deadliest fighter" in six months."

black belt. It's pathetic really, but this is what happens at times. Of course, to be fair to some of those who do drift away, they become disillusioned with their instructors who might be greedy or exploitative in other ways. There are those who feel that after a couple of years they have achieved a modicum of skill or fitness, possibly to the level they wanted when they began and so they go. Others leave because of the pressure of work, or family commitments and so on. Of course, many people regard karate training as a form of entertainment or fitness training and when it becomes too painful or demanding they move on to something else.

Q: Have there been times when you felt fear in your karate training?
A: I have never been so frightened that I was paralyzed or anything like that, but I have certainly felt real apprehension at times. When I was a 7th kyu I faced Terry O'Neill in the team event at the British Championships; that certainly caught my attention—I lost the fight! But you should remember that part of training in karate should be to overcome fear and develop a sense of grace under pressure. When I was a beginner most of the members of the dojo I joined were bigger, stronger, and a lot more aggressive than I was. One or two were well-known hard cases in the town where I lived. They worked as laborers while I was still at school, getting ready to go to university. When I first began sparring I was scared of them, they could easily have hurt me quite badly if they had wanted. I took some quite nasty knocks, but nothing permanent. Actually, I think the greatest fear I have felt in karate occurred when I hit a friend of mine with a back kick in the mouth

during a friendly competition between our dojos. He dropped to the floor and when the referee turned him over a gout of blood came out of his mouth. I thought he was dead. I have never felt so bad before or since, and my feeling of relief when he eventually stood up was profound.

Q: What are your thoughts on the future of karate-do?
A: I hope that Olympic recognition does not mean that karate will go the way of judo and turn totally into a competition sport where

"I think that what is generally considered to be "traditional" karate will survive alongside sport karate."

winning Olympic, or other medals becomes the be-all and end-all of the training. Actually, I think that what is generally considered to be "traditional" karate will survive alongside sport karate, and possibly traditional karate will survive more in the West than in the Orient.

Q: Do you have any general advice you would care to pass on to karateka everywhere?
A: I would like to end this interview with the words that begin my book *History of Shotokan*. It is a quote from the 1st century B.C. Roman teacher Publilius Syrus, "*Vincit qui se vincit*—He conquers, who conquers himself." O

Masters' Techniques

Harry Cook faces an attacker (1), who attacks with a punch to the face which Cook blocks using kakuto uke (2). He then follows with a counterattack to the neck (3), and a knee to the head (4).

An attacker grabs Sensei Cook's right wrist (1). Cook turns his wrist, using a technique from seipai kata to release the grip (2), then attacks the aggressor's chest with an elbow (3), grabs the head and applies a throwing technique for the finish (4).

Sensei Cook, unaware of a potential attack (1), is grabbed with a bear hug from the back (2). As soon as he feels the pressure, he moves his right foot forward (3). Using a technique from seienchin kata, his uses one elbow to break the attacker's grip, and then another to attack the opponent's ribs (4). This allows him to circle around (5), and apply a bent arm-lock to control the aggressor (6).

RAY L. DALKE

An Original American Samurai

HE IS THE REBEL *WITH* A CAUSE OF AMERICAN KARATE—AND THIS LEGENDARY MARTIAL ARTIST IS AS SHARP WITH HIS WORDS AS HE IS WITH HIS FISTS. KNOWN FOR NEVER PULLING ANY PUNCHES—EITHER IN OR OUT OF THE DOJO—8TH DAN RAY DALKE IS A TRUE ICON OF A BYGONE ERA WHERE STUDENTS WERE ALLOWED TO SPAR AND TRAIN WITH THE BEST MASTERS IN THE WORLD. SHOULDER TO SHOULDER WITH SUCH NAMES AS KANZAWA, ENOEDA AND SHIRAI, RAY DALKE FORGED HIS TECHNIQUE AND SPIRIT UNDER THE DEMANDING ATTENTION OF JKA GREAT, HIDETAKA NISHIYAMA. HIS BREAK FROM THE JAPANESE KARATE ASSOCIATION (JKA) TO FORM THE AMERICAN JAPAN KARATE ASSOCIATION (AJKA) WAS AN ATTEMPT TO PROVIDE A VOICE FOR THOSE WESTERNERS WHO, AFTER TRAINING FOR MORE THAN 40 YEARS, HAD NO VOTE IN THE DIRECTION THAT THE ART WAS TAKING IN THE UNITED STATES. AFTER MORE THAN FOUR DECADES OF UP AND DOWNS IN THE WAY OF BUDO, DALKE KEEPS WALKING THE SAME PATH, IMMERSING HIMSELF IN THE PRACTICE AND DEVELOPMENT OF HIS BELOVED ART, WITH NO CHANGES IN HIS MIND ABOUT WHAT KARATE IS OR IS NOT.

Q: Tell us about your background in the martial arts.
A: I have been training for over 40 years. I did three years of judo and also dabbled in others arts such as kenpo karate with Ed Parker before training Japanese karate. I formally started my karate training with Dan Ivan, who used take us down to Ed Parker's school once in a while for training. Dan was my first instructor and things back then were pretty open among teachers and students. After Ivan, I went to train with Hidetaka Nishiyama in 1961 and I have been with him every since.

Q: What was your first impression when you saw Nishiyama?
A: Back then was a different time and you looked at people differently—but he was something very special. I had heard about karate and how you could kill someone with a karate chop—so he was a novelty. He was someone you could look at and realize he could really destroy you with his bare hands. I was looking for a self-defense method that could teach me to fight. I didn't realize it was shotokan or anything else, because back then we did-

"When I saw Nishiyama perform, I knew right away that I had something very special here. It was something that I adapted to and enjoyed instantly. I knew as soon as I started that it was something I would never stop doing for the rest of my life."

n't know about styles at all. Nishiyama sensei was just there and he showed up and he looked neat. Then he coached and he was a tremendous teacher. He was so unique. I had not been involved with any Japanese teacher before; and Dan Ivan was just another long-haired greasy biker like I was back in the old days. I thought that the Japanese were the only ones that did karate and then I found out Dan was part of the Army Criminal Investigation Division (CID). I thought it was pretty cool you could be a bad guy and still be a good guy!

In the beginning, when I saw Nishiyama perform, I was not quite sure about him as he could not speak English. It was broken English and I couldn't understand what he was saying. I thought that *zenkutsu dachi* and *kiba dachi* were all the same so instead of trying to understand him I just copied him. Then as his English got better he was better able to explain the dynamics. Just prior to this Nishiyama and Dan Ivan had split up and Nishiyama had opened up a dojo through Oshima. Then Dan Ivan said to me, "Ray, Nishiyama can take you further than I can and that is probably the right thing for you to do. I knew right away that I had something very special here. It was something that I adapted to and enjoyed instantly. I knew as soon as I started that it was something I would never stop doing for the rest of my life.

Q: Why did some students leave Oshima sensei and go with Nishiyama?

A: It's not we "left." Some people felt more comfortable with the modern approach to teaching that Nishiyama was using and we decided to stay with him. At that time he introduced a lot of scientific and physiological basis for the concepts and techniques he was teaching. The JKA finally explained why you were doing what you were doing and supported it with science and logical reasoning. Nishiyama opened up our eyes to a new concept of karate training. So some students decided to go with Nishiyama sensei and other stayed with Oshima sensei. To me, Nishiyama knows more about karate—the physical, the mental, the spiritual—than anybody I've seen so far. And I have seen a lot, trust me.

Q: Were the karate moves natural for you?

A: I think I was very comfortable because I was a good athlete. I played ball and all types of sports and I was a real good at it. Also during my youth I did a lot of boxing. I was looking for something so that I could fight—I was a little guy who only weighed 120 pounds. It was a good thing that I was dumb—I just didn't realize how really dumb I was. I was small but I didn't know it! I had a big ego, you know a 120-pound body and a 220-pound mouth. My mouth was always getting me in trouble and I wanted something that would get me out of it. I knew then that I couldn't fight the big guys, so I wanted something that could eliminate them and I didn't care what. So I was very careful whom I got in a fight with.

Q: How was the training with Nishiyama back then?

A: When Nishiyama sensei taught us how to punch, he never just counted, he lectured on the physics behind the movement, the opponent's vulnerability, and the right spirit to fight. All this taught us a lot more than just how to make a fist and punch. But the training was savage. It was really brutal. Nishiyama was the main man back then and several top guys would come and train with us. Okazaki would come and train, Yaguichi, Mikami, Enoeda, Shirai, and Kanazawa—these were our training sparring, partners. Kase sensei was more of an instructor. We got a chance to get after these guys and they were not very gentle men. But we believed that this was a very special thing that could enable a small man to defend himself. Pretty much like the assassin in the Manchurian Candidate—to be able to kill someone very quickly. Not fight them but kill them and that was kind of what we were looking for. Everything we trained for was based on that mindset.

I was looking for some direction and I was an uneducated street kid with a sixth grade education and it was a nice way to educate me. Then over the years my education developed and Nishiyama seemed to me to be intelligent; he seemed to be a deliberate man with no hesitation, and he carried himself as an athlete and as someone special. We never sparred with the man; he just had our respect and that will never change. We just trusted his word—it was a different time back then, American philosophy was very different. We were going through the Berlin crisis and we had the Cuban crisis. We were just out of the second world war by only 10 years or so. We were getting into Vietnam and back then if you put the Americans into a corner you had to watch out! Now you put them in a corner and they look for the nearest door to escape! Things were just different back then, a different society. I don't think the karate has changed at all, it's still the same. The people have changed so the message has to be a little different now. If you want to win in both karate and life you must be very determined and very deliberate.

Q: Was there any thing in particular that Nishiyama did that really impressed you?
A: It wasn't any one thing that he did, it was what he was able to make you do that made him so great. For instance, training before a world championship until 1:00 AM in the morning so that we couldn't get to the bars to have a beer afterwards. And we started at 7:00 AM! That was very common and the main thing is that he made us do it. We did an hour of non-stop basics and then an hour of combinations then two hours of free sparring and then another hour of sparring and combinations. It was really brutal. You can't do that with the students today. But this was a different time.

Q: Do you go to Japan for your instructors' training?
A: No, I didn't go to Japan for that training. I did my instructors' training in Los Angeles with Nishiyama. It was with Nishiyama, Yaguichi and whoever the guest instructors were at that time from Japan. It was five days a week. That was really hard training. I always wanted to become a karate instructor. The JKA instructors I saw were intelligent and educated and that appealed to me. We only went to Japan to compete against the Japanese— so we did train in Japan but not in the Instructors Training Program.

Q: How did you react to that type of militaristic training?
A: For the Westerners at that time it was a novelty. People thought that if you did karate you could kill people. Nobody knew the difference between

karate, judo or aikido. But a big portion of the Westerners really adapted well. The group that I came up with were adventurers—they were die-hard guys like John Gelson who trained with Kubota and Tony Tulleners. They were fighters. Of course, the white collar guys had a difficult time with it. Nishiyama, although he was a white-collar teacher, always talked about some blue collar stuff. We went through situations where people were just smashed, and you would get up and feel terrible, get the blood cleaned up, and get back on the floor. Then you would get knocked down and you would hear get up off the floor again. You were told you weren't hurt and the truth was that we weren't hurt. We had a bloody lip or a broken nose or knee dislocated or whatever but remember we were looking at the Berlin Wall and the Cuban Missile Crisis, so our bumps and bruises seemed trivial by comparison.

"We went through situations where people were just smashed, and you would get up and feel terrible, get the blood cleaned up, and get back on the floor. Then you would get knocked down and you would hear get up off the floor again."

Q: Can you compare the spirit you had to the Japanese samurai spirit?

A: Oh yes! We had that for sure but that is also the basic Western philosophy as well. You know, if my buddy goes down I will be right there to pick up the sword, and if I go down he will be there to pick it up. The only thing some of us would have said was if we were told to jump off a 10 story building some of us would have said you first and if you survive we will do it. We were not foolish. We weren't that far over the edge but we were pretty serious. We were all intent—no one was doing it to be fancy. We were all doing it for the same reason because all these situations were going on at the time in our country. People were uptight and we were becoming more of an armed society and we wanted to be more prepared so we didn't have to carry weapons.

"Nishiyama sensei taught me to think and organize my thoughts—how to organize my life. I didn't have a hell of a lot in common with most people. I had a limited education so I wasn't going to sit down and discuss physics with anyone."

Q: When did you start to teach?

A: I started almost right away. What I learned the class before is what I would teach in the next class I taught. I was from the beautiful city of Vancouver, Canada, and I was living in a Mexican barrio and I was dying to get out but I didn't know how to do it. It was a ghetto on the east side of LA. I had no education and I was extremely frustrated. But Nishiyama sensei taught me to think and organize my thoughts—how to organize my life. I didn't have a hell of a lot in common with most people. I had a limited education so I wasn't going to sit down and discuss physics with anyone. I opened my first dojo in 1960 with Dan Ivan and that is where I met Chuck Norris for the first time. I recall he had just got out of the Air Force—I am not sure of the year—but it was around 1960 or something and we were the first karate school out in that area. What I found out was that my way of communicating with people was to sit down and talk to them. What it came down to writing articles, I would copy an article on baseball or whatever and then just replace the words "baseball" with "karate." Pretty soon I was able to do bigger articles and that is how I learned to write and to organize things properly.

Q: After all these years, how has your karate changed?

A: It has changed tremendously and that is just from maturity. Techniques that I once studied so hard, so feverishly, I don't study anymore. I don't have to worry if my back heel is down, or if my shoulders are down, or if my wrist is straight. I just don't have to worry about these things anymore. I always knew that karate would only work if the body is in perfect condition, if everything in your technique is perfect. It would only work if everything came together as one whole unity as the contact is made, and that would generate tremendous force. In fact, Nishiyama mentioned to me that he would watch me as a young man perfecting everything. Of course, I didn't realize what I was doing. He said I was always trying to align all my body parts in the right position. That was a process I repeated over and over again, and I'm talking of six or seven hours a day. Not a long time ago, Yabi runs over to watch me and Nishiyama sensei, in front of everybody in class, says, "Yabi what are you doing?" And Yabi answers, "Sensei, I'm trying to watch Ray and learn to do it the right way!"

Nishiyama used to say that Yabi was always better, but now it has all changed and that was really nice to hear from your instructor after forty years. It finally paid off! When Yabi and I go to the dojo now, you see two old men out there just joking around with each other. One day he came over out of line and was watching me do a knife-hand block and a back stance and Nishiyama sensei said, "What are you doing?" Yabi replied, "I'm trying to learn a back stance the right way." Suddenly, we were both in trouble so I right away let my toes go out and my butt go out and said, 'Don't look at me!" Back then I was sweating the details but now I just relax. The difference between then and now is that back then there was no moment in time I could relax. Everything had to be quick, fast, sharp, and correct. Now I really enjoy it and I feel like I have a lot of power—real shocking power— and I don't worry about it anymore. I am really comfortable with my karate.

Recently, I was telling my students that I really got a lot more mentally flexible when I was in my 40s, when I moved away from the student-sensei relationship. Its not that I don't have a sensei, or that I don't respect him or anything like that; I do still listen and I listen feverishly—but at 40 I didn't want to be patronized any more and patted on the head like a good little boy. I wanted to grow and in that regard it was time for me to move on and I did. All of a sudden, I began to relax and feel natural and let karate and me become one.

Q: Do you think there is still pure shotokan or goju being taught?
A: No, not really. Everybody adapt things differently. And what's the definition of "pure?" The bottom line is that you better be practicing the art and not just trying to learn how to fight. If you're trying to learn just to fight, you better look around because there are because some pretty tough guys out there. What are you going to do at 50 years old? Are you going to fight or are you going to be practicing karate? Truthfully, style has nothing to do with defending ourselves against a drug-crazed biker. It doesn't matter because goju-ryu can take care of it, wado-ryu can take care of it, and

shotokan can take care of it—they can all do the job. The bottom line is we all meet at the same place but how we get there is different since there are multiple paths. I like shotokan because I have never studied the others styles deeply. I have dabbled in them but never studied them profoundly. But when it gets down to fighting we are not talking about styles anymore, we are talking about the athlete and his technique. It don't care if that technique is goju, shito, wado or shotokan.

One of my guys got hit up in Canada by a guy doing a flying hook-kick and it just about knocked him out. The guy scored an *ippon* on him, knocking him out of the tournament. It was a shotokan guy, a tall, skinny German kid. When I look at that, it isn't shotokan, but it was a good fighting technique. Any of the arts teaches a person not to hesitate and that is what I have found out through experience. The people who continue to practice will not hesitate in a real confrontation. Therefore a person who is defending his life will not hesitate if he trains properly in any style.

Q: What is your opinion of kickboxing, the UFC, or other combat sport such as muay Thai or savate?
A: Well, I think that they are all good sports if that is what you want to do and get hammered around. I like boxing and collegiate wrestling and am amazed by some of the pro athletes today—some of those guys are serious business. I just can't imagine fighting Shaq O' Neil at 315 pounds and over seven feet tall. It is wonderful to get old because you realize that you just pick fights with someone you can whip—like that old lady over there. Seriously, though, there wouldn't be any amount of money that would get me to fight those guys in the ring. But to defend myself against them on the street is a different thing and I wouldn't hesitate a second—because I would be way ahead of them as far as acting quickly and without thought. I think that is what karate has taught me. I wouldn't hesitate even a second to use my most dangerous techniques if my life is at stake.

Q: Today people refer to karate as a sport? Do you agree with that?
A: No, not real karate. If it were just kicking and punching then you would have to stop training at 35 or 40 years of age. Real karate is self-defense. They have these new rules out but let me tell you, I would hate to be punched by Frank Smith once and then have to go another 3 or 4 minutes with him. The way we used to score an *ippon* in the old days was very different of what it's considered today. I saw a guy in Moscow a couple of years ago get drilled by a French shotokan guy—a very a small guy, actually—and he was out cold on his back with a body punch and the referees gave him

the match! Competition has become so subjective. You got these referees deciding whether there was too much contact or not. When we fought in the '60s it was all contact—I don't want to exaggerate that but it was a really rough go. We had legs broken, teeth knocked out, fingers broken, and ribs broken—but this was not real contact.

I look at these guys who do toughman contests and no-hold-barred and these guys are really tough. And they are the guys I keep my eyes on in a bar because if they get really rowdy I am going to go home and have a beer in my living room. That is what I think decent people should be doing, saying "I don't want to fight." But that is what these type of guys are doing if they aren't fighting in the ring—they are fighting in

"It's like the CIA and the rest of the security services; they teach you not to get into a fight and to be aware and keep your eyes open. Karate is just not about dominating a physical confrontation, it is about winning the mental ones as well."

bars and looking for someone to give them a go. This is what I have trained my whole life to avoid and I can't do this by just being a fighter. I fought a West Coast champion and I was doing pretty good until the last punch of the first round and man, I got hit. I lasted one more round and that was it. Like Mike Tyson said once, "Everyone's got a plan until they get hit and then everything changes." And that is the truth. This is why I think traditional karate has a good chance of making it right now, because people are looking at it and saying well I can do that, and I know I can't do that TV stuff and jump in the air and do that fancy stuff, but I can do this and learn to defend myself. It's like the CIA and the rest of the security services; they teach you not to get into a fight and to be aware and keep your eyes open.

"I see good athletes excelling but they are not all doing good karate. Of course, there are exceptions but they are not the norm."

Karate is just not about dominating a physical confrontation, it is about winning the mental ones as well.

Q: Do you think that Western karate has caught up to Japanese karate?

A: Oh yes! We caught up to them in 1966 and 1967. Nishiyama's students caught them a long time ago. I remember when they brought in a guy from Japan to fight 10 of us and he couldn't get through us and he was the JKA Grand Champion. The idea was that they would bring in one guy to beat 10 Americans, but that didn't happen. I really felt sorry for the Japanese champion because he really got beaten badly. It was in the late '60s or early '70s. Physically and technically we are as good as they are, but culturally and socially we are not there—we are not even close to them. They have a great heritage and Budo culture and mind. In all these types of things we are just not even close to them.

Q: How do you see Japanese karate these days in the United States?

A: I see it so watered down that it really is ineffective as a self-defense. I have coached fighters on teams that were so good in sport karate that I couldn't coach them on how to do real karate, but I had to coach them on how to fight in a competition and I couldn't teach them the real fighting art. If you can't teach them the fighting art then you don't have a base. They couldn't understand the "why," and that is something that Nishiyama always did. He is great at explaining "why" we stand that way and "why" this punch is better, and "why" that kick is better. We stayed with him because we were learning every single minute and I don't see that happening much today. I see good athletes excelling but they are not all doing good karate. Of course, there are exceptions but they are not the norm.

Q: What was the instructors' training program like?

A: Nishiyama sensei taught it and Yaguichi assisted him on Tuesdays and Thursdays because Yaguichi did not want to teach. We would have to kick over a rail for an hour non-stop. Then we would do kata for an hour and then we would have a regular class. Then after the class we go out and do 250 of each of the four kicks for an hour, and then we would prepare our reports for the week or study. Then if we weren't doing that then we were cleaning the dojo. I will never forget one day when I came without a tie and Nishiyama was at the door and he said, "Where is your tie?" I just smiled and answered, "I am a cowboy from Fontana." He said, "Go get it or you can't come in." I had to go to my buddy's place up the street and knock on the door and get a tie. When I came again Nishiyama said, "Good. Don't forget it again or you can't come in."

Of course, I forgot it again and he took me out and bought me a tie. It was the absolute worst looking tie in the world and he made me wear it. I can't even describe how ugly it was. We were going to a meeting with Norman Wilson, the athletic director at UCLA, and I had a crew cut. You know, all those beautiful woman around the University and I was really pale at the time because I never got out of the dojo since I was training all the time. I could just see people looking at me and saying to themselves what an ugly tie that guy is wearing. Let me tell you I never forgot my tie thereafter.

The training was seven-hours a day, six-days a week and we would start at 6 AM with the beginner's class and then the intermediate and then the advanced and then the team class after that. I remember he would make me sit there in the chair until 10 PM and then I could go home. I had an hour's drive home I would get home at 11:00 PM in my old Volkswagen station wagon and I would even sometimes sleep in a sleeping bag in the back of it if I was to tired to drive home. Of course, the next day I would be there and do it all over again.

Q: What is your opinion of *makiwara* training?

A: I think it is very important, and this is very hard to understand because it doesn't offer squat for timing since the makiwara is a stationery object. But if you know how to train with it, it offers a lot for developing correct distancing. If you are too close you will feel it and if you are to far you will be able to tell. The most important thing is that it forces you to connect the small and large muscles in a split instant, which is what the concept of *kime* in technique is all about. We don't have anything to test our technique on since we are punching the air, so it becomes imperative to have something to hit that helps to have a good strong mental attitude to visualize the opponent. Its use helps to develop trust that the techniques will work. It pulls the entire body together, not only physically but also emotionally and mentally as well, because you can't be thinking about anything else, only that one spot.

The makiwara training is like hitting pads in football, sliding into second base in baseball, and running from wicket to wicket to cricket. It is just a portion of karate training but not the end-all of the training; it just a small part of it. It just simulates what will take place on impact if we hit someone. It teaches to transfer energy from the punch to the person getting hit. What is totally important in traditional karate is that the body must totally and completely stop so that the opponent absorbs all the energy and it does not come back to you. I believe that makiwara will give you that ability.

I boxed before and I hit the bag and it is great for timing, but what I do is hit the makiwara about 50 times and then go and hit the bag again and man, there is an incredible difference! You can feel it inside your body. It is very obvious because what we are simulating is the focus and the makiwara gives us this as well as the kata—and I explain this in the new videotapes that I'm finishing. It's important to get that focus so that every muscle in our body snaps at the same time, and that takes a long time to develop connecting all the muscles at the same moment. I used to hit it with a back-fist and knife-hand strike, and I can hit it pretty hard, but it hurts a little more the next day now than it did back then. We used to do a lot of makiwara training back then in the old days. I don't punch the bag as much as I hit the makiwara.

Q: How do you teach differently than the way you were taught?
A: I think that you have to relate so the students can understand. It's important that they realize that *kihon, kata,* and *bunkai* are just training methods like in football where they hit the pads or run sprints or run routes. These are just training methods and we have to take all of the mystical stuff out of it so that we can develop our technique. When you look at it, karate is a great art just from the fact that it conditions the entire body. I get a lot more out of doing a couple of kata than I do out of going for a walk with my friends.

Q: How does your training differ from lower belts?
A: Well, my training is very precise and I do a lot of kata these days. I don't need a big dojo to train in. I trained in the kitchen when I was a little younger; I would practice opening and closing doors with my foot for balance and if there was a couch there I would be constantly kicking over it to develop my *hiki ashi.* I am horrible around mirrors and windows as I am always practicing and correcting myself. I will be practicing combinations

when I am in the garage working on my car or wherever it is that I am. Karate is always on my mind every minute of every day—it's always there. I don't think there has been a day that I haven't done karate since the day I started. Even when I was in the hospital having my hip replaced I was practicing in the mornings doing my basic blocks and punches in the bed.

"Karate is always on my mind every minute of every day— it's always there. I don't think there has been a day that I haven't done karate since the day I started."

But to answer your question, it really depends on if you're a young instructor or an older instructor. When I was young I would practice a lot on my conditioning and timing and distancing but as an older instructor I can't do that as much but I still work on catching the right timing or whatever, and I will work with a couple of guys which helps me to keep it warm. I would hope that my instruction would give my students enough information to really learn from me. If someone was only at my dojo to learn to fight I would be screwed, but if he comes to learn the art then I can teach the art.

As an example, we all teach a front kick the same way, foot up, kick out, back and down—but if they never seem to have enough balance maybe we could consider teaching them to hold the wall until they can do it right and then move on and let them do it without holding the wall. If they are allowed to hold the wall they can instantly have that balance, then they can start to study the technique and find out how and why it actually works. Then when they go home they can study the kick because they have something to really work on not just balance. This forces them into self-practice.

*"When I started to study kata I noticed different katas worked different things.
I think that kata is a very tricky way of developing the body. "*

Q: What is the proper ratio between kata and kumite for practice?

A: I think it should be 30 percent each and all the rest should be 10 percent. We don't do a lot of bunkai out of the kata but we do a lot of combinations which we call kihon. I think in every class we do a little of each but what I do is show it in in kata and then in kihon and then in kumite so it all works together. The timing is all relevant. So if we are working on timing then I will show this in a kata and we will practice it, then I will show it in kihon and we will practice it again, and then in kumite we will work this idea

again. If we do one thing in kata it must relate to kihon, and then it must relate to kumite.

Q: How important do you think kata bunkai is?
A: There is so many different interpretations of bunkai—that is one of the things I learned when I went through the JKA Instructors Course. Every instructor has a different interpretation of the technique. For example, Sensei Nishiyama rarely ever taught bunkai—in fact I can't remember when he did teach it. I think that kata is a wonderful way to develop the practitioner. For example, a front stance is a great way to develop the quads and hamstrings and the cat stance is a great way to develop the back leg. Every kata has its strong points and if one doesn't have a way of working the triceps or hamstring we have another kata that does work those areas.

I used to help coach football a little and I would watch the way they would coach the guys and I would ask what this was for and what that was for and they would say it develops this muscle or this skill. Then when I started to study kata I noticed the same thing—different katas worked different things. I think that kata is a very tricky way of developing the body. You know without the proper form you have nothing. I remember a Chrysler ad that said, "Form is efficiency." I will never forget it. I have a race boat and when we built it we were looking for the most efficient way to make it go fast.

Q: Some people think that it is necessary to go to Japan to truly understand karate. Do you agree?
A: I would agree with that. Not for the training but for the culture. I know a lot of people that just go to the JKA dojo and get the crap beat out of them and that is bad. I think it's good to go there and savor the culture. I have been told by Japanese that if Japan loses the world championships then the Westerners won't follow the Japanese way anymore. Well, the people who talk like that don't really know the Western mind because we are not that way. The culture it is a wonderful experience for us, but for many years I've been as much as told to my face that a non-Japanese could never truly know karate. Well, I don't think that is true. As far as tradition goes, of course they see things different than we do in the West. But that doesn't keep me from feeling that I've achieved whatever they think I was incapable of as a non-Japanese.

Q: Some Western karate sensei have trained for a very long time. You pre-viously mentioned that the Japanese organizations don't like to give up control. How do you feel about that?

A: Well this has caused a lot of pain in the U.S. in the past, and Europe is now experiencing that too. There is always a top position—a place for the leader. We don't want to be the top man but with all the years we have done this we don't want to be at the back of the bus either. The problem is that some of the Japanese instructors never expected us to stick around as long as some of us have, which is more than forty years in my case. I think they figured we would stick around for 10 years maximum and then quit. This has forced some of us to form our own small groups—groups where we are prepared to share the top with each other. Maybe we don't have a large group but we have a very serious one.

I look at Nishiyama and he sees me in class and I am 62 years old and he says I look pretty good and he never said that before. That is what I have always striven for—to get that nod of approval. I don't give that nod very often to my students but I do give it when they deserve and I am prepared to share the top with them if they deserve it. If some guy has done karate for 25 years he is no punk and he deserves it. Lesley Safar was Okazaki's top student and he left. Sharing the top position always comes back to another thing called money, and you know that is a pretty important thing especially when you are a professional and you have a wife and family. Then that's a big issue. If it is an international organization and I am an 8th dan or a 9th dan and they say I have a lot of experience, then I deserve a piece of the cake as well as them.

I underwent their training and I broke my body and I wouldn't have been the person I am now if I didn't. Be careful because I don't just credit them for it, I also credit myself for hanging in there. But they will not share with us. We get crumbs off the crust while they get the big portions of the pie. What was really not fair was when they brought in junior instructors and put them in front of us and that is when some of us just said, "It's enough." I have been training twice as long as this guy and you are putting him up as my sensei? Don't do that and look at us as equal to a junior Japanese. That is pretty hard for a guy like me to swallow and it was really hard for a guy like Frank Smith. It is just too bad that guys like Frank Smith quit karate 15 years ago because he had something to say but he kept his mouth shut.

Me? I didn't keep quiet. I said over and over again, "What you are doing is wrong." I told Okazaki sensei that I didn't want to drive the bus, but I was not going to sit at the back of it either. I paid my dues for four decades and spent my time yet you want me to bring in Mr. Yaguichi to test my green belts? No way! Who pays my rent? It boils down to business. And it is not we walked out, we just decided that it was time to stand up and do what was right.

Q: What did Okazaki say to that?
A: He said that I didn't understand the politics. I said, "OK. Then I want a promise from you in writing that when I can't pay my rent next month you will pay it for me." He said, " No. You are supposed to run your own business." Well, I told him that if I couldn't test my own belts then I couldn't run a business. So that was when I had a parting of the ways with both Mr. Nishiyama and Mr. Okazaki. There are guys I went through instructors training school with who think they are part of the Japanese hierarchy—but because they are not ethnic Japanese they will learn where they really stand one of these days. Some of them are 67 years old and they can only test students up to 3rd degree brown belt. It is a business but the Japanese make all the money.

Q: I guess in Europe they starting to have that problem, too.
A: Yes, it is true. I hope that Nishiyama sensei is a multi-millionaire but don't stop me from being able to support my family at a very basic

"It is unfortunate that friends can't train together, but because I spoke my mind and stood up for what is right and fair, I am called a bad guy and a rebel in the dojo down there."

level because you want to make another million. Don't stop me from growing my students and my school. For all their talk about philosophy, this is not the true Budo way. We are brothers, not servants, and they are not lords presiding over a medieval fiefdom. Yabi said to me one time, "You know, I really missed training with you." It is unfortunate that friends can't train together, but because I spoke my mind and stood up for what is right and fair, I am called a bad guy and a rebel in the dojo down there.

"My toughest fights were little guys like Mikami. He was a tough guy, really tough. Enoeda was tough, too, and so was Shirai. I was the only one who got a draw with him and he was pissed!"

Q: Do you regret any of the decisions you made early in your training?

A: Absolutely not. It had to be done. Everyone has to leave home sometime. As I said to Yabi, "I really regret not hanging out with you guys." He answered, "But, Ray you grew so much, and honestly when you came back in the dojo we were all just curious to see what you would look like after all these years away and you look better then every body. Even Nishiyama said he was totally surprised and never expected you to look like you do. Sensei's secretary said sensei is quite proud of you." I just said, "What did you expect? I had such a great teacher but I had to grow." You know it is like the father that says to his son that he can't leave the house. But then you do leave home and then after 10 years or so you come back and the father is so proud and he says, "Look! This is my son the success story!" That is exactly what it is like. They said to me don't you remember saying to Nishiyama that, "You will always be the sensei but I just can't be under you?" Now, it's different. I can be under him because I am an old man and I don't give a damn!

I think that we get along better now then we ever did. It was really strained because of the politics and the business end of it. At the dojo, the training is great now, and I am the one that can play with him.

Q: After all these years of practice what is the meaning of karate for you?
A: I think it all changes. I have always felt that if I got as good as I could in the art, then everything else would fall into place. I think what you start with and what you end up with are two different things. I think that age has everything to do with it. In the beginning it takes on a shallow look; it is about just kicking punching and beating someone up. When I trained at Dan Ivan's we would train and then go to the bar and try out some of the techniques and sometimes they worked and sometimes they didn't, and if they didn't you would get your ass kicked. Then as the years go along, you try to change yourself and the technical takes over. Then you have the strong years.

When I was in my 20's you just couldn't tire me out and I would train 8 hours a day. Then in my 30's I felt extremely strong—I truly believe they were my strongest years. In my 40's I pushed away from being the instructor and started to relax a bit more and my body became really flexible—almost to the point that I felt like I was doing tai chi. The real change happens between 45 and 55. You just relax and let things come to you. That's the secret—relax and let things come. I really fell in love with a lady and I have been with her for a long time now. Now at 60 I think I have gone to the mountain and I realize that some of these big monstrous guys could fall on you and hurt you and all these old masters better realize that they just can't cut the mustard that way anymore. It's when you reach that point that you come back to what karate is really about—self defense.

You can just play with it when you are in your 20's and you will realize it is just a toy like baseball. Then in your 30's, you get pretty confident in your own ability and you keep it going. If I had not kept going I wouldn't have realized that karate is what can make you deliberate and not hesitate in a moment of danger. If you hesitate you lose, and I am thinking of our modern society and all the guns and that stuff. Sometimes I am training with Nishiyama sensei and Yabi, and we are working out together and I do something and then Yabi says, "How the hell did you do that?" I will answer, " I don't know. I just did it." The truth is I don't know how I did it. It's like you come full circle. You start not knowing how to do anything and then you learn all these techniques and kata and after years of training you don't know how you did what you did. It is like your reaction when something falls in front of you and you catch it before it lands on the floor. You wonder how you reacted that way. But you don't know you just did it.

I think that if I hadn't trained in karate all these years I don't think I could have done some of these things. But now fighting is just out of the question although defending myself is definitely an option and I will do it with no hesitation—if the time comes it will be very deliberate. It seems that you have to become old enough to be able to be aware of this. When I was a young man I was there with all the big guys and the other day someone asked me how did I deal with all those big guys? Right there I just realized that I really was a small kid! I have fought some real tough little guys sometimes, but almost everybody was much bigger than me. My toughest fights were little guys like Mikami. He was a tough guy, really tough. Enoeda was tough, too, and so was Shirai. I was the only one who got a draw with him and he was pissed! They had to break us up because he elbowed me on the break and knocked all my teeth lose and I caught him in the back of the head and then they had to break us up. That was here in L.A. and there was Enoeda, Kanazawa, and others as well. They were really good but we didn't know we had five years of experience and they had about 10. That was when Frank Smith got his jaw broken.

Q: What happened?
A: Keinosuke Enoeda hooked him and then swept him with his front leg, and then he roundhouse-kicked him right in the face with the same leg and Frank went down. There was blood all over. It was a very nasty mess! After that Frank got serious, very serious. He changed a lot. After that, in fact, we all got serious and realized that it wasn't a game anymore and that is how we played it after that—hard, brutal, and with full force. We didn't care anymore. Every fight was a war. When we went to class we never knew if we were going to live or die. It was very serious from then on.

Q: Did you ever compete in open tournaments with people like Joe Lewis, Mike Stone, or Chuck Norris?
A: No, we never did. We weren't allowed to. But people like Lewis, Norris and Stone used to come and watch our training sessions and they said, "You guys are crazy!" And they were right. We had our gi's covered with blood from sparring—but only after thousands of punches and kicks as a proper warm-up. We understood them. For them karate was something different. For us the training was a war, and we didn't care who was in front of us—Japanese or Caucasian.

Q: Have you ever felt fear in your training?
A: I have never felt fear that I couldn't control, but in every class I went into the fear was always in the back of my mind. You knew you could get seriously injured. The very moment you got into a class it put you into a totally different state of mind. When I look at some of these Europeans, I can see

they are not doing karate for sport, I can see it in their eyes. The karateka from Kosovo is doing karate for real and when you look at him, right into his eyes, you can tell. The philosophy of the training is different.

Q: Who would you like to have trained with more if you could have?
A: I would really liked to have trained with Mikami and Shirai. I hear Shirai is really good and he is my age. Mikami has really fluid, clean movement and he is a really mean and amazing fighter. Of course, I kind of liked that attitude when I was a kid, but now I don't like see the point. I stayed with Nishiyama sensei because he was the teacher but I liked Shirai very much because he carried himself well—and I don't think he was a bully. That has been my thing during all my life—I just don't like bullies. I trained with Yaguichi and I fought a lot with him—not for me to learn but for him. I did learn a lot about the body being soft. Nishiyama sensei's way was just to go in straight, hard, and fast. Now that I think about it, this was a good way for me because I am small and I just had to keep going and keep coming at you! So I guess that is what I learned from Nishiyama sensei. But from Yaguichi I learned a lot more about how to play and move around. It was a different approach. Mikami had a lot of speed and a lot of really neat techniques that I felt I could use because our bodies were similar in many ways. But Shirai was pretty special to me.

Q: What have you learned through karate?
A: It has taught me patience as it is found in the Japanese culture. I remember asking Nishiyama sensei when I could take a test and he answered: "Wait a little more." Over 25 years later, it has really taught me patience and it's like a snake, just waiting there for when you go all the way. Nothing ends in the first round and it has been a wonderful thing for me. It has allowed me to talk to people that I wouldn't have talked to. It really has given me a meaning to my life and it gave me a direction to follow. The secret is that you have got to just hang in there. There were a lot of tough times and a lot of kicks in the balls—and there are times when you've just got to stand-up for yourself. Sometimes you won't have a lot of friends and sometimes those friends are so far behind you that can't see them, but you just got to hang in there and keep going. These things sort of annoy me, but I still think I've had the best training and instruction anyone could have had. O

Sensei Ray Dalke faces his opponent
(1). Using his right hand to cover the
angle he enters (2), and applies a sweep
to his opponent's lead leg (3), followed
by a gyaku-tsuki jodan (4). He then
sweeps with his left leg (5), bringing
his opponent down to the ground (6),
where he finishes him with a punch
to the chest (7).

Sensei Ray Dalke in kamae *squares off against his opponent (1). His opponent tries to sweep Dalke's lead leg, but he avoids it by retracting his foot (2). Using this to get attack momentum (3), he applies a* mae mawashi geri chudan *(4), to his opponent's stomach (5), then spins into a* tettsui uchi *(6). Pivoting over himself, he delivers a sweep to his opponent's lead leg, bringing him to the ground (7), where he finishes him with a straight punch (8).*

Sensei Ray Dalke faces his opponent (1). When the aggressor attacks with a oi tsuki, Dalke reacts by ducking under the attack and delivering a gyaku tsuki chudan (2). He then grabs the opponent's lead leg (3), takes him to the ground (4), and finishes him with a tsuki to the face (5).

Sensei Ray Dalke squares off against his opponent (1), who attacks with a jodan tsuki which Dalke sidesteps (2). Dalke follows with a side kick to the face (3), and an inside sweep to the opponent's lead leg (4), which unbalances and takes him to the ground (5), where Dalke finishes him with a punch to the head (6).

Fumio Demura

Leading by Example

Although Fumio Demura has been a martial arts superstar for more than three decades, he has managed to keep traditional karate values in his life, and loyalty and respect in his personal and professional relationships. A superb technician, a great martial artist, and one of the finest performers and weapons experts in the world, he is credited with being the first professional karate performer to incorporate lights, music, costumes, and martial arts into the same routine. His technical prowess is breathtaking—as is the trademark precision of his punches and kicks. Easy-going and affable, he is one of the most accessible karate masters to learn from. Author of several books on karate and kobudo, Sensei Demura is known worldwide for his movie work in films such as The Karate Kid, Rising Sun, and The Island of Dr. Moreau.

The All-Japan Karate Champion in 1961, Demura came to the United States in 1965 to share his knowledge and spread his teachings in his own unique exuberant way. In so doing, he managed the difficult task of preserving the old values passed to him by his Japanese master without compromising his traditional beliefs. Living in Southern California since his arrival, Demura was a close friend of martial arts legend Donn F. Draeger, who also knew acclaimed authority Dan Ivan, the man who brought Demura from Japan in the mid-60s. Simply said, Fumio Demura is the type of person that people naturally follow.

Q: What's your rank in karate-do?
A: Rank is something I really don't care about, but because you asked I hold a 7th Dan in shito-ryu itosu-kai karate-do. I still consider myself a 5th degree, though, like most traditionalists. I was a 5th degree for over 25 years until my teacher told me that my own students were going to outrank me, and gave me the 7th degree black belt.

Sean Connery with Sensei Demura

"I went to high school to study drama because I wanted to be an actor."

Q: Why don't you dwell on rank?

A: Basically, because I consider myself a Master Ryusho Sakagami student. I don't look at myself as a master at all. Today everybody wants recognition; everybody wants to be called "master." They say, "They don't give credit to me." I really feel embarrassed by all this for the sake of karate.

Q: What did Sensei Sakagami mean to you?

A: Everything. Master Sakagami had a big influence on my life and was like a second father to me. While he didn't physically train me so much, I learned a lot from him in other ways. Sincerely, I would say that he "created" me in many different ways. I really liked his personality and his way of doing things.

Q: Did you study other arts?

A: Yes, I did. But because of my attitude towards rank, I never tested for belts in them.

Q: When did you start training in karate?

A: It was a long time ago! I started training because of illness. As a child I got a severe infection in my tonsils which left me very weak. The doctor said I should exercise. When I was 8 years old I started taking kendo lessons under Sensei Asano. When he had to move away, he gave me a letter of recommendation for Ryusho Sakagami to begin karate training. But in fact I didn't take it seriously until I was around 12. I also studied aikido, kyudo, and judo during my high school days. I went to high school to study drama because I wanted to be an actor. But once I finished school, my father disapproved so I had to go to the university to study economics because that's what my father wanted.

Q: How did you come to study kobudo?
A: Thanks to Sensei Sakagami, I was able to receive my training from Kenshin Taira, a kongou-ryu kobudo master who died in 1973. Master Sakagami invited him to become a teacher in our dojo and he accepted the position and came to live in Master Sakagami's house. Master Taira influenced a lot of people because he was moving around all the time in order to teach. Due to his age, Sensei Taira was a little hard to communicate with—but his skill and teaching abilities were fantastic. He was a typical "old style" sensei and taught just one way, which never ever changed. He was very, very special. Master Sakagami was also a kendo and iaido teacher. I took iaido and kendo classes from him, but I also trained kendo under Sensei Taisaburo Nakamura.

"I have always believed that failures can make you grow and improve if you know how to make a stepping-stone out of them."

Q: Were you outgoing as a child?
A: My personality was very different from now. I was born in Yokohama and I had four brothers and two sisters. I was very bashful and it was almost impossible for me to go in front of people. From the physical point of view I was very weak, I had a problem with my tonsils. Fortunately, martial arts changed all that!

Q: How was the training during the old days?
A: Very difficult! The training was harder and very demanding. We used to train the basics everyday for hours. Just basics!

Q: It is true that you failed your first test for white belt?
A: Yes, I did! In fact, that made me realize a lot of things. That embarrassed me so much that I decided to set goals and put more time into training. Since them, I have always believed that failures can make you grow and improve if you know how to make a stepping-stone out of them.

Q: How hard was it to win the All Japan Karate Championship in 1961?
A: That tournament was very hard because every style, association, and school was there—goju-ryu, shotokan, shito-ryu, wado-ryu, and more. It

"I remember that when I arrived in the States, I had to fight a great battle against frustration because of my poor English."

was very difficult to win because the best fighters in Japan were competing in it. I was very nervous. I had fought in other small tournaments but never in a big one like that.

Q: When did you decide to come to the United States?
A: The final decision was in 1965, but in 1963 I was helping Sensei Sakagami with a lot of demonstrations and I met Donn F. Draeger. Mr. Draeger was assisting his jiu-jitsu teacher, Takaji Shimizu, and I was helping Sensei Sakagami. I had no idea that meeting Donn would change the course of my life. We became good friends and he later introduced me to Dan Ivan. I remember that when I arrived in the States, I had to fight a great battle against frustration because of my poor English. I recall crying in bed for more than two days because I couldn't communicate. It was very difficult for me to adapt to a new culture and language. But Ed Parker gave a great opportunity to demonstrate my art publically at the 1965 Long Beach International Karate Championships, and that boosted my confidence and self-image.

"Thanks to Sensei Sakagami, I was able to receive my training from Kenshin Taira, a kongou-ryu kobudo master who died in 1973."

Q: Who was your first connection in California?
A: Dan Ivan. He used to travel to Japan a lot and we became friends. He brought me over and later offered me a partnership that lasted for a long time—not only in martial arts but in other businesses such as real estate. I would say that Mr. Ivan, along with Mr. Parker and Mr. Curtis Wong, helped me very, very much.

Q: Did you ever meet Bruce Lee?
A: Yes. He was very nice to me. Bruce had a very strong sense for everything related to martial arts. He always wanted to learn more and was never satisfied with what he had. I remember that after my book on nunchaku came out, he would call me up with questions about the weapon, which he was studying at that time.

Q: Dan Ivan is a shotokan stylist and you are a shito-ryu practitioner. How did you combine those two styles?
A: Well, out of respect for him I learned all the shotokan kata and taught them so the school would have the same curriculum. Once we separated our schools, I went back to teaching strictly traditional shito-ryu and kobudo. I don't recommend mixing styles. I tried to do it with shotokan and shito-ryu and it was impossible—it just didn't work. If you really understand

"Bruce had a very strong sense for everything related to martial arts. He always wanted to learn more and was never satisfied with what he had."

both styles' principles, they don't mix. There are a lot of reasons why many of today's modern innovators are going back to the traditional systems.

Q: You were one of the first to use music to display traditional karate in a modern way. Were you criticized by your peers in Japan?

A: Very much. Even my own instructor criticized me for using music and giving demonstrations in a park. I was really upset. I kept asking myself if I was doing something wrong. Then my mother, Masu, whom I consider to be the greatest inspiration in my life, came to the United States and saw me perform. That gave me a lot of power and strength. She basically said that everyone was jealous because of my new position. She told me that people were paying for watching the demonstrations and that I had to give them a great show. The final turning point was at the WUKO World Championships in Long Beach, California in 1975. I gave a great demonstration in front of all the great masters from Japan, including the President of the WUKO, Mr. Sasakawa. I received a standing ovation, the biggest of the whole tournament. I guess that day they understood that I was not prostituting the art but drawing more attention to it. That's why I didn't understand the initial criticism at all. I really like the feeling of history and respect that the traditional approach provides.

Q: What are shito-ryu's strong points?
A: The founder, Kenwa Mabuni, studied under two major teachers, Yasutsune Itosu (Shuri-te) and Kanryo Higaonna (Naha-te). He combined the soft and circular approach of Naha with the hard and more linear techniques from the Shuri system. He also added part of tomari-te, creating a very versatile karate method. You see, style does not matter; it's the instruction that counts.

"Kata should not change at all. It is the traditional part of karate. Karate is an art. In the past it was used for combat and fighting."

Q: Would you recommend the multi-style training approach?
A: No, not for beginners since this can be very confusing. At an advanced level I think it is very positive to learn something from other arts; the more you know about something, the more you can appreciate it. It doesn't mean that you have to like everything but at least understand it and have some respect for it.

Q: Do you think traditional kata has to be changed to adapt to modern times?
A: Kata should not change at all. It is the traditional part of karate. Karate is an art. In the past it was used for combat and fighting. Perhaps a master altered part of the kata for certain reasons, according to his practical combat

"In 1963 I was helping Sensei Sakagami with a lot of demonstrations and I met Donn F. Draeger. Mr. Draeger was assisting his jiu-jitsu teacher, Takaji Shimizu."

experience. To me, though, the kata has to be kept intact in modern times. Training methods and sparring techniques may change, but not kata.

Q: How do you perceive the modern approach to karate?
A: I think that people want too much, too quickly. They want to run before knowing how to walk; or learn advanced techniques without mastering the basics. You can't have a strong house without a strong foundation. The stronger the basics, the stronger the house—it's as simple as that. Unfortunately, a lot of practitioners don't understand. Competition has a good and a bad side. The worst thing is losing sight of your training just to

win a trophy. Sometimes, the trophy gets to be the most important thing and that's not right. The student loses so much when they think like that.

On the other hand, the good part is that competition can help the student learn about goal-setting. This allows the student to go through a learning process which includes a viable system of performance grading at the end of the process. I know that the end doesn't always seem to work, but what is important is that the student went through the process by increasing their training, focused their minds, et cetera. I would like to see all karate practitioners understand that competition is just a small aspect of their total training—it is not the ultimate aim.

"I would like to see all karate practitioners understand that competition is just a small aspect of their total training—it is not the ultimate aim."

Q: As a karate sensei and kobudo teacher, do you feel both arts are related?

A: Of course they are! I always say that they are like the two wheels of a bicycle. They work under the same principles. A full study of kobudo is not for everyone but I strongly recommend some weapons training to everyone. My approach to kobudo is different from that of my instructors, though; in the beginning I use it more for supplemental training.

Q: Which do you consider to be the best kobudo weapon?

A: I don't think there is a "best" weapon. They help you to develop different things. In fact, the kobudo weaponry is divided into three different cate-

"Sometimes people think that I'm doing great things for others, but in fact that's what a martial artist is supposed to be doing—helping others."

gories; long weapons like the bo; short weapons like the kama, sai, and tonfa; and hiding weapons such as the nunchaku.

Q: But didn't you always feel very comfortable with the nunchaku?
A: Yes. I consider the nunchaku to be a very good weapon. Unfortunately a lot of people misunderstand its use—maybe because of Bruce Lee's movies. They think you really need that much movement and swinging, when in real-life situations one simple swing is all it takes. There is no traditional kata in nunchaku training, but people made their own for practice and to structure the techniques—which I feel is very acceptable.

Q: You've have been involved in the movie industry, working with celebrities such as Sean Connery, Burt Lancaster, Wesley Snipes, and many more. But you received the majority of your recognition for your work in *The Karate Kid*.

A: I've been very fortunate. But as result of all that work, and seminars and videos, I had a heart attack. That made me take a look at my lifestyle. I used to leave the dojo for long periods of time on travel, but now I try to focus more on school and doing a little bit of movie work. That's it and I'm happy. I like to help people. Sometimes people think that I'm doing great things for others, but in fact that's what a martial artist is supposed to do—help others. That's what martial arts are all about.

Q: What is your personal training like now?

A: I guess everybody goes through the same process. When we are young we try to show how tough we are and we do a lot of kumite. When we get older and our body start to hurt, then we start to appreci-

"Martial arts training is not easy, but if you believe strongly enough in yourself, you can achieve anything."

ate kata. I emphasize more kata and kihon in my personal training. Sensei Sakagami always told me that the original Okinawan kata were easier on the body, because they put less stress on the joints. I didn't appreciate the truth of this until years later.

Q: What's your message for all martial artists?

A: Never give up. Martial arts training is not easy, but if you believe strongly enough in yourself, you can achieve anything. For me, that's the greatest part of being an instructor. I don't care about the money. If I help my students to become better human beings, that is the greatest reward. O

Masters' Techniques

Sensei Demura is caught in a headlock (1). He gets out by simultaneously stomping the foot and striking the groin (2-3). He then reaches for the hair with the left hand (4-5), and grabs the right leg with the right hand (6-7). He drops his enemy (8-9), and drives his middle knuckles into his nose and solar plexus (10-11).

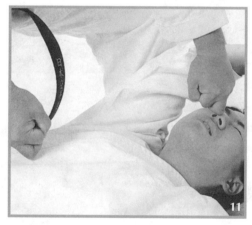

From an on-guard position (1), Sensei Demura counters a knife lunge from an attacker (2), by side-stepping (3), and blocking with the inside arm (4). He then circles the weapon arm and catches the wrist (5). Turning the body with his arm (6-7), Demura then elbows the attacker in the back (8).

William Dometrich

Western Master of the Eastern Way

ONE OF AMERICAN MARTIAL ARTS MOST KNOWLEDGEABLE AND RESPECTED TEACHERS, WILLIAM DOMETRICH IS A LIVING ICON OF TRADITIONAL KARATE VALUES AND A DIRECT LINK TO ITS MOST FABLED MASTERS. BORN MARCH 15, 1935, IN CLARKSBURG, WEST VIRGINIA, DOMETRICH READ AN ARTICLE IN 1950, IN READER'S DIGEST, ABOUT A MAN NAMED MAS OYAMA WHO HAD KILLED A RUNAWAY BULL ON A BEACH NEAR TOKYO, JAPAN. HE LATER READ AN ARTICLE IN TRUE MAGAZINE ABOUT KARATE AND KUNG-FU ENTITLED, "THE SCREAM AND THE EAGLE'S CLAW." HE JOINED THE U.S. ARMY AND WAS ASSIGNED TO THE JAPANESE OCCUPATION FORCE ON KYUSHU ISLAND, AFTER SERVING IN THE KOREAN CONFLICT. THERE, DOMETRICH WAS INTRODUCED TO KARATE BY A U.S. MARINE WHO HAD BEEN STATIONED IN OKINAWA AND BEGAN TRAINING IN CHITO-RYU UNDER ICHIRO SHIRAHAMA, A DIRECT STUDENT OF STYLE-FOUNDER TSUYOSHI CHITOSE.

Q: Sensei Dometrich, what is your current position in chito-ryu karate-do?
A: I'm the founder and head of the United States Chito-Ryu Federation. Originally a part of the Japan Chito-Kai and International Chito-Kai Federation, the U.S. Chito-Ryu Federation declared its independence in 1994, 12 years after the death of Doctor Chitose. Currently I try to cooperate with all chito-ryu organizations and teachers.

I started the first chito-ryu class in the United States in West Virginia in 1955, opened the first Cincinnati karate dojo with Harvey Eubank and Ray Hughes in 1961. I founded the United States Chito-Ryu Federation at the request of Doctor Chitose in 1967, and visited Japan and received 7th dan and the title of *kyoshi* from Doctor Chitose in 1971. I gave a demonstration in 1998 before the Japanese Imperial Family and received my 8th dan (*hanchidan*). In 1999 I received the title of *hanchi* from the Dai-Nippon Budodu Kai, the most prestigious martial arts organization in the world.

"When I inquired about karate one of them said that Dr. Chitose was the most outstanding karate teacher on the island of Kyushu."

Q: How long have you been practicing martial arts?

A: For 48 years now. When I was 15 years old, in 1950, I read about karate and was fascinated. I decided that the only way that I could get to Japan to study this unique art was to join the military—and that's what I did. When I got to Japan I saw a judo demonstration by some Japanese police officers. When I inquired about karate one of them said that Dr. Chitose was the most outstanding karate teacher on the island of Kyushu.

Q: How many styles have you trained in?

A: One, chito-ryu. I have, however, had many opportunities to train with some of the top instructors in other styles such as shito-ryu, goju-ryu, shotokan and other styles over the years, which I feel has enhanced my chito-ryu training.

Q: Sensei, who were your first teachers?

A: Tsuyoshi Chitose, Ichiro Shirahama and Hidika Ito.

Q: What set Dr. Chitose apart as a great teacher?

A: Compared to some of the other teachers I have seen, it was like he was in a different time zone. He was extremely sharp, even into his 80s, and would see things that others missed. He had a fantastic intellect and was talented physically as well. He had tremendous power and his hands were like vice grips. When I was at a tournament with Mr. Okazaki and Mr. Nishiyama in Philadelphia, Richard Kim came up and asked me who my teacher was. When I told him it was Dr. Chitose he said, "Mr. Dometrich, I will tell you something you most likely don't know. Back during the height of the Japanese Empire, during 1934-1936, Dr. Chitose was considered the greatest master of kata in the world." Almost as an afterthought I asked, "Who said he was?" Mr. Kim answered, "Gichin Funakoshi himself."

Q: Were you close to him out-side of karate?

A: He became more of a father to me than a teacher. He was a very kind man and had a wonderful smile. But a lot of times when you were training, if you made a mistake several times in a row, he could give you that look which let you know that you should never make that mistake again and should pay more attention. He was just a great individual.

Q: Did he emphasize self-defense in his training?

A: To a certain degree. More so than a lot of the more modern Japanese styles do now. Dr. Chitose was born in Okinawa. When he went to grade school one of his first teachers was

"I think that the masters who came from Okinawa did a lot of self-defense training."

Gichin Funakoshi. I think that the masters who came from Okinawa did a lot of self-defense training. I think that some of the later styles in Japan concentrated more on the sportive aspect of the art.

Q: Would you tell us some stories about your early days training karate in Japan and the U.S.?

A: I have few! When I was in Japan the first time I heard about a very tough Japanese karateka who lived on the western side of Kyushu. While I was in Japan I never had the opportunity nor the misfortune of meeting him. I met him during he summer of 1963 when I was in Toronto, Canada. He was a perfect gentleman, which surprised me greatly. After we arrived at his dojo and he changed into his karate gi, I met the terror of Kyushu. His entire being underwent a complete transformation. Standing before me was a serious, dedicated, no-nonsense karate sensei, and for a long time I had a fear of him. His name was Masami Tsuruoka, the father of Canadian karate. I feel the training was harder then, than it now is. There were little or no breaks, and minor injuries were neglected. I feel that the technique currently is better

"I now realize that some of the most effective techniques are not that impressive looking nor photogenic."

than it was then, but the spirit of the old dojo was fantastic. Joe Lewis, who is in my mind the equivalent of an American Choki Motobu, was a product of this hard and spirited training. Once a sensei, who wishes to remain anonymous, was going to break a board which was approximately 2"x 2" x 6' long with his shin. One of the instructors there yelled, "If you break it into four pieces that would really impress me." The sensei had two students hold each end of the stick and kicked it with his right leg. It split lengthwise. He then kicked it again with his left shin and it broke into four pieces. "Like that?" he asked the other instructor. I also saw this same instructor follow a student out of the dojo which was surrounded by at least three feet of snow. The student had dropped his car keys in a snow bank. He had looked for five minutes and could not find them. The sensei walked to the large snow bank, plunged his hand in withdrew it a second later and handed the student his lost keys. "How could you do that?" the student inquired. "How come you couldn't?" the sensei answered.

Q: How did Westerners respond to traditional Japanese training.
A: Most of the early Americans in Japan responded to traditional Japanese training very well. They were Marines, Paratroopers, Army Rangers, and Navy UDT, the forerunner of the modern U S Navy Seals. Many of them brought karate to America in the late '40s and early '50s and are still training. The training in the United States and Japan also has undergone a great change over the past forty years. It is more technical now with much more kumite. Many years ago we did a great deal of kata and self-defense training and very little kumite.

Q: Were you natural in karate? Did the movements come easily to you?
A: I was by no means a gifted karate student, although I learned the basics fairly easily. I had a very hard time, however, of getting the movements to flow and in the development of *kime*. Over years of training I slowly developed the ability to develop more power and better movement.

Q: How has your personal karate changed and developed over the years?
A: My techniques now look softer than they did years ago but they are really more powerful. I have come to realize that a great many of the techniques which impressed me when I started, no longer do. I now realize that some of the most effective techniques are not that impressive looking nor photogenic.

Q: What are the most importance points of your teaching days?
A: I am still teaching as much as time and old injuries allow me too. Today when I teach I attempt to view my teaching from my student's eyes; in this way I become a better teacher. This is something I never did years ago.

"He became more of a father to me than a teacher. He was a very kind man and he had a wonderful smile."

Q: With all of the technical changes during the last 30 years, do you think there is still a pure shotokan, chito-ryu, et cetera?

A: One of the basic tenants of Buddhism is that all things are impermanent; life is in a constant change from the day we are born until the day we die. I believe that a great majority of the traditional Okinawan and Japanese styles in America are being well taken care of by traditional American and Japanese sensei who live in this country. Their various *ryu* are progressing at a reasonable rate in the US. Of course, there are always those few select individuals who study a little of this and a little of that making green belt in one style and brown belt in another and soon proclaim that they are the master of their own style.

Q: Do you think different *ryu* are important?

A: Yes I do. The various *ryu* are like a modern road map which allows us to glance into karate history and see how karate has evolved into what we practice today.

Q: What is your opinion of kickboxing and other events such as the UFC?

A: I don't follow them, so I have no knowledge on which to base an opinion, as I am busy training in traditional karate. I feel that it is OK if people like them and want to follow them. Don't misunderstand me, I'm not saying they are wrong but for me I prefer the older disciplines based on Japanese Budo. I believe they provide a long-term education for the individual's character. This helps people to improve as human beings, not only as fighters.

Q: Do you think that karate in the West has caught up with Japanese karate?

A: In some areas we have done wonders, so my answer is yes. But we still have many years of hard training ahead of us before we totally catch up.

Q: Do you feel that there are fundamental differences in the physical capabilities of Japanese karateka in comparison to European or American karateka?

A: Yes. Many of the American instructors I know have a broader overview of karate than their Japanese counterpart. The Japanese, however, in many cases are better trained in the basics than many Americans. Many of the Japanese will work a few basics for months or years. Most Americans always want to learn something new.

Q: Karate is now often referred to as a sport—would you agree with this definition?

A: We have taken something which was never meant to be a sport, and have made a sport out of it. In this context I guess we could call it a sport. No sport can be a Budo nor can a true Budo become a sport. So karate has split into two factions, Budo and sport.

"Each day of practice brings us closer to perfection which means we have not yet mastered the art of karate."

Q: Do you feel you still have further to go in your studies?

A: Certainly I have a long way to go, after all I am not dead yet. In chito-ryu karate we have no masters. Each day of practice brings us closer to perfection, which means we have not yet mastered the art of karate. My teacher Chitose sensei trained almost up until the time he passed away in 1984. "Each day I don my karate gi and train, I learn something new," he personally told me when he was 84. I hope to follow in his footsteps.

Q: How do you see Japanese karate in America at this time?

A: I think it is very strong because of the dedicated teachers who have devoted themselves to its teaching. I know of many dojo around the United States which are almost equivalent to the old Japanese and Okinawan dojo of decades ago. We are making progress.

Q: Do you think it helps karate physically to train with weapons?

A: For the more advanced students I feel that kobudo offers great benefits. I feel that beginners should spend all of their time training in karate basics.

"Tradition and self defense are the most important.
Sport will come in third in my opinion."

Q: What is your opinion of makiwara training?
A: I favor it. My dojo has several makiwara and next year we hope to install additional ones. It is the forge of traditional karate.

Q: Do you think the practitioner's training should be different from his teaching schedule as instructor?
A: Yes I do, but please let me qualify that. An instructor teaches many students of different abilities and skill levels and grades. He must continue to train in his many kata daily, many of which the majority of his students may not know. Because of this he needs to train in his basics but not neglect his more advanced techniques while doing so.

Q: When teaching the art of karate, what is the most important element: self-defense, sport, or tradition?
A: Tradition and self-defense are the most important. Sport comes in third in my opinion. Of course this varies from instructor to instructor.

Q: Kata and kumite: what is the proper ratio in training?

A: The answer to this will vary from school to school and instructor to instructor. I personally feel that the mix should be that for every hour of kata you should do a half hour of kumite.

Q: Some people feel that going to Japan to train is highly necessary; do you share this point of view?

A: With all of the good, traditional karate schools in the United States I do not feel that it is necessary, especially for the newer students who are just beginning their karate training. For advanced students I think that a trip is very worthwhile.

"People are looking back at the teachings of the old masters and thinking that perhaps we've strayed from them, and are wanting to learn them."

Q: What are the major changes in the art since you began?

A: Instruction has improved tremendously during the past forty-some years. The tournament concept for sport karate has matured around the world. There are many very mature traditional karate schools in the U.S. and the Western world. I think traditional karate is going to come back very strongly. Karate is more well-known now. The popularity is because of sport karate, there's no doubt about it. I have no problem with sport karate because that is one aspect of karate training. But as we see in professional sports, a lot of athletes have bad attitudes towards the referees, toward the other players, and toward the judges. I just hate to think that this particular attitude will bleed over into karate sports. I think that karate sports should be based on courtesy, first and foremost. People now are very interested in the history of karate, going back as far as two centuries. People are looking back at the teachings of the old masters and thinking that perhaps we've strayed from them, and are wanting to learn them. I think the future holds great promise for traditional karate as well as sport karate.

Q: Who would you like to have trained with if you could pick anyone?

A: Kenwa Mabuni, the founder of shito-ryu. With his vast knowledge of traditional karate kata and its history I feel that to have had the opportunity to train with him would have been a great honor.

"A truly dedicated student should find a qualified teacher and then make a commitment to study their chosen style and to perfect the style they have chosen."

Q: What would you say to someone who is interested in starting to learn karate?

A: Try to research various elements of the martial arts prior to joining any martial arts school. With the various Web sites they may want to start there. I would also tell them to visit several schools, more than once if at all possible, prior to making their decision. Most importantly, I would tell them not to be impressed by flashy techniques, lots of trophies in the window, or be taken in by promises. Choosing a qualified instructor will be the most important thing they will do as a new martial artist.

Q: What is it that keeps you motivated after all of these years?

A: Two people, Doctor Tsuyoshi Chitose who passed away in 1984, who inspired me greatly, and my wife Barbara Ellen who continues to inspire me to this day by her deep understanding of the spirit of Budo.

Q: Do you think it is necessary to engage in free-fighting to achieve good fighting skill in the street?

A: While it is not the most important thing on the teaching agenda, I feel that some sparring training helps the student to relax, increase their timing, and helps improve their distance awareness. All of these are necessary in any street confrontation.

Q: What is your opinion about mixing karate styles like shotokan and goju-ryu, uechi-ryu, and shito-ryu? Does the practice of one nullify the effectiveness of the other or can it be beneficial to the student?

A: Personally, combining various styles of karate and then coming up with "shoju-ryu" or "uecto-ryu" is a bad idea. A truly dedicated student should find a qualified teacher and then make a commitment to study their chosen style and to perfect the style they have chosen. This commitment, if it is a true commitment, will be a life long commitment. Now I would like to add that I have no problem with high black belts or their students taking clinics from other well-qualified black belts. After the clinic ends, however, always return to your original style.

"Now that I am older, I realize that I no longer have a philosophical outlook. I just train. It is like breathing, I just do it."

Q: Modern karate is moving away from the bunkai in kata practice how important do you think bunkai is in the understanding of kata and karate-do in general?

A: To tell the truth, I am mildly surprised at this question. In the Midwest area of the United States I have found that a great many of the traditional karate teachers are now stressing bunkai training to a greater extent now than they did ten years ago. They also train the *kaisetz* applications of the kata, the *te-gumite* methods and others. But to answer your question, I am positive that without bunkai training, karate kata training becomes merely a form of ballet and the students will never truly grasp the essence of traditional karate-do.

Q: What is your philosophical basis for your karate training?

A: In the beginning there was none over the years, however, my philosophical outlook has developed and broadened, then one day I woke up and realized I was a Buddhist. Now that I am older, I realize that I no longer have a philosophical outlook. I just train. It is like breathing, I just do it.

Q: Do you have a particularly memorable karate experience which is an inspiration for your training?

A: I have a student who has been with me now for over thirty-five years. I have many who have inspired me, however, I would like to talk about this student. He is truly an inspiration to all who have come to know him. He moved to Florida in the early '70s, taught karate in his back yard, and finally built the largest chito-kai karate dojo in the United States. He built the dojo with a few of his students. He paid for everything out of his own pocket. He does not charge his students dues, and he taught them for free. He has had heart attacks, diabetics and has lost part of his foot. He still trains to the best of his ability. His name is Art Rott and he is now 83 years old. He inspires me greatly. He is an example for everybody to follow.

Q: After all of these years of training and experience can you explain the meaning of the practice of karate-do?

A: This is really hard to do because you can explain ideas, but it is impossible to describe an experience, but I will attempt it. Karate has become to me the same as breathing or eating. I just do it. I have made many good friends through my karate training. I feel that overall, my physical fitness is much better than most people my age. It is a great stress reducer. Karate training to me is like life, you just do it, you don't think about it. I don't approach karate training with a calculating mind. I know it's difficult but we must strive to do karate without thinking about other additional things such as fame and money. When you train in the martial arts and try to calculate everything, then you're defeated from the very beginning because you reasons are the wrong reasons. The arts of Budo are very special, but at the same time we must try to not make them special. Just do them naturally, as part of life. It's not good to have false and unrealistic hopes when we train, because in the end we'll be very disappointed with ourselves. Train for the sake of training, that's the point!

Q: How do you think a practitioner can increase their understanding of the spiritual aspects of karate?

A: Learn to practice *zazen* properly, then do it. The idea of the art of Budo is to forget yourself and throw everything you have into practice. It is simple, there is nothing more to it. And one day you'll understand. It's something that has to be experienced, not told or explained.

Q: How much training should a senior karateka be doing to improve and get better at the art?

A: This depends upon the senior's age and health. I try to practice a little each day whether I am at the dojo or not.

Q: Is there anything lacking in the way martial artist are taught today, compared with those who were taught in your day?

A: We have only a few very spirited karateka today, however years ago everyone had very great spirit. If we didn't I do not think we would have survived.

Q: What are the most important qualities of a successful karateka?

A: The first is the desire to study karate. The second is the ability to find a qualified teacher. The third and perhaps the most important, is never quit. Loyalty, spirit, a never-say-die attitude, and intelligence are the most important attributes of a student. Unfortunately, is very easy for the students to get bored with the art, but in many cases they are bored with themselves. This is very common today not just in karate training but in society itself. People, after a short time, trade families, change jobs, et cetera. In Budo, discouragement is part of the training, there is nothing wrong with being discouraged. The important point is not to misunderstand it and quit practice, but to keep training as usual. It takes times, but in the end you realize that there was no reason to be discouraged. This is the reason why karate-do practice should bring meaning into your life in the sense that it shows you who you really are, and how you should react to the circumstances surrounding you.

"In Budo, discouragement is part of the training, there is nothing wrong with being discouraged. The important point is not to misunderstand it and quit practice, but to keep training as usual."

Q: What advice would you give to students about supplementary training?

A: I would encourage them to use supplementary training and training aids to assist them in obtaining karate skill. I would also remind them to not overtrain and never forget their kata.

Q: There is very little written about you in magazines, et cetera—you obviously do not thrive on publicity. Why?

A: I really don't know. Fame is fleeting so why chase it. I would prefer to dedicate myself to try to get more articles in magazines around the world about my teacher Dr. Tsuyoshi Chitose, who was a major teacher in Japan, but unfortunately is not so well-known here.

Q: Who stands out among the karate men you've met?

A: I have to first start out with Dr. Chitose, of course. I think another great man who has almost been passed over by history has been Marami Suroka.

He's my big brother, my *sempi*. When he was younger and I was younger, he was the one who always tried to keep me straight, back in the late '60s and early '70s. Mr. Nishiyama is a terrific karate man. As far as historians go, I'd have to say Patrick McCarthy—he's just unbelievable. But one person who has always been very kind to me and also a very good friend is Fumio Demura—he helps everybody. Because of that I think Sensei Demura will go down in history as one of the greatest karate masters ever.

Q: Have there been times when you felt fear in your karate training?
A: Yes, on many occasions. Fear is part of Budo training. Feeling fear is irrelevant, what is important is how you control, redirect and use this fear to overcome difficulties.

Q: What are your thoughts on the future of karate-do?
A: I think that traditional karate is in good hands and will continue to be in good hands in the future. We now have many qualified, dedicated, and motivated instructors throughout the world. The seed has been planted and it will continue to grow. Personally, in my school we do more Budo, actually. We do some sports, but not very much. We're primarily interested in the development of the individual as a better, kinder person. We feel that karate is great for good health, for stress reduction, and we cover self-defense aspects of the martial arts much more than the sportive aspects.

Q: Has your wife played any part in your pioneering role in American karate?
A: She is the power behind the throne, so to speak—no doubt about it. Without her I wouldn't have anything. She's the one who maintains the *honbu* dojo—the mother dojo—here in the United States. Without her we would really be hard pressed. I owe her more than words can ever express.

Q: How would you like to be thought of in the world of karate.
A: Just as an average guy who didn't have a lot of natural talent but who worked very hard and was very loyal to his teacher. Also as someone who trained hard and achieved his goals through hard work. Anyone can reach their goals if they work hard.

Q: Sensei, do you have any general advice you would care to pass on to karateka everywhere?
A: Always be loyal to your original instructor and never, ever quit. O

Facing his opponent (1), Sensei Dometrich blocks the punch (2), strikes and kicks simultaneously (3), attacks the knee (4), strikes to the head (5), and finishes by locking the neck (6).

Teruo Hayashi

In Pursuit of Karate Excellence

HAYASHI SENSEI IS ONE OF THE WORLD'S MOST RESPECTED AND ADMIRED KARATE MAS-
TERS. BORN IN NAHA, ON THE ISLAND OF HONSHU, OCTOBER 1924, HAYASHI TERUO
STARTED IN JUDO AND EARNED HIS BLACK BELT AT AGE 16. HE REACHED HIS 3RD DAN
IN JUDO AT 23 YEARS OF AGE AND WAS CONSIDERED ONE OF THE MOST PROMISING
YOUNG BLACK BELTS OF THAT GENERATION. HOWEVER, ONCE HE WATCHED KARATE HE
BECAME SO IMPRESSED THAT HE GAVE UP EVERYTHING TO STUDY IT FULL TIME. TODAY HE
IS THE CHIEF INSTRUCTOR OF JAPAN KARATE-DO HAYASHI-HA SHITO-RYU.

SENSEI HAYASHI STARTED HIS KARATE TRAINING IN OSAKA, JAPAN, UNDER KOSEI
KUNIBA, AN ORIGINAL SHITO-RYU KARATE-DO STUDENT OF KENWA MABUNI, WHO ALSO
RECEIVED INSTRUCTION FROM CHOKI MOTOBU AND FUNAKOSHI GICHIN. LATER ON,
HAYASHI WENT TO STUDY UNDER THE GREAT MASTER OF THE GOJU-RYU SYSTEM, SEKO
HIGA, FROM WHOM HE LEARNED A GREAT DEAL OF PRACTICAL KNOWLEDGE OF THE
NAHA-TE METHODS. THIS INSPIRED HIM TO TRAVEL TO OKINAWA FOR FURTHER STUDIES.

IN OKINAWA, HE PRACTICED SHORIN-RYU WITH CHOSIN CHIBANA AND THEN
ANOTHER SHORIN-RYU METHOD UNDER CHOJIN NAGAMINE AND MASTER NAGA. HE
ALSO STUDIED KOBUDO UNDER MASTER HOHAN SOKEN, SHINKEN TAIRA AND KENKO
NAKAIMA, WHO NOT ONLY TAUGHT HIM KOBUDO, BUT ALSO A KARATE METHOD
CALLED "RYUEI-RYU." SENSEI HAYASHI DECIDED TO NAME HIS KOBUDO METHOD "KEN-
SHIN-RYU," WHICH MEANS "HEART," AND IS ANOTHER WAY OF SAYING "RYUEI-RYU."

KNOWN INTERNATIONALLY AS "THE WEAPONS MAN," BECAUSE OF HIS IMMENSE
SKILL AND KNOWLEDGE, HE BECAME RESPONSIBLE FOR REFEREEING TOURNAMENTS OF
THE WORLD UNION KARATE-DO ORGANIZATIONS, OR WUKO. SENSEI HAYASHI IS
RECOGNIZED AS A GREAT MASTER WHO DEVOTED MOST OF HIS LIFE TO A SELFLESS DEDI-
CATION IN PURSUIT OF KARATE EXCELLENCE.

Q: How did you start training in martial arts?
A: I remember that I was strongly attracted to martial arts at a very young
age. I began training in judo and I got my black belt at 16. I was 20 when I
went to the military service and I served as a co-pilot in the Air Force during
the war. For a long time I could not train openly since all martial arts systems were prohibited by the Americans—but nobody could prevent me

*"When I reached 3rd dan, many people considered me
one of the most promising students of my generation."*

from training privately with my friends. When I reached 3rd dan, many people considered me one of the most promising students of my generation. Almost three years later I was introduced to an unknown martial art called "karate." After training for a while, I fell in love with the art and I gave up everything else. I decided that I wanted to be a full-time karate student.

Q: Who was your first teacher?
A: When I was 18 I went to live in Osaka. I started with Master Kosei Kuniba and then I studied the goju-ryu style under Master Seko Higa. He taught a great deal and I progressed very consistently for a long time. But then I decided to go to Okinawa to train. The main reason I did this is because I believed Okinawa to be the cradle of the martial arts, and I wanted strongly to go to the source of the knowledge. Now I know I was right because I was astonished by the amount of knowledge that I received there. I studied shorin-ryu under Choshin Nagamine, and I was formally introduced to the art of kobudo which I studied under Hohan Soken, Shiken Taira, and Nakaima Kenko, who also was a karate master of a method called "ryuei-ryu."

"In fact, I incorporated much of the ryuei-ryu theory into my own style."

Q: Did Nakaima Kenko train you in empty-hand karate methods?
A: Yes, he did. As a matter of fact, it was very difficult for me to be accepted into his dojo. Ryuei-ryu is a family art imported from Southern China over three generations before I went to Okinawa. The reason I went to him was because I was looking for a kobudo teacher. At the time, it was almost impossible to find a master who would teach an outsider, which is what I was. When I found Nakaima Kenko, his only student was his son and he had no intention of breaking that tradition. I sat in front of his house for many hours and begged for months until he decided to accept me as a disciple.

Q: What method did you study under him?
A: Well, he taught me mostly the *kama* and the *sai,* and the empty-hand method of karate. In fact, I incorporated much of the ryuei-ryu theory into my own style. My other two kobudo teachers were Hohan Soken, from whom I studied the bo and kama, and Shiken Taira who gave me a lot of knowledge in several other kobudo weapons.

"Each master had his own specialty since they were transmitting the knowledge in the same way they had received it from their instructors."

Q: Why did you study under so many masters?

A: Well, this is a very complicated question. To begin with, each master only knew two weapons perfectly, and it was mostly in the form of kata. Each master had his own specialty since they were transmitting the knowledge in the same way they had received it from their instructors. When I arrived in Okinawa I realized that if the students of karate didn't do something, all these systems were going to die. So I committed myself to perpetuate these arts and when I returned back to Japan I kept all the information intact, but I updated some things and I tried to evolve a more practical and realistic way of training. Unfortunately, kobudo practice has degenerated around the world. You can find people who just took a couple of classes and became self-proclaimed masters. Then they teach and give certification and ranking! Some of them just take a short trip to Okinawa and return as a 5th dan. I think this is really a shame and personally I just don't want to have anything to do with that.

Q: Do you think that training in different disciplines is beneficial?

A: Let me put it this way: it is very important to go deeply into one art and study everything related to it such as body movement, mechanism in the delivery of the techniques and body awareness, and to educate your body about the finer points, applying the proper energy, et cetera. When you truly understand your art after many years of practice and research, then you can look into something else and immediately have a greater appreciation of it because of your level of understanding. If you practice many styles without a base and without going deeply in one, you'll become a "jack of all trades, master of none." It is only after many years of training that you can research other methods effectively.

Q: You have a great reputation as a fighter. In fact, it is well known that you used to travel and challenge other teachers.

A: Yes, but let me explain this. Let me start by saying that no modern martial artist should ever degrade his art by trying the techniques out in the street or by going to challenge any other school master or martial arts method. Times are very different now. What I used to do, some say was brave, others foolish, but in fact it was an honored tradition known as dojo *yaburi*. You fight against the lowest rank until you defeat the dojo's senpai. Then and only then, do you have the right to challenge the sensei himself. Probably, because of this practice, I became infamous and very good at kumite. Some didn't accept my challenge and would not let me get inside the door. Others, of course, did. Anyway, upon reflection I realized the reasons for my street-fighting were wrong.

"Every time I got hurt, I used to go back and train much harder; so by the time I'd fight again I'd be able to win."

Q: Did you ever get seriously injured during any of these matches?

A: Yes. Numerous broken ribs, a broken leg, a broken jaw, knee injuries, et cetera. But I always thought that if I was injured it was my fault for not being skillful enough to block or avoid the attacks properly. Every time I got hurt, I used to go back and train much harder; so by the time I'd fight again I'd be able to win. Please, don't assume that all my matches were against one person. On one occasion I fought ten men. I suffered head cuts but I was happy to find out that karate was and is a very good self-defense method.

Q: Did you defeat all of them?

A: No! I laid most of them out—but then I ran away!

"I train hard every day. I've seen very good martial artists that stopped training after the 40-year-old mark. The secret is to keep training hard."

Q: Is it true that Kuniba Kosei asked you to be his successor?

A: Well, he asked me on his deathbed to lead his organization until his son, Shogo Kuniba, reached a level of maturity sufficient to assume the leadership. So I did. I became the president of seishin kai until 1970. After that, I passed Sensei Shogo Kuniba the mantle of leadership and decided to go on my own with hayashi-ha shito-ryu kai.

Q: How do you keep yourself in such a good shape?

A: I train hard every day. I've seen very good martial artists that stopped training after the 40-year-old mark. The secret is to keep training hard. Of course, you're going to lose some speed and power in your technique but you can make it up with superior experience and knowledge about both the mental aspects and the real way the techniques work. You must focus on developing what I call "fighting soul." On the other hand, there is no way of bypassing the basic school of learning the technique; there is no way around it.

In order to achieve this there is something every practitioner has to understand—your body changes and your karate changes with your body. You become softer as you grow older. Some young practitioners don't understand that everybody's karate has to be different, must be different, as the karateka gets older. It would be stupid for a 50-year-old practitioner to try to keep doing the same karate that he did when he was 25. It's against nature and common sense. For instance, take the principle of kime; it takes more time for a young practitioner to achieve the correct kime in the physical motion. For an older and more experienced karateka the time for the right kime in shorter. Some techniques can be very effective for young people, but they are impossible for an older practitioner to make work.

There are other kinds of skill the real karateka should aim for when he gets older. Many people ask me if I have changed my karate. Well, sometimes the question is confusing so I have to be very careful when I answer. I did change my karate because I have changed myself both physically and mentally. I'm more experienced now than 20 years ago and have a broader perspective of things. My perception of life and of the world has evolved, therefore, yes, I have changed and these changes definitely affect the art I'm teaching. On the other hand, I don't teach karate to please the student. I teach the art the way I think it should be taught. Period. But as a teacher, I need to find better ways to communicate and pass the knowledge, depending on whom I'm teaching at that time. Students have different backgrounds, education levels, understanding, et cetera and you have to adapt accordingly.

Q: What's your opinion about grading?
A: Well, in the old days the whole purpose was increasing one's own skill. We cared about karate training, not about rank. Belt ranking came from judo. We used to train hard and if we got a dan along the way, fine, but it was never the goal of the training. I'm totally against the concept of selling grades as is happening all over the world. I think this is a shame for the karate world. Students get advancement in grading because the monetary connotations of what they represent.

"I don't teach karate to please the student. I teach the art the way I think it should be taught. Period."

Q: Do you believe in the use of ki?
A: Well, we all have the energy but I don't like to spend time theorizing about it. I try to steer clear of that mysterious approach to karate training. The real skills come from correct training methods, strong conditioning and endless repetition. Too many stories have been around the art for too long; this master used to puncture an oil drum with his toes, that master's dojo had footprints on the ceiling, et cetera. I think it is more important to develop a fighting spirit which allows us to keep fighting against all the odds in life. That's why my classes are very hard. Good hard training is what I consider important. If you develop a proper understanding of the art with correct technique, timing, and kime, using your body accordingly,

"Training should not stop once you remove your gi. Without the right spirit your karate will be of little use."

you'll be able to not only cope with different opponents, but also different situations in life. I do believe that a student must be strong, not only physically but also morally. I don't accept lazy people or those who lack willpower as students. It is important for the student to learn the true Budo mind and spirit. I understand that this is very difficult since the description of Budo is very confusing.

Q: What is your best advice for karate practitioners?
A: Always train in the basics. This is something I noticed during all the past years; some top-competitors have very weak basics, they lack kihon. And after the competition years, it is very hard for them to progress in the true art of karate-do. There is nothing wrong with training these basic competition techniques and becoming a champion, but the art of karate is not a sport, it deals with self-defense and this is another subject altogether. You can't build a house with just two or three tools, you need a variety of tools to accomplish that goal. On the other hand, training should not stop once you remove your gi. Without the right spirit your karate will be of little use.

I would recommend striving to be intelligent. I'm talking about the proper attitude towards learning. One person can be intellectual and not intelligent. Of course, the academic aspect helps in karate training but it is not absolutely necessary. In the same way that a high education doesn't imply that the person has a high IQ, being academic in the art doesn't mean that you truly understand what you're doing. I understand that after many years of training the trick is how to get motivated to do the same things that you have been doing for so long. Fortunately, there are a lot of methods to achieve this. What is important is understanding how to achieve more with less training. This stage is reserved for those who have trained for many years. After a long time practicing, less training can bring more results than more training at an earlier stage. Nevertheless, the main point is to keep training and keep constantly seeking the right attitude.

Q: Are you against sport competition?

A: No, not at all. To a certain extent, competition helps to improve your fighting ability—but in my time karate was full-contact karate; it was knock-out karate. I like contact karate because it is a very good method of making you cautious and it forces you to have your eyes open. The competition system is improving but there is still a long way to go in order to achieve the right scoring system that encompasses both the Budo and the sport aspects.

For instance, the *ippon shobu* system makes a fighter very careful, they have to be more precise and the technique more powerful. This is more realistic because when you fight for your life you fight more carefully, too. Competitive kumite has changed a few things—for instance, the concept of *"mai"* or "critical distance." In the past we used to fight each other from further away. The idea was to make the opponent enter into our *mai* to deliver a decisive blow. These days, the fighting distance in competition is shorter because they know that even if they get hit they're not going to die from it. The real dimension of danger has disappeared. Nevertheless, and at least to me, both aspects are very closely linked and constitute what we call "modern karate."

In Okinawa, the art is practiced as a method of self-exploration, as an internal research, without focusing on fighting. And this is perfect for those who look for that particular goal but for those who look at karate as a fighting art, competition is necessary. On the other hand, the real purpose of karate training in not to get dan or compete against your fellow student but rather self-improvement as an individual, finding your own way in the martial arts. Karate doesn't have to be your whole life but a major part of it. The philosophy and the training will help the practitioner to cope not only with difficult situations but also to show the proper respect to every human being. And that is tremendously important.

Q: What do you feel is wrong with karate today?

A: There are too many so-called self-promoted karate-do schools who will issue certification and rankings to non-qualified instructors. This practice not only dilutes the quality of the art but actually degrades karate-do to the public. Karate-do training should constantly pursue higher technical perfection. The practitioner should reflect how their achievements have enhanced society as a whole. Karate-do should be a lifelong endeavor which is enjoyable and beneficial, and not seen as a personal burden. O

Morio Higaonna

The Master, The Warrior

HE IS A MASTER, HE IS A WARRIOR, HE IS ONE OF THE MOST CHARISMATIC KARATE INSTRUCTORS IN THE ENTIRE WORLD. BORN IN 1940, THE SON OF A POLICEMAN, SENSEI HIGAONNA'S AMAZING KNOWLEDGE OF BOTH KARATE AND GOJU-RYU HISTORY HAS CONFOUNDED PRACTITIONERS FROM ALL STYLES AND DISCIPLINES. THE CHIEF INSTRUCTOR AND FOUNDER OF THE INTERNATIONAL GOJU KARATE FEDERATION, HE HAS SPREAD THE TEACHINGS AND TRADITIONS OF ORIGINAL GRANDMASTER CHOJUN MIYAGI TO ALL CORNERS OF THE WORLD. HIS POWER, SPEED, AND QUICK SMILE ARE SECOND TO NONE, AND THE CALLUSES ON HIS HANDS SHOW HIS LETHAL DEVOTION TO KARATE-DO.

FROM OKINAWA TO JAPAN, FROM JAPAN TO CALIFORNIA, AND THEN BACK TO THE FAR EAST AGAIN, HIGAONNA'S SPIRIT HAS BEEN FORGED IN THE FIRE OF TRADITIONAL KARATE TRAINING AND SHAPED BY THE HAMMER OF HIS INTENSE WILL AND DEDICATION. MANY OTHER TEACHER DON'T HESITATE TO SAY THAT HIGAONNA'S STUDENTS ARE THE BEST ALL-AROUND KARATEKA IN TERMS OF RESPECT, TRAINING SPIRIT, AND SAMURAI COOPERATION. HE IS A LIVING EXAMPLE TO ALL KARATE PRACTITIONERS OF HOW THE ART CAN SHAPE A MAN INTO A WARRIOR. HIS GOAL, THOUGH, HAS NEVER BEEN TO GLORIFY HIMSELF, BUT RATHER TO PRESERVE AND PERPETUATE THE TRADITIONAL TEACH-INGS HE LEARNED IN CHOJUN MIYAGI'S FAMOUS GARDEN DOJO.

Q: When did you start to train?
A: My father taught me the basic techniques of shorinji-ryu, but he didn't feel very comfortable doing so. Later on I went to train under Shimabuku, not the famous isshin-ryu master, and other teachers until I end up with An'ichi Miyagi.

Q: There are some wild stories about you as a teenager.
A: I used to skip school and steal food. I'd rather spend the day at the beach than go to school. I was really shy, but also a difficult child.

"I started under An'ichi Miyagi who was running Grandmaster Chojun Miyagi's school—the original garden dojo. I felt in love with goju-ryu on the very first day."

Q: How you were introduced to goju-ryu?

A: It was Shimabuku who recommended goju-ryu. He thought that me being stocky would fit very good into the style. So I started under An'ichi Miyagi who was running Grandmaster Chojun Miyagi's school—the original garden dojo. I felt in love with goju-ryu on the very first day. I started to train up to six hours a day!

Q: What was Aichi Miyagi like?

A: He started to train under Grandmaster Miyagi right after the war in 1948. He joined the school with three other boys who, considering his weak body, expected him to quit right away. Yet An'ichi was the only one to stay and keep training at the dojo! Grandmaster Miyagi used to teach the history of the art to An'ichi—the oral traditions and the philosophy—but not before he had finished the chores of fixing the house, cleaning the garden, et cetera. After the grandmaster's death, his wife decided to keep the dojo open with An'ichi as the instructor. Later on, the garden dojo was closed and everyone moved over the new dojo named the "Jundokan" operated by Eichi Miyazato.

Q: Why did you leave Okinawa and go to Japan?

A: Master An'ichi joined the Merchant Marines and left the dojo to travel all over the world. I decided to move to Tokyo in order to study at Takushoku University and teach karate. A teacher there was one of my old classmates named Ryujo Aragaki. When he left I took over the teaching. It was a great time for me—just teaching and training the whole day!

Q: Some say that An'ichi sensei was only a child when he trained with Chojun Miyagi sensei, that he learned only part of the system, and that his character was questionable.

A: If it wasn't so funny this would make me very angry. It's also very ironic, but please let me explain this in detail and clarify it once and for all. People seem unwilling to accept my word that my teacher is the little-known

An'ichi Miyagi, but willing to accept the claims of one of my former students that his teacher was Chojun Miyagi the founder of goju-ryu. This despite the fact that he would have been barely more than an infant when Chojun sensei died. They ignore the truth but accept the ludicrous. The fact of the matter is very simple. When, full of nervous excitement and with the money my mother had given me clenched in my fist, I first went to the garden dojo of Chojun Miyagi sensei as a boy of 16, I was told by Koshin Iha, a student of Chojun Miyagi sensei, "If you want to train seriously An'ichi will teach you." He has taught me every since; I only have the one teacher. At first I was not particularly impressed by An'ichi sensei. Although his movements were very smooth and powerful, I was more impressed by the naked power of the younger students, Saburo Higa particularly. You could feel the rush of wind when he kicked and punched and the physique he developed from *sanchin* training was awe inspiring. It was only as I progressed and began to understand Chojun Miyagi sensei's goju-ryu that I became aware of An'ichi Sensei's mastery of it.

"I know other instructors have claimed to be my primary teacher and this is ridiculous. I know who taught me and even now, when I need my kata checked, I return to the same source, An'ichi Miyagi."

People should check their facts before they speak publicly. When Chojun sensei died on October 8th, 1953, An'ichi sensei was in fact 22 years old; his birth date is February 9th, 1931. His formative years, from 1948 until 1953 were spent in intense personal training with Chojun sensei on a daily basis, at times he was the founder's only student. How better to learn goju-ryu karate than to acquire it from the founder at a young age and spend the rest of your life perfecting your skill!

I know other instructors have claimed to be my primary teacher and this is ridiculous. I know who taught me and even now, when I need my kata checked, I return to the same source, An'ichi Miyagi. There is no doubt in my mind, so why would there be doubt in the minds of others? Of course when I started karate all the *sanpai* taught us. Training was very different

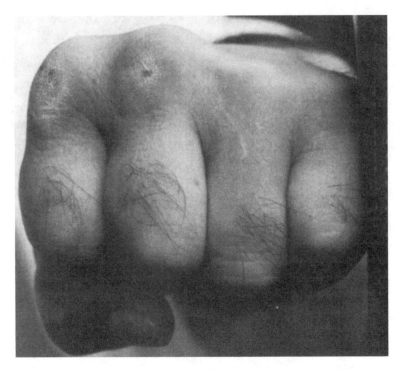

"I train on the makiwara for over an hour, then move to kata training and the heavy bag."

then; it was more like an extended family arrangement, older brothers helping younger brothers. If you really stretch the point, all of them could say that they taught me. However, it's true that others would offer their advice from time to time even as I got older. For example, Miyazato sensei checked my *sanchin* perhaps two or three times in all the years I was at the Jundokan, but my teacher was, and is, An'ichi sensei. I have to say that Miyazato sensei was always kind to me personally but had a habit of saying unkind things about people behind their backs which always made me feel uncomfortable.

Q: I was hoping that you would address the question of your training at the Jundokan after the garden dojo of Chojun sensei closed.
A: It seems like only yesterday that An'ichi sensei would call at my house and ask me to help him repair makiwara at the Jundokan dojo, or clean up the yard and the equipment. It was at the Jundokan that An'ichi sensei really

started to teach me seriously. He explained to me every tiny detail he had learned from the founder about our method and I was fascinated by his knowledge.

When I think of it I experience the thrill and excitement again of my training in those days. An'ichi sensei gave everything he had when training, and expected us to do the same. Unfortunately this led to disagreements with Miyazato sensei. Miyazato sensei felt that An'ichi sensei was much too tough, and his iron discipline, together with the physical demands he made on students, would lose us members and therefore income.

"When I think of it I experience the thrill and excitement again of my training in those days. An'ichi sensei gave everything he had when training, and expected us to do the same."

Q: Why did you leave the Jundokan?
A: There were a number of reasons for leaving the Jundokan. An'ichi sensei was not shown the respect he deserved. Also, when Miyazato sensei would change details of the kata, An'ichi sensei would protest and a heated discussion would then take place which was very unpleasant. I didn't like the board that was displayed publicly with the names of those who had not paid their dojo fees. I thought this was demeaning. And then there was the matter of the loan that was taken out to build the Jundokan. An'ichi sensei paid for the Jundokan building lot to be cleared with his own money and didn't expect to recover anything. However, the actual building costs were paid for by a loan guaranteed by Harno Kochi and this, I understand, was never repaid which angered An'ichi sensei a great deal. He left to join the Merchant Marine and the Jundokan changed a lot for me as a result but I stayed on even after that, for a while at least.

Q: Is this where the accusation came that An'ichi left Okinawa to avoid paying his debts?
A: Exactly! In fact things were the other way around. He spent a lot of his own money on the Jundokan then left to join the Merchant Marine in order to earn a decent living—life was still very hard on Okinawa at that time.

"Because I teach so much I have a responsibility to train as hard as I can to pass on my knowledge in as pure a form as possible."

When the source of this allegation—that An'ichi sensei had left Okinawa to avoid paying his debts—was confronted recently he denied saying anything of the sort!

Q: This allegation seems to have become something of a cultural tradition in Okinawan karate society. Gichin Funakoshi's critics claimed, also in the absence of any credible evidence, that he left Okinawa to avoid paying his debts. Perhaps this is an inevitable result of being a successful karate master, particularly if you train students that became internationally famous.

A: You may be right. An'ichi sensei told me that Miyazato sensei was upset when he heard that my Yoyogi (Tokyo) dojo was busy because he assumed that I was making a lot of money. In fact, all the fees went to the owner of the dojo and I only received a small salary and a place to sleep. The salary was only paid for the days I taught. If I went away for a *gasshuku*, for example, I was not paid. I didn't realize what the problem was, or that there was a problem about money or anything else until in July 1981, when Ryosei Aragaki asked me to come back to the Jundokan. I told him that I had made up my mind and I couldn't change it. Then in August 1981 at the championship in Osaka I was asked to attend a meeting and was surprised to find Miyazato sensei there.

He complained that when I went home to Okinawa I never went to see him. I really didn't understand what he was talking about as I had no reason to go and see him. While I respect him as a student of Chojun sensei, he wasn't my teacher or anything like that, and I really didn't know what to do under the circumstances. Mr. Arimoto who was also at the meeting said that I should apologize to Miyazato sensei, so I did, and thought no more about it.

Q: I know that you have rather strong views on the subject of dan grades, but have publicly said very little. May we hear your opinion?

A: Dan grades have only become important because they cause so many problems. Chojun Miyagi sensei refused to award dan grades and the martial arts didn't have dan grades until judo adopted them. I was given third dan by Miyazato sensei at the first grading I attended when I was little more than a kid and it meant nothing to me, then or now. I never wore the belt. I agree that for students they are a way of measuring progress, but at a high price. They cause discontent, squabbles, and lead to excessive pride in self, which is the opposite of what martial arts training should develop in a student. Every one has different standards, so inevitably there are differences between the level of students from different dojo even when they have the same grade, and then the politics start. I believe that there should be black belts and white belts only, and that the focus should be on training, not on accumulating rank.

"I am pleased to say my training has hardly changed over the years."

Q: On the subject of training, could you please tell me something about your own?

A: I am pleased to say my training has hardly changed over the years. Recently I started to study meditation with Sakiyama sensei who is a famous Zen priest. Every day I run, practice *hojo undo*, kata, and also meditation. My family is as supportive as ever so I am free to train for at least six hours each day.

Of course, you must remember that physical training is just the gateway to mastery of the mind. That's why you must strive to achieve true humility through training. If you don't, it's difficult, if not impossible, to rise above the purely physical because your mind is forever clouded by thoughts of material things, pride and scorn for others, and similar negative feelings. Good karate makes good people, and I feel a responsibility to pass on what was given to me as a way of thanking my teacher, An'ichi Miyagi, and, hopefully, produce more good karate people by doing so. Because I teach so much I have a responsibility to train as hard as I can to pass on my knowledge in as pure a form as possible. If you do not train hard you should not teach!

Q: How is your training these days?

A: Good. I train quite a bit. When I was in Okinawa I didn't train as much as I would have liked to, but now I'm back to a lot of training and I feel really good. I do a long warm-up using some conditioning drills. Then I move into the *hojo undo* which are special exercises named *chisi, sashi,* and *onigi game*. I train on the makiwara for over an hour, then move to kata training and the heavy bag. Three days per week I meet my instructor and we practice *kata* and free-sparring using gloves and headgear. I practice around three hours of kata per day.

Q: Do you teach what you train?

A: Karate teaching and training is not something easy. Everybody starts very passionately with lots of illusions, but due to the hard training only a few people continue. In the mid '60s karate was so popular that my classes were literally packed with students. I used to drill these students through kihon— but after a while not very many were left. In karate training, those who stick with it go through a process of self-analysis. They start questioning a lot of things about themselves and their reasons for training. The answer becomes a reflection of themselves. As a result, this leads to more focus, determination, and overall inner peace.

Q: As a teacher, did you have any problems adapting from the Japanese students' mindset to the American students' mentality?

A: Not really, but it is true that you have to know how to properly communicate with the different cultures. For instance, in Japan or Okinawa, people don't ask questions, they just repeat what you tell them to do. In the West, everyone want to know "why," so you have to explain. That's the reason why I teach more applications in the West than I do back in Japan or Okinawa. Of course, once the student reaches the black belt level he doesn't need an explanation for everything. The problem in the West is that many people think of themselves as masters because they know kata applications when, in fact, they can't properly perform the kata itself because they waste too much time asking instead of doing.

Q: You traveled extensively in China in order to research the original training. What did you discover?

A: A lot of very interesting things! I contacted different Chinese masters who helped me to dig into the roots of the goju-ryu system. In one of my trips, the city mayor invited 15 or 16 old masters who performed kata from

"I'm against changing the essence of kata. I always say that kata is like a printed letter. They are portraits of the basic techniques and history."

sanchin to suparimpei. We all agreed that our techniques had evolved from the Chinese white crane and tiger styles.

Q: Are the kata the same as the original Chinese?
A: Pretty much. I'm against changing kata. I believe that kata is not just something that someone made up. They are hundreds and thousands of years old. There is a lot of information in each one of them. Few people know that there are certain kata to be practiced in the morning and others to be performed in the evening in order to get the most from them. I understand that a lot of knowledge has been lost through the years but it is my responsibility to keep this important information alive for the generations to come.

Q: So you are against personal interpretations of kata?
A: I'm against changing the essence of kata. I always say that kata is like a printed letter. They are portraits of the basic techniques and history. If you change the essence of kata, you lose all this.

"If you simply retire after doing only competitions, and have strictly focused only on winning against an opponent, then karate has no meaning at all."

Q: If kata is a printed letter, what is kumite?
A: Kumite is handwriting, and everybody has their own penmanship! In sparring, you have an opponent and it's a little bit easier because you adapt to the movements of your adversary. In kata there is only space and time and you. There is no opponent— nothing to grasp—you have to imagine and aim for a spiritual opponent.

Q: Do you consider karate an art or a sport?
A: Karate is a martial art that uses no weapons. This doesn't mean that I reject the sport aspect since I feel that's one part of the whole art. However, karate is deep. If you simply retire after doing only competitions, and have strictly focused only on winning against an opponent, then karate has no meaning at all. Karate is for all your life. We can continue training until we are 70 or 80 years old. The real purpose of karate is not to beat someone or to win against someone. Karate is a pacifist philosophy of self-discovery.

Q: Why did you create the Okinawan Goju-Ryu Karate Federation?
A: My whole idea is to preserve the teachings and philosophy of Grandmaster Chojun Miyagi and spread them all over the world. That is why. It was not a matter of ego or power. I only want to protect and pass-on these teachings.

Q: You are very much into physical conditioning. Is the traditional method better than modern approaches such as weight training?

A: Not necessarily, but the traditional conditioning methods allow the practitioner to work the muscles in the body as a unit, not in an isolated way as weight training does. The traditional way was developed to help karate technique, so the training methods fit the karate structure and the way of moving the human body.

Q: Why do you train so much on the makiwara?

A: When we punch the makiwara, we are not only conditioning the knuckles but developing power, speed, and body coordination and punching mechanics. Everything comes together in makiwara training. On the other hand, if your body is not conditioned, it is very easy to hurt yourself when you hit someone. Just don't forget to start slowly and add power and increase speed as you improve in kihon.

Q: What does the term "do" mean to you?

A: *Do* is the way for the men. I never let passion or feelings rule my behavior. I try to stay clam and face problems like Grandmaster Miyagi did in the Second World War. He didn't have any food at all, but yet he stayed calm. This is very hard to do, but it shows a lot about your spirit. Karate is spirit. Karate is life. Karate, for me, is like a cloud with nothing substantial to grab onto. You can do karate all your life and still find new meanings and new answers—that's why I practice every single day.

Q: Do you practice *zazen* and meditation?

A: Yes I do. For me, being focused on what I do every day is very important. I don't think about tomorrow when I train. I train today; I do my best today—then I'm happy. If tomorrow I'm alive when I wake up, then I will do the same thing. I try to be extremely concentrated on the "now."

Q: What do you expect from your students?

A: Everybody has different reasons to train karate. Some look for health, others for sport, and some for self-defense. There are many things yet to be discovered in goju-ryu. So I expect my students to keep researching the art so one day they can find the answers through their own personal investigation. Karate training has to be done with heart and sincerity. It brings your body and mind together. That's the real karate. O

Masters' Techniques

As the opponent attacks, Master Higaonna reacts with a left-hand block and straight punch to the face (1). He then begins a combination composed of an uppercut to the chin (2), a finger jab to the eyes (3), and a palm strike to the chin (4), followed by a knuckle pressure-point to the neck (5), that controls the head (6). This allows him to push his opponent to the ground (7), where he finishes with a downward heel kick (8).

Master Higaonna faces his opponent (1). As the opponent attacks with a front punch, Higaonna side-steps and applies an outside block (2), followed by a shuto uchi (knife-hand attack) to the neck (3). Replacing his left hand (4), Higaonna delivers a haito uchi (5), that serves as the entry (6), for a take-down with a finishing downward heel kick to the solar plexus (7).

Dan Ivan

Karate's Enduring Spirit

A HALF-CENTURY OF BUDO EXPERIENCE IS CONTAINED WITHIN THIS OLD-WORLD GEN-
TLEMAN WHO IS RESPONSIBLE FOR BRINGING SOME OF THE GREATEST JAPANESE KARATE
MASTERS OF ALL TIME TO THE UNITED STATES. A CRIMINAL INVESTIGATOR WITH THE
U.S. MILITARY OCCUPATIONAL FORCE IN JAPAN AFTER WWII, IVAN WAS ONE OF THE
FIRST WESTERNERS TO FORGET THE HATRED OF THE WAR AND TO BUILD BRIDGES BY
STUDYING KARATE WITH HIS FORMER ENEMIES. IGNORING THE HARSH WORDS OF
EASTERN AND WESTERN CRITICS WHO QUESTIONED HIS OPENNESS, IVAN'S STRENGTH
OF CHARACTER AND STRONG PERSONAL MORALS ENABLED HIM TO FORGE FRIENDSHIPS
WITH MANY OF THE TOP MARTIAL ARTS MASTERS OF SHATTERED POST-WAR JAPAN THAT
LAST UNTIL THIS DAY.

NOW, A HALF-CENTURY LATER, IVAN IS LOOKED UPON AS AN EXAMPLE OF UNDER-
STANDING, PATIENCE, AND TOLERANCE. HUMBLE, CHARMING, AND KNOWLEDGEABLE,
IVAN IS AN AMERICAN ICON. HIS TRAINING UNDER SUCH NOTABLES AS ISAO OBATA,
GOGEN YAMAGUCHI, GOZO SHIODA, AND RYUSHO SAKAGAMI—JUST TO NAME A
FEW—MAKES PRACTITIONERS AROUND THE WORLD, WHO WOULD GIVE UP THEIR FIRST-
BORN FOR 10 PERCENT OF THIS MAN'S EXPERIENCES, LOOK AT HIM WITH HEALTHY ENVY.

NOW IN HIS 70S BUT STILL FIT AND VITAL WITH A SHARP, INQUIRING MIND, IVAN
ENJOYS SHARING HIS EXPERIENCES AND KNOWLEDGE WITH THOSE LUCKY ENOUGH TO
COME IN CONTACT WITH HIM. WHEN YOU MEET THIS OUTSTANDING MARTIAL ARTIST
AND FINE HUMAN BEING YOU WOULD BE WELL ADVISED TO STOP TALKING, LISTEN, AND
LEARN FROM A MAN WHO IS ONE OF THE MOST TREASURED MARTIAL ARTISTS OF THE
WESTERN WORLD.

Q: How long have you been practicing the martial arts?
A: Formally since 1948, when I was stationed in Japan. Prior to that, in 1945,
I had WWII military unarmed-combat training which peaked my interest. In
those early years I earned black belts in karate, judo, aikido and kendo. I've
heard people in Japan say that I was the first foreigner to do this in the four
major Budo arts. In karate, my training was mostly in shotokan, shito-ryu, a
little goju-ryu and wado-ryu, plus a taste of some lesser known arts.

*"In aikido, my sensei was Gozo Shioda, head of Yoshinkai;
a man small in stature but with fantastic technique."*

Q: How many styles have you trained in and who were your first teachers?
A: My very first teachers were from the Kodokan—most notable were
Mifune and Ito, both 10th dan, Meijin, then my close friend, Sato, a close
friend, and Ishikawa, a two-year judo champion in Japan and many others.
In karate my first instructor was Isao Obata, first disciple under Master
Funakoshi; also I started goju-ryu with Gogen Yamaguchi, but stopped
when the Kodokan asked me to. In those early years after the war,
Yamaguchi and others were struggling and not yet well accepted—while
Obata was. At the JKA it was Chief Nakayama and Sensei Kase. Most significant to my shotokan training was Kenji Yamamoto from Hosei University
and one of JKA's main sensei; this was after about two years with Obata
who really gave me my foundation. Over the years, many other JKA sensei
added a lot to my knowledge. One of my greatest sensei and an inspiration
to me was shito-ryu master Ryusho Sakagami. This man was a dictionary of
kata and a great but humble person. Also, a tough old sensei, Yamada, who

"Kicking with precision was different than street-fighting kicks, and learning to punch with a bare hand was different than boxing with gloves—but overall, it was enjoyable."

taught the Yakuza and also professional bodyguards. He brought a whole different dimension to karate than did the others. I can't forget another prominent goju-ryu master—Izumigawa. I know I am probably forgetting someone, but I learned from so many because of my military situation. I was stationed in different parts of Japan due to my assignment as a criminal investigator.

In aikido, my sensei was Gozo Shioda, head of Yoshinkai; a man small in stature but with fantastic technique. He and his staff helped me and other agents in our office to cope with handling criminal suspects in a more humane way. My kendo training was with the Japan Kendo Federation and their instructors. Kendo was at the time the most organized group. Sensei Saeki, who was a descendent of a true Samurai family, was my main teacher and mentor. There were many other arts and sensei that I had the privilege of training with. In the beginning the physical movements were not all that difficult for me. Kicking with precision was different than street-fighting kicks, and learning to punch with a bare hand was different than boxing with gloves—but overall, it was enjoyable.

"I realized no man can ever learn it all because there are so many fascinating angles to all these arts. You should concentrate on one and make it your foundation, but other arts have much to offer."

Q: How did Westerners respond to your traditional Japanese training?

A: In the early days, there was a lot of hostility in Japan against Americans; however, in the dojo it was not too apparent. As a matter of fact martial arts helped to bridge this hostility. I recall being called a "Jap lover" because I hung out with my new friends and sensei. I am sure that they were also getting the same treatment for hanging out with me. Eventually, all this passed. Westerners loved Japanese martial arts. There were not a whole lot of us, but those who did train really took to it. There were eventually more men taking karate than judo, and fewer took kendo; but as time went on, Westerners begin taking iaido, even more than kendo.

Q: How has your personal karate changed and developed over the years?

A: Like anyone else, my first years were cramming in all the training I could, jumping in with both feet, not really stopping to analyze techniques. Then, as the years went on, I began to realize the dynamics and principles of proper kicking and striking. You learn that when something is executed the right way, you can cause more damage with your technique.

Even today, after producing over 135 videos of masters in all arts, Chinese, Korean, Japanese, Okinawan, Philippine and others, I realized no man can ever learn it all because there are so many fascinating angles to all these arts. I wish I had another one or two lifetimes ahead of me. There are many new things to do and try in so many different arts. You should concentrate on one and make it your foundation, but other arts have much to offer.

Q: What were the most important points of your teaching days?

A: At first, I began teaching to have someone to train with. There were hardly any martial artists around. Then I had a wake-up call. I realized that men, women, and children were coming to me and I was responsible for them. If you are sincere and you are teaching properly, they will come to you, and, like it or not, you are guiding and influencing their lives—a major responsibility that I took seriously. I actually changed from having personal selfish goals of doing karate—now I had to do it for my students.

Q: With all the technical changes during the last 30 years, do you think there is still "pure" shotokan, shito-ryu, et cetera?

A: Different styles or *ryu*, add competition and interest. Each style feeds off the other and learns from the other, so it's good. From fifty years ago, I see many styles that you could only distinguish from the kata, but the basics are very similar. We don't want to become too generic, so lets keep our separate styles that include our history and traditions. Purists in the martial arts, especially karate, are rare and becoming almost extinct. Influences today change the way we teach, and what we teach; however, there are still a handful of sensei that flow with the times and still manage to maintain the true art with the right spirit and attitude.

"Purists in the martial arts, especially karate, are rare and becoming almost extinct."

Q: What's your opinion of full contact karate and kickboxing, and other fighting events such as the UFC?

A: They're all great. Out of a class of a thousand or more, you may have one student who aspires to go into kickboxing. It's not for everyone, is hard work, and takes a certain personality, just as boxing does. Almost thirty years ago, I had a partner and we promoted full contact karate. It was not accepted at the time, so we dropped it. Today, however, the rules have improved, and you have Indonesian muay Thai and other forms of kickboxing that I find far more interesting than conventional boxing. Plus, you have

"The salvation of the traditional martial arts of Japan, China, and others is in their ethical teachings and their cultural education."

some real talented fighters; but remember, this is not for everyone. We see what happened in the UFC—it opened our eyes to other arts such as jiu-jitsu and grappling. And the UFC spawned other arts which are really interesting spectator sports, all derived from martial arts. Again, this is not for the normal student who just wants to get in shape, do something interesting, and learn self-defense.

Today, from what I hear, the K-1 fights are the most interesting because they don't stay on the ground for too long. Remember, worldwide, boxing went pro, and Greco-Roman wrestling never did because people won't sit still for that much mat work—they don't understand it and can't relate to it. As far as the UFC-type events, I think they are great spectator sports, and for those few martial artists who are the right age and have the right conditioning, they can compete in it. Whereas many of the eclectic, nontraditional arts have faded. The salvation of the traditional martial arts of Japan, China, and others is in their ethical teachings and their cultural education. They offer more than fighting and so will continue in popularity and advance in members. Japanese karate has it problems, of course, but in general it is doing great.

Q: Do you think that Western karate has caught up with Japanese karate?
A: If you monitor the world karate events, you'll see that the Japanese no longer dominate the sport. This is regulated competition, of course, but if you look at true Budo and non-sport karate, I think you will find Japan still has the edge. Karate has evolved into a sport, like it or not. And as a sport it has attracted far more students. But there are still a rare few schools out there that disregard this part of training and teach the old way, which is technique, self-defense and personal development. The winners in this

struggle are those that can do it all—the sport and the traditional training—even though it is a very difficult balance to strike.

Q: Do you feel that there are any fundamental differences in karateka from different ethnic or cultural backgrounds?

A: All of us—all races—have the same body. The deciding factor is your size, your physical conditioning, and your length of training. There is one area that the Japanese might have an edge—the college years. In Japan, karate is part of the curriculum at most colleges and universities. A young man can train every day, two to four hours, for his entire four years in school. So, for the 18 to 22-year-olds it is an advantage because you won't find many schools that keep up this regimen.

"Makiwara or bag training is something you must do, otherwise you never know that your wrist might be weak and your hand might collapse when you punch; or if you don't kick properly you can twist an ankle."

Q: Do you think it helps karateka to train with weapons?

A: Training with weapons is another dimension—another road to take for more dexterity and coordination. It is part of the total art and stimulating to practice.

Q: What's your opinion of the makiwara and other supplemental training devices?

A: Makiwara training has been replaced by the heavy bag. Remember, the makiwara was invented because in early times, and in poor times in postwar Japan, they didn't have money or equipment. Makiwara or bag training is something you must do, otherwise you never know that your wrist might be weak and your hand might collapse when you punch, or if you don't kick properly you can twist an ankle. Supplemental training—weights, running, swimming, and other sports, is good to help build your body. Don't

"It's hard to teach and train at the same time. If you train alongside your students, how can you correct them?"

forget, we live with TV and automobiles and generally live a soft life; so we should exert ourselves at every opportunity. Besides, young people have growing bodies. So the more varied exercise they get, the better.

Q: Do you think a sensei's personal training should be different from what he teaches?
A: It's hard to teach and train at the same time. If you train alongside your students, how can you correct them? And this is the responsibility of the sensei, to correct his students. Some training can be done with them, but as a sensei you must make separate time for yourself to portray the technique or kata to the class. Get rid of your bad habits or your class will emulate them. Definitely, both things have to be taken care of separately.

Q: What is the most important element of karate teaching: self-defense, sport, or tradition?
A: Lot of basics and sparring techniques are probably first, then kata, and then sport techniques for those in the class that attend sport tournaments. Too many groups are striving to win tournaments and are neglecting good, solid training which improves your overall ability. Kata should take up about a third, or maybe only a fourth of the training; the rest should be kumite, basics, and self-defense.

Q: Some people think that going to Japan to train is highly necessary; do you share this view?
A: Going to Japan to train is highly motivational due to the atmosphere and the entire attitude. And you can find good old-fashioned dojo there and solid training; but as far as being highly necessary, perhaps it is not that way anymore since we do have some very capable sensei here, both American and

Japanese. Karate changed in a major way after World War II, when myself and other G.I.s were stationed there. Early training was more combative, since Japan had just come out of about a fifty-year war. The attitude was a more severe war mentality, training was more serious and it took year for us to quit training and teaching as if we were going into life and death combat. Today, there are countless deadly techniques not taught or even known by modern sensei—both in Japan and around the world. Kids and women are now widely accepted; this was not allowed after the war because what we taught was for men that might have to face mortal enemies. Today, sport has emerged strongly and allows all ages and sexes to participate. But I do long for the old days of true Budo.

"Early training was more combative, since Japan had just come out of about a fifty-year war. The attitude was a more severe war mentality."

Q: Who would you like to have trained with?
A: Actually, I sought out who I wanted, so actually there are perhaps only a couple of men I wish I had developed a relationship with that I didn't. One is Grandmaster Ueshiba and the other is Grandmaster Funakoshi. Both were present at many events being held in those early days, but I never had the privilege of taking any classes with them. When I was new to the arts in the 1940s and '50s, these masters were pointed out to me, but I was too stupid to be impressed—and it was only after many years that I realized these men were founding icons.

Q: What would you say to someone who is interested in learning karate-do?
A: If you are interested in the art, visit some schools and observe. See the quality and look closely at the physical skills of the students; but just as importantly look closely at their attitude and manners. Listen to the facts, not a sales pitch. Karate is growing, and there are good schools out there turning out good students. Overall, the true sensei—the traditionalist—survives and thrives. If they fall by the wayside, they are not ready to be sensei or perhaps just not capable. A good school depends on a good sensei. A lot of lumps and bruises will happen along the way, but stick to it. What's your

"Mixing karate styles won't hurt, but you absolutely must concentrate heavily on only one for more efficient advanced in knowledge."

alternative, watching TV? Do it—bring in the whole family. There's room for everyone in karate and that's what makes it so special.

Q: Do you think engaging in free-fighting is necessary to achieving good street-fighting skills?

A: Free-fighting is really important, whether you do it with equipment or without. It gives you speed, timing, and distancing that you can use if someone attacks you. Good free-fighters can simply outmaneuver the average person that comes swinging and kicking wildly.

Q: What is your opinion about mixing karate styles?

A: Mixing karate styles won't hurt, but you absolutely must concentrate heavily only on one for more efficient advanced in knowledge. As time goes on you will find many similarities in the arts—the single biggest difference is kata. In fact, today in major tournaments and events you will often see a shotokan stylist doing a goju kata, or shito-ryu student using a shotokan technique. Overall, more knowledge is good for you if you get solid roots in one system first.

Q: Modern karate is moving away from bunkai, or applications, in kata practice. How important is bunkai for understanding kata and karate-do in general?

A: Kata bunkai is good and necessary. Translating a kata is something very challenging. Most of the challenge is in asking yourself, "What the hell is this move for?" Simple blocks, strikes, and kicks in kata are easy to see and understand; but frankly there are many moves handed down from centuries ago that are perplexing. Over the years I have watched many so-called "high-ranking masters" perform many different bunkai to the same kata. And this is not wrong. You can devise applications any way you want in many cases, keeping in mind that whoever originated a particular kata was influenced by certain weapons of his era and certain circumstances in fighting. Some of these circumstances are lost to us today, so we do the best we can.

Q: What is the philosophical basis for your karate training?

A: That's a hard one. My motivation and even my philosophy was to elevate my physical and mental stature. Martial arts does that while you're training without having to think about it. One day, despite all the hard knocks, you feel mentally and physically stronger—and this is something to be cherished no matter what your age or status in life. Personally, I didn't have much of a spiritual view of karate until after decades of training. My brain works slower than others perhaps, but it took me years to realize that karate was more than fighting movements, and that I was much stronger mentally than physically. You can meditate, read up on lives of the masters, and so forth, but the

"My motivation and even my philosophy was to elevate my physical and mental stature. Martial arts does that while you're training without having to think about it."

spiritual aspects have to grow on you. I don't think you can just look for it and find it. It has to exist as a seed within you that can grow later on. Besides karate being an invaluable aid in working the streets of Tokyo, it also was motivational to feel my improvement as the years went on, and also to see my students achieve status in the martial arts world. Things like these inspire me even today.

Q: What keeps you motivated after all these years?

A: As you grow older and as you teach, your training becomes less intense—or at least you have less time to train—so you do what you can because you can't keep the same pace you had when you were young and unencumbered with teaching or raising a family. Make a little time every day, or every other day, even if you are training alone, work the muscles for kicks and strikes, and do some kata. Your lifestyle, age, and available time will dictate how much

"The practice of karate offers you a path to achievement in a deep, personal sense—it's something you have that can't be taken away."

you'll be able to do. A mistake many people make is that because they can't do what they did before, they drop out. This is not wise. The practitioner has to make adjustments and do the best they can. The motivation for training in the first place is different. During my prime training years, the world was coming out of a depression and a war, and hardships made hard men and women. Today this condition doesn't exist; so with few exceptions, students are a lot softer mentally and physically. Nevertheless, they can still be as dedicated and sincere about their training and achieve impressive results if they have the right sensei. The practice of karate offers you a path to achievement in a deep, personal sense—it's something you have that can't be taken away. Even away from practice, this attitude always stays with you. It may be not evident for a long period of time but it will emerge when you need it the most. At my age, watching the skill of good practitioners is so inspiring. Martial artists of all styles are truly fascinating to watch if they are skilled. Remember the recent Olympics? Although you may not be a high diver, watching them was great—and to see our American heavyweight in his wrestling win over the Russian champion was great. So my motivation is staying in the best condition I can at my age, and watching and associating with good sensei and students.

Q: What are the most important attributes of a student?
A: A student needs to be prepared to learn even before the actual learning process begins; this is one of the most important aspects in traditional martial arts training. Of course, the key words are "dedication" and "hard work." It sounds cliche, but that's what it takes: dedication and hard work over and above anything else you might do. One of the most important qualities for a

student is the ability to listen and try really hard—to master one simple technique at a time, not try to advance too fast and overlook basics. Training becomes hard as you go along; more is expected of you as you advance in grade. As the pressure mounts you must meet this challenge as you would in any sport. Karate differs from all other activities because you should always be working against yourself, not others; so if you slow down or stop, you will find it harder to continue again.

"Karate differs from all other activities because you should always be working against yourself, not others."

Q: Have you ever felt fear in your karate training?
A: Not really fear, but often apprehension. In my earliest years in Japan, before I was confident that my former enemies, the Japanese, wouldn't bust my head in training, I was definitely wide-eyed and cautious.

Q: There has been very little written about you in magazines. Why do you obviously not thrive on publicity?
A: Maybe it's my prior military experience of working undercover on criminal cases, and then working military intelligence—being inconspicuous and overlooked was vital to survival. But then again, I never liked loudmouths and braggarts, so it's my nature to be happy in the background. But I've had my share of publicity. When I was younger I was in over a dozen martial arts magazines, including *Inside Kung Fu* and *Black Belt*, and I wrote hundreds of articles on the martial arts. But fame and publicity are fleeting—your inner soul and your spirit are what endures. O

Masters' Techniques

Facing an attacker (1) Sensei Ivan blocks the punch to the inside (2), comes over the top of the elbow (3), presses on the attacker's stomach to unbalance him (4), knees to the stomach (5), and then hooks the leg and clotheslines across the chest, sending the attacker tumbling to the ground (6).

Grabbed from behind by an assailant (1), Sensei Ivan spins around, breaking the grip (2), traps both arms with an overhook (3), smashes to the attacker's face (4) and then knees to the stomach (5).

Hirokazu Kanazawa

Master of the Karate Spirit

ONE OF MARTIAL ARTS MOST REVERED TEACHERS, SENSEI KANAZAWA'S JOURNEY FROM SCHOLARSHIP TO KARATE MASTERY IS A STORY OF PHYSICAL SKILL AND SPIRITUAL ACHIEVEMENT.

SENSEI KANAZAWA WAS THE SECOND PERSON TO GRADUATE FROM THE JKA INSTRUCTOR TRAINING PROGRAM, AND IS CONSIDERED BY MANY TO BE ONE OF THE MOST SKILLFUL FIGHTERS OF ALL TIME. TEMPERED BY YEARS OF STRICT AND DIFFICULT PRACTICE, HIS BODY REFLECTS THE DECADES OF GRUELING KARATE TRAINING AND CONDITIONING. USED BY MASATOSHI NAKAYAMA AS A MODEL FOR KARATE TECHNIQUES IN THE CLASSIC BOOK DYNAMIC KARATE, KANAZAWA IS AN LIVING EXAMPLE OF THE POWER OF KARATE-DO AT ITS HIGHEST LEVEL.

AN ORIGINAL THINKER, KANAZAWA CREATED HIS OWN ORGANIZATION, SHOTOKAN KARATE INTERNATIONAL, IN 1975 AFTER TEACHING IN HAWAII AND BEING THE JKA'S CHIEF INSTRUCTOR IN GREAT BRITAIN UNTIL THE MID-'70S. IT IS SAID THAT TRAINING WITH A TRUE MASTER IS THE ONLY WAY TO FULLY UNDERSTAND KARATE-DO. HIROKAZU KANAZAWA IS ONE OF THOSE RARE TEACHERS WHO POSSESSES THE ABILITY TO PASS BOTH THE SPIRITUAL AND PHYSICAL ESSENCE OF THE ART TO YOUNGER INITIATES.

Q: Many karate practitioners consider you a rebel. Why?
A: I don't know. The karate that I teach is a product of more than thirty years of spiritual and physical research into the true meaning of martial arts. Perhaps because of my training in tai chi and kobudo, some karateka look at me differently. Also, it may be due to my very personal perception of karate—I teach for everybody, not only for the young and the strong. For me, karate is unlimited. I always said that karate is a form of self-administered therapeutic massage. It is not just a sport.

Q: How did you begin in tai chi?
A: I began when I went to Hawaii, but it was not regular training. Later on, I met Mr. Yang, who is a member of the family tree of the Yang family style of tai chi. He is very famous and his organization is probably the best in Japan. I met him when he came to the JKA to learn karate. I had the feeling that he

127

"After I started training in tai chi, I began to really understand how to keep and develop a healthy body, mind, and spirit."

was already practicing another martial art but he didn't say anything. Later on, I discovered that he was a master in tai chi. I began training under him around 1957 and I haven't stopped since.

Q: Do you have any rank in tai chi?
A: In Yang tai chi there are only seven degrees and I hold the highest. I received my certification many years ago.

Q: Has tai chi helped you to improve and understand your karate?
A: I don't practice tai chi for tai chi, but for my karate. After I started training in tai chi, I began to really understand how to keep and develop a healthy body, mind, and spirit. In the beginning, tai chi was very difficult, I couldn't use any tension at all and had to force myself to relax all my muscles. You see, I was trying to do tai chi with karate power, and it was painful trying to move with no force at all. My body felt really uncomfortable but after a couple of years of training I began to understand and developed a natural softness that still retained the real strength in the technique.

Q: Were you initially frustrated with tai chi?
A: Of course. During my first year of training even my stomach used to make weird noises. Mr. Yang told me once that the reason was that I had no internal power and my body was protesting! You see, the human body changes and your martial art has to change with it. And I think this has to be done using internal power because it strengthens the internal organs. There is a point in every karate practitioner's life where the punch's unifying force must no longer be rooted in the muscles but in the internal organs.

I am much older and I will honestly tell you that my body is not as supple as it used to be and does not respond as quickly as it once did. This is a physiological reality and is perfectly normal—that's why I adapted my karate to the needs of my body and why tai chi has been of a great benefit to me. I have many students who did not start karate until they were 50 years old and they all do quite well. They could not fight the young men

"Unfortunately, karate today is neither a sport nor a martial art, and that's very confusing for the students."

with hard contact, of course, but then that is not their approach. By the same token, young men need to train differently.

Q: Have you attempted to combine karate and tai chi?
A: I don't think that is a good idea. I feel it is better to study them separately. But even although they are opposites, the study of both brings a more balanced view. Tai chi has allowed me to step outside of karate in much the same way as you need to step outside your house to fully appreciate it. From the inside, you do not have a complete view of it. This act of stepping outside afforded me a chance to see karate from an entirely different point of view and to appreciate it even more.

Q: You also train in Okinawa kobudo, correct?
A: I train in bo, sai, and nunchaku. I have always said that tai chi is very much like the nunchaku movement. When you're using the nunchaku, your arms must be relaxed and soft—"empty" is the right word—no tense muscles. In nunchaku training if you move the weapon with tension, then you lose power. The same is true in tai chi.

129

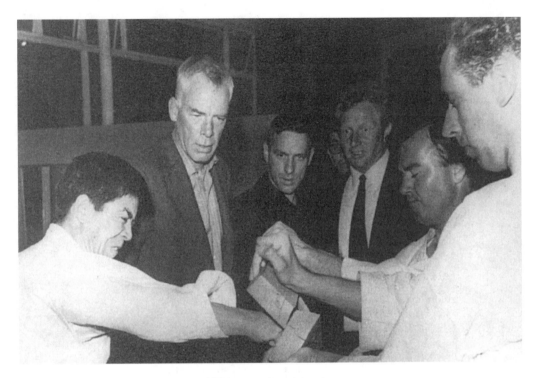

With actor Lee Marvin

"I never wanted to be independent—that's not in my spirit. But I had to defend myself. A samurai must not be frightened—even of death."

Q: How did you start your kobudo training?
A: I started in Okinawa, and when I returned to Japan I tried it for myself. At that time I knew the basics only. My teacher told me that there was no kobudo kata. So I devised some kata myself. Many people twirl the nunchaku, but this doesn't allow real power to develop. In kata training one learns concentration and how to develop smoothness in motion in order to create devastating striking power.

Q: Was kobudo ever practiced at the old Japan Karate Association?
A: No, never. But it is interesting that there is some evidence of Master Funakoshi Gichin using the sai for training.

Q: Do you think weapons training should be a part of every karateka training?

A: Maybe it is not important for everyone, but it is for me. I truly consider karate and kobudo part of the same family. Therefore, if I learn kobudo I will better understand the history of karate.

Q: Do you like the direction karate is currently taking?

A: I believe it is quite a confusing period for students. They really don't know if they are practicing a sport or a martial art. Sport is an aspect of karate but it is not everything. Unfortunately, karate today is neither a sport nor a martial art, and that's very confusing for the students. I think it would be better if sport karate evolved separately from the martial art side.

Q: Why did you split from the JKA and create Shotokan Karate International?

A: I never wanted to create my own organization. That was never my goal. When I was in Europe, making plans to go to Montreal University in Canada to teach for a few months, I sent a letter of

"So I decided that if the JKA was against me, I had to defend myself."

resignation to the JKA—not as a JKA instructor—but as the director of a section of the JKA. I just didn't feel I could function in that capacity while I was out of the country. Three months later, when I returned to Europe, I received a letter from the JKA informing me that I was summarily dismissed.

Q: How did you feel?

A: I was completely shocked. But I said to myself that I wouldn't go back to Canada but would struggle on in Europe. Giving up would have been against the Budo spirit of everything I had been taught. So I decided that if the JKA was against me, I had to defend myself.

"We must look to the different roots. That's why I decided train in Okinawan styles. After all, they are the root of karate."

Q: Did you think Shotokan Karate International would last?
A: In the beginning, many people said that it would only last a couple of months. Fortunately, as you can see, we are still going strong! But I want to emphasize that I never wanted to leave the JKA. Some people said that I deserted Nakayama sensei, but the truth is that I never wanted to be independent—that's not in my spirit. But I had to defend myself. A samurai must not be frightened—even of death.

Q: Is any style "pure" shotokan?
A: No. Pure shotokan does not exists. The JKA practices a type of shotokan—but it is the shotokan of the JKA. Oshima sensei practices a shotokan but again it is *his* shotokan. Each master has a different view, a different brain, a different comprehension of things. This is normal.

Q: Do you train in any karate styles besides shotokan?
A: I have been fortunate to study different *ryu* under other great teachers. I sometimes invite instructors of different styles to teach at my dojo. Likewise, I visit other ryu's dojos and occasionally teach. I've been lucky! I researched shorin-ryu, uechi-ryu, goju-ryu, and others, because I really believe that no karate style is complete. We must look to the different roots. That's why I decided train in Okinawan styles. After all, they are the root of karate. Unfortunately, some organizations forbid this. This close-minded thinking is driven by politics, not karate.

Q: Do you watch martial arts movies?
A: I think they are OK. Some are good while others are bad. Bruce Lee and Jackie Chan have been good as far as making the art popular and attracting students. Unfortunately, many people watch Bruce Lee and think that they can be just like him in a couple of months. That's impossible! On other hand if you teach too seriously, the correct Budo, young people lose interest. So there is a balance.

Q: Do you recommend makiwara training?
A: Yes, I do but with conditions. As a young student, I used to punch the makiwara more than 1,000 times daily, which is not correct. This kind of training is very impor-

"In history, there was always a trend to improve health exercises for self-defense techniques. I haven't changed karate, I just kept it within the historical tradition."

tant for karate but only with 50 or 60 full-powered blows per hand. It's important to develop power, speed and kime. I remember my knuckles were split open to the bone during my early training sessions. Once I went to see a doctor who cleaned the wounds and wrapped my hands! My senpai almost kicked me out of the dojo!

Q: Did you modify the karate you were taught?
A: Not really, but I did try to go back to its roots. Not to *kung-fu* but to *kong-fu*. Kong-fu was a healthy exercise for mind and body. Daruma developed Zen exercises for internal power. This is very hard training and the students should never stop or they will never understand. In history, there was always a trend to improve health exercises for self-defense techniques. I haven't changed karate, I just kept it within the historical tradition.

Q: Why do so many karateka develop problems in the lower back?
A: The main reason is the lack of adequate self-care. Most practitioners limit their self-care to karate training. But you must take the proper

"Karate is not always enjoyable because it is never easy to do the right thing. Karate is for the self."

precautions before a problem arises. Performing karate like a machine, without the proper relaxation, correct posture and breathing, will cause problems. That's the reason why I make my karate "self-chiropractic." Karate should improve health, not cause injuries.

Q: What do you think about karate going into the Olympic Games?

A: Sport is good as long as it is regarded as a recreation that you can leave and then go back to karate Budo. Competition by itself is bad for the art, because you will understand nothing. Sport is open and enjoyable. Karate is not always enjoyable, because it is never easy to do the right thing. Karate is for the self. In sport we win over an opponent—in karate, we win over the self. In Budo, a good kata performer must be a good fighter and vice versa. To realize the spirit of Budo, one must be good at both kata and kumite—both sides have to be taught. The positive and the negative balance is very important. Good things always come in twos. In sport karate, one is only good at kata or kumite. Kata must look good for the referees, but at the same time must not be changed for aesthetics to create an extra flourish.

Q: Do you believe that it is important to go to Japan to study karate?

A: Not for the technique but for the philosophy, the attitude, and the spirit.

Q: What are your most important teaching points?

A: Breathing, movement and timing—but breathing is first. The very first thing we do in this world is to breathe—but 90 percent of the population do not know how to breath correctly. If your breathing is wrong, your body will be wrong and your mind will be wrong also. There is a very strong connection. You control your spirit with your breathing and should always be thinking and trying to learn more about this most vital aspect, since it is the very core of life. I always stress the philosophical and health aspects of karate and try to explain the reason behind the techniques.

For instance, when I'm teaching the *tsuki* I do not show a punch to hit someone, I relate the movement to the person's *hara*—his center. I explain in the tsuki, that you should always push the head straight because it will promote good health by sending blood and oxygen into the head, which nourishes the cells. Utilizing the correct breathing, the hara, the concentration, and the impact produces a slight vibration on the verte-

"If your breathing is wrong, your body will be wrong and your mind will be wrong also. There is a very strong connection."

bral column, which communicates to the brain and produces a sort of massaging effect. Remember that basic movements must be good for health; if not, then they are not good for human life. I can give you an example. Performing the *fumikomi* in the *tekki* kata flexes the base of the spine which uses the whole correctly. The base of the spine is a nerve center which stimulates the internal organs.

Two hundred years ago, *bushi* was OK. It was a matter of being strong without caring about health or anything else because there was a continuous life and death struggle. One had to be strong and have no fear in order to face daily life. Now, things have changed in society, and it is more important to be healthy in body and mind. Our character must be more peaceful but still having the same *bushido* spirit.

Q: Did your understanding of breathing change your physical techniques?

A: Yes. In the beginning I did not teach so much about breathing, but I adhered to a power style—quite a natural thing when I was young because at that age you favor strength. But with time and thought, I have come to a

"The bottom line is that if you don't train extensively in the basics, you cannot reach the higher stages of martial arts."

realization that winning can be done using only 60 percent of your power—100 percent is not necessary if you have good technique. If I use 60 percent correctly and then use 40 percent of my opponent's power against him, the total is still 100 percent and the combination will result in more damage to him. This approach is the result of my tai chi studies.

Q: Have you modified any of the basic karate techniques?
A: Not really, but my *tsuki* has developed considerably since my younger days—but it happened subconsciously. I was not thinking about it, it just developed. I now have a double kime—a physical focus first, and then a speed focus, which delivers more shock. I did not realize what I was doing until it was pointed out to me by Matsuda Ryuchi, a very famous authority on Chinese martial arts. He mentioned that my punch was from Chinese kempo—but I was unaware of that. The same happened in other aspects. For instance, some people think that I have changed kata, but I never did. After five years of kata training, two people can practice the same movement and look identical—but after ten years differences emerge. They may think that they are doing the same movement, but since the body, character, and thoughts are different it is only natural that the kata will be different.

Q: How do you feel about full-contact sports?
A: There are schools where the students start free-sparring almost immediately. With this way it might be possible to improve quickly, but you will never reach the higher levels. The bottom line is that if you don't train extensively in the basics, you cannot reach the higher stages of martial arts. Some people misunderstand the meaning and use of the basics. You see, full

contact karate, like Western boxing, is both good and not good. If you are young and strong it is very good but, of course, for older people and children it is not good. The kihon are just the basic techniques, but a thorough grounding in those will teach your body to instantly understand what is required in combat. The idea is to merge the body and mind. You should be able to perform any movement without thinking. This is the real meaning and purpose of the kihon.

Q: You are in great physical condition. How do you train?
A: If I could train as I like, I'd be in even better condition, but sometimes is impossible due to meetings, visitors, business, et cetera. I believe a good karateka must use his body and his mind, so I study and read also. This gives a practitioner a much stronger quality—a balanced personality. As far as food, I think a lot depends on the mental attitude. If you eat something and think, "This is not good for me," then your body won't make proper use of it. But even if you eat curry, for example, and think, "This is good! It's great for my body," then you'll derive something positive from it.

I also think that control of the *hara* helps your body to use the food properly.

"The kihon are just the basic techniques, but a thorough grounding in those will teach your body to instantly understand what is required in combat. The idea is to merge the body and mind."

Q: Do you weight train?
A: No, but it might be beneficial for other people. There is good training equipment for the martial artist if they know how to use them properly. It is important to understand that the body changes and one loses the power of the muscles as you age. You cannot retain physical power forever. At some point you must develop the power of the internal organs. When you're older, the power of the spirit is what shapes your karate.

137

Q: You mentioned that kumite it is very important to harmonize oneself with the opponent. What does this mean?
A: I know this is a very difficult concept to understand until the practitioner is able to experience it himself. The basic idea is to establish harmony within yourself—harmonize your breathing, your movements, and your power. This will lead you to harmonize with the opponent. With this kind of harmony your opponent will be unable to find a good moment to attack you and it will be very difficult for him to beat you. Only then will you be able to use and combine *sen no sen*, and *go no sen*. You must work in harmony with your opponent and not against him.

Q: What's your advice to practitioners?
A: I would like to see them work to understand the real spirit of karate—the breathing control and the cultivation of *hara*. They are difficult to put into words but can be found and experienced with thought and by applying oneself. My philosophy is to always be true to myself and to others. I can honestly say that I fear nothing, not even death—and I do not mean this in a big-headed or conceited way. I simply always try my best in everything I do, so I will be satisfied when I die. I think the reason that people fear death is because they want to accomplish so many things that are left undone—they feel their life is unfinished.

Tournaments are OK, but the practitioner has to understand more than only sport. Usually the practitioner is disappointed when the point goes against him because winning is everything, and he understands nothing else. A person like this is very dangerous to society because he respects only himself. If you respect your opponent, you'll never start a war. Everything connects to karate. True Budo is good for society.

Q: Do you have any karate secrets?
A: There is no secret other than hard training. When I started karate training, the first year included a lot of running. The dojo at Takushoku University was so small that the loser of the race were eliminated from karate class! This built spirit. You must never forget that the purpose of training is to master the art of karate, and to do so one has to develop perseverance, patience, and imagination to survive the ups and downs of being in the dojo. This is the real spirit of karate. O

Facing his opponent *(1)*, Sensei Kanazawa deflects the attacking *yoko geri (2)*, to to his left side *(3)*, creating an opening *(4)*, which allows him to finish his opponent with a *powerful* ushiro geri *to the face (5).*

Masters' Techniques

Sensei Kanazawa (left) faces the aggressor (1). As his opponent assumes a position to attack with a front kick (2), Sensei Kanazawa adjusts the distance and blocks the kick (3), sets himself (4), and finishes with a final double hand counterattack to his opponent's neck (5).

Sensei Kanazawa squares off with his opponent (1). The opponent attacks with a mae geri chudan that Kanazawa blocks with both hands (2). Deflecting the incoming leg to the side and simultaneously counterattacking to the opponent's neck with a shuto uchi (3), Kanazawa safely moves out of the aggressor's attack range (4).

Taiji Kase

Karate's Timeless Master

Taiji Kase is one of the top karate-do instructors in the world. Born in Tokyo on February 9, 1929, and a direct student of Master Funakoshi, Sensei Kase displays a very personal expression of the art. His performance in traditional kata is flawless and his skill in kumite is second to none. Years of practice and hard training have forged this icon of Japanese karate into a living embodiment of kime or fighting spirit.

He is constantly traveling all over the world and was one of the first instructors sent to the West when the Japan Karate Association decided to spread the art of the empty hand to every corner of the globe.

The spirit and the privilege of being part of the first, legendary Shotokan dojo built by Funakoshi in 1944, and destroyed by the American forces one year later, still spices every action and movement performed by Sensei Kase. It is his trademark and a memory that he cherishes. When he demonstrates any of his exquisite Shotokan kata he looks like a reincarnated kami, invoking some timeless elemental spirit. He is a master whose spirit and technique are as timeless as Mount Fuji and as deep as the Sea of Japan.

Q: When did you begin training in karate-do?
A: When I was 6 I began training in judo, since my father was a judo teacher. Judo was much better known during the war, but I started practicing karate in 1944 at the shotokan dojo, where Master Funakoshi was imparting his knowledge of the art of the empty hand. I remember one day I was in a bookstore and I saw a book written by Master Funakoshi. Of course, I knew about judo, aikido, and kendo, but karate was something new to me. I decided then to go to his dojo. This dojo was destroyed by the American Air Force in 1945. This is a very important memory to me because many other great karate instructors never had the chance to train and learn from Master Funakoshi at his original dojo. I'll keep that memory until the last day of my life and beyond.

143

"We didn't think about tournaments or sport. It was touch and kill, very much like katana training. This was the true age of Budo!"

Q: Who else was there with you?

A: I remember that Master Tsuomu Oshima, who now resides in California, was also training there with me. My university was Senshin, and Sensei Oshima went to Komazawa. I used to collect Sensei Funakoshi to go to training. Both the atmosphere and the spirit at the old dojo was very special—very different from the other schools. I firmly believe that there was some kind of magic there. The training we did then with sword was perfectly applicable to the empty-hand methods of karate. You have to remember that we were living in a time of war so the martial spirit was everywhere. We didn't think about tournaments or sport. It was touch and kill, very much like katana training. This was the true age of Budo!

Q: Did you only train under Sensei Funakoshi?

A: Well, Sensei Egami and Sensei Hironishi were also my teachers. They helped Funakoshi Yoshitaka in assisting Funakoshi Gichin. I remember that around 1946 Sensei Hironishi was helping Gichen Funakoshi. I also trained under Yoshitaka, his son.

Q: What do you remember about the son of Master Funakoshi?

A: He was really fast and strong. His movements were truly powerful—like a tiger! He was good at everything. Unfortunately, at 38 he was already very sick. Sometimes he had to stop in the middle of the training and go to a corner to rest. Then he would apologize and return to train—even harder. He had been told at 12 years old that his illness had no cure. I guess he wanted to reach a higher spiritual level by training without limits. I truly believe this was the reason for his extraordinary ability and skill in the art.

Q: Some of these names are related to the shotokai branch, right?
A: Yes. For instance Shimoda, Ohtsuka, and Obata can be considered Funakoshi's first generation students. Hironishi was second generation. I guess this is the reason why I have a very good relationship with shotokai people. We were together, so I never saw a reason to stop our relationship.

Q: What has changed in you and in the art of karate-do since those times?
A: A lot of things! I have changed a lot and the art has also changed. I guess all these changes have been for the good. I have been practicing karate for almost 50 years non-stop, every single day. But there is something that has not changed during all these years and that is the mentality and the training spirit found in Master Funakoshi's dojo. This spirit is still inside of me. From the technical point of view, the art of karate has greatly evolved over the years but I think that part of the old spirit has been lost. And that is not good. I believe that spirit has to be kept within the art because it is the real spirit of karate-do.

"I have been practicing karate for almost 50 years non-stop, every single day. But there is something that has not changed during all these years and that is the mentality."

Q: You were personally trained by Master Funakoshi. How do you remember him?
A: I met him when he was 70 years old. He had a very structured mentality concerning the art and was concerned about how it should be taught to the new generations. Sensei Funakoshi was continually changing and improving the art. I would say that he liberated karate from the precepts of Okinawan karate. On the other hand, he was a very honest and calm man—very kind and with a deep spirituality.

Q: Do you think Master Funakoshi would approve of the karate-do evolution during the last years?
A: First of all, Sensei Funakoshi was constantly changing and making innovations to the art. I am sure he would agree with the evolution, but it is very important to try to understand his mentality. He was from Okinawa and

"Competition might impoverish the art because practitioners tend to standardize the way they train, therefore creating a competition style."

when he moved to Japan he saw how other martial arts systems like judo had great recognition from the government and the people. He wished the same thing for karate-do. He wanted karate-do to be part of the Budo arts. For Master Funakoshi, karate was not a sport but a way of life. He always advised us to practice and keep practicing all the time. I really think Sensei Funakoshi would be very proud of all his students and how the art he brought to Japan from Okinawa is being practiced around the world. However, it is important to distinguish three different stages in the development of shotokan karate—the Okinawan, the Japanese and that of Yoshitaka Funakoshi.

Q: You mentioned that Funakoshi did not believe in karate as a sport. What do think about the fact that karate is probably going to be accepted in the Olympics?
A: I agree with the idea of karate becoming an Olympic sport. The sport aspect is a small part of the whole art—a small but important part nowadays. Karate competition is very fashionable these days and it has allowed the art to spread. In itself, that's not particularly bad but it may bring some consequences if we don't keep an eye on it. Competition might impoverish the art because practitioners tend to standardize the way they train, therefore creating a competition style. Fighters end up losing their personality and their training becomes competition-orientated. On the other hand, karate is not only Budo, but Budo is a big part of karate that has to be kept. It can be used to develop human relationships. This is why the sportive side of karate is good. But it is only good as long as the techniques are kept in the right context and the karateka understand the tradition that links his spirit to the other parts of the art. I'd say that the sportsman has to respect the Budo.

"Sport karate is useful during your youth but the art of karate is for all your life. Karate is karate, boxing is boxing, and tennis is tennis. You shouldn't modify techniques just to score a point."

Q: What do you mean?

A: It's important to keep the right attitude and approach to training while you develop the sport, but if you begin to modify the karate techniques in order to be better in sport competition—and you forget about the right *zanchin,* the right posture, and the right combat spirit—then sport karate will ruin real karate. Sport karate is useful during your youth but the art of karate is for all your life. Karate is karate, boxing is boxing, and tennis is tennis. You shouldn't modify techniques just to score a point. Your technique and spirit have to be strong, never lacking in concentration. I don't see a problem in doing sport competition and preserving the real spirit of karate in every technique you use in combat. This is the right way. Real karate is not just jumping around and grazing your opponent. It's concentration and bang! Game over. You have to think about a life-or-death situation. Karate is a martial art which is practiced bare-handed. You try to render an opponent unable to fight by using a single technique. Period.

Q: You were one of the first JKA instructors sent to spread the art around the world and one of the pioneers in the famous Instructors Course. Is the JKA Instructors Course as hard as it used to be?

A: Not anymore. I still teach some of the classes every time I go back to Japan but these courses are not that taxing when compared to the old ones. In the old days they were very hard, very exhausting and tough. There was an unbelievable spirit in the air with Sensei Kanazawa, Sensei Shirai, Sensei Enoeda, et cetera. Classes today are very hard, but not that hard. After training there we were sent to different countries to teach the art of karate-do. I believe that JKA karate is the most researched and refined karate there is. The instructor training program allowed the students to devote themselves to the art, to completely immerse themselves in study and training. This is what made JKA karate so strong and the true reason why JKA teachers had such a high technical level.

Q: Did this personally affect your evolution and development as a karateka?

A: Well, not only myself but other instructors like Enoeda sensei, Shirai sensei, Kanazawa sensei, et cetera, who have been away from Japan for three decades! Our distancing from Japan meant we had to set our own standards—either to improve or deteriorate as karateka independently. We are always exchanging ideas and I believe our standard has greatly improved. I always look for reality training for myself and my students. I like to analyze the technical and psychological levels of karate and the way it is expanding. I am daily searching for new techniques that are more relevant to the way I see the art these days. When karate was developing there were many gaps to be filled. Master Funakoshi knew that the influence of other methods was essential and that's why I'm trying to incorporate them. I truly believe in a healthy karate. Unfortunately, these days I see too much tension in the practitioners. They become so excited that they forget to relax their muscles. Trying hard is all they do and by the time they develop speed, their muscles are too tense. Therefore they can't relax properly in order to use their natural energy and muscle relaxation to build up speed in their techniques. Modern practitioners need to develop a sense of balance between the soft and hard side of karate.

Q: What did Sensei Nakayama mean to the art of karate-do?

A: Very much. He was a turning point in the evolution of the art and his dedication and work should be recognized by every practitioner around the world. He opened a lot of new doors for karate, not only for shotokan practitioners but for students of any karate style. Master Funakoshi was a true gentleman and the person taking over should be the same. Nakayama sensei was a great man and a gentleman as well. Unfortunately, since he passed away the JKA has split and all the great teachers that once were together now are working in different directions. It's sad but there's not much you can do about it. The old top instructors like Sensei Nishiyama, Sensei Okazaki, Sensei Shoji, or myself—we are living out of Japan so a problem was created as far as choosing a leader. The rest is history.

Q: Sensei, you mentioned once that you were "doing your own karate." It is possible to personalize the art of karate?

A: I definitely do my own expression of the art. It depends on my body, my mentality, my spirit, and my attitude. It is based on the way I look at life itself. Everybody is different and after many years of practice and understanding of the principles of karate your own expression of what you have learned will see the light.

"Everybody is different and after many years of practice and understanding of the principles of karate your own expression of what you have learned will see the light."

Sensei Oyama began his training in shotokan but he experienced different arts and decided to add certain things. Later on, he created the kyokushinkai system. Don't misunderstand me, this is not something that can be done overnight. It takes many years of training and above all, a deep understanding of the fundamental principles of karate and yourself. I don't think the style is that important. For instance, Sensei Tagaki practices shotokai. The technique is different but the spirit is the same. The essence of the art is the same, it has not changed a bit. This is what is really important.

"It's like playing piano; you can play Mozart or Chopin but if you are a lousy pianist, forget about it!"

Q: Have you practiced other karate styles?
A: I have a lot of friends that practice and teach other styles, and let me tell you that at a certain level it is not the art but the person that's important. The styles converge, they share the same principles but it's up to the practitioner to make it work.

Q: What does kata training mean in your perception of karate-do?
A: For the beginners, kata is just a form, an external mold—but when you've trained for many years your understanding expands and kata becomes something else quite distinct. Also, you preferences in kata change with your age and evolution. Some kata may be very difficult for me but easy for you and vice versa. It is the person's ability that causes the difficulty. Unfortunately, in most cases, the kata we see are not real. The judges in competition only look at rhythm. I believe everyone, including myself, should talk to each other about the different aspects related to kata. I think

some people are losing the kata internal meaning just for competition purposes. And that's definitely something wrong.

Q: Master Shigeru Egami developed shotokai, which differs from the system practiced and taught by Nakayama Sensei. What is your opinion of Egami Sensei?

A: The shotokai style seems strange to anyone practicing the more orthodox systems of karate-do. The kata are the same as shotokan but are performed in a soft, slow and fluid fashion, reminiscent of tai chi. Egami Sensei was one of the senior students of Master Funakoshi and he was an excellent technician. In fact, he was the model for the kata in the second edition of Funakoshi's book, *Karate Do Kyohan*. In the early '60s, Egami Sensei began his researches on the internal aspects of the martial arts and came upon his unique soft karate. He felt he was continuing his karate development in a way Funakoshi Gichin would have approved. He was an excellent karateka. Sensei Egami found something, but perhaps it was too difficult for him to transmit this to his students. He was very concerned with the "do" of karate-do.

Q: What is your advice for the karate practitioners around the world?

A: I would recommend that they train hard, every single day. Always keep in mind the right spirit and attitude in training. Don't forget about striking a balance in training between kata and kumite because that is the real secret. I am very old but I still train as much as I can accordingly to my age. You never stop learning and this is something that you have to carve in your mind from the first day. From day one to the last day of your life you are always learning. In the end, it is not about the styles of karate—there is just karate. O

Takayuki "Tak" Kubota

The Master of Inner and Outer Strength

TAKAYUKI KUBOTA IS ONE OF THE MOST FAMOUS AND RESPECTED KARATE MASTERS IN THE UNITED STATES. BORN ON SEPTEMBER 20, 1934 ON THE JAPANESE ISLAND OF KYUSHU, HE DEMONSTRATED AND PERFORMED HIS BREATHTAKING STRENGTH AND CONDITIONING EXERCISES AT ED PARKER'S LONG BEACH INTERNATIONAL CHAMPIONSHIPS IN 1966.

IN ADDITION TO TEACHING HIS VERY AGGRESSIVE STYLE OF GOSOKU-RYU KARATE, SENSEI KUBOTA HAS BEEN ACKNOWLEDGED AS THE MOST ACTIVE AND INNOVATIVE KARATE INSTRUCTOR IN THE FIELD OF LAW ENFORCEMENT TECHNIQUES. ALTHOUGH HIS HAIR HAS GRAYED SOME SINCE HIS MEMORABLE LONG BEACH DEMONSTRATION IN THE MID-'60S, HE STILL LEADS HIS CLASSES WITH THE SAME INTENSITY AND DEDICATION HE DID THEN. AS FAMOUS FOR HIS WORK IN MOTION PICTURES AS FOR HIS KARATE EXPERTISE, HIS CREDITS INCLUDE APPEARANCES IN FILMS SUCH AS THE CLASSIC TORA, TORA, TORA, AND THE KILLER ELITE.

SOMEONE SAID ONCE THAT IF YOU THREW ALL THE TOP MASTERS IN THE WORLD INTO ONE ROOM AND HAD THEM FIGHT, KUBOTA WOULD BE THE ONE WHO WALKED OUT. ENOUGH SAID.

Q: Why do you have so many foreign students training in your Glendale dojo?
A: I guess it became almost a tradition. They are students of other top instructors in different karate styles such as shotokan, goju-ryu, shito-ryu, et cetera, in their own countries. I think they are attracted by the versatility of what I teach. I honestly don't know the main reason, though. The only thing I do is provide them with the best training and welcome them. I believe in many ways this is great. You can find students from France, Italy, Hong Kong, Mexico, Korea, and more—it's like visiting the United Nations!

Q: When did you start training?
A: During World Word II, many Okinawans came to my home in Kyusho and my family helped some of them. Two of these men were experts in *to-de* (it was not called karate in Okinawa at that time) and taught the towns-

"I teach gosoku-ryu karate. I like to say that it may not look too classy but it is very effective."

people in return for their assistance. Their names were Terada and Tokunaga. When I was only 4 years old, my father began to teach me the very basics of karate-do— kihon, kata and a lot of makiwara training. My training was very hard; everything evolved around number 500: 500 kicks, 500 punches, 500 stance changes, 500 hits to the makiwara, and 500 minutes of kata. Everyday was very much the same. My father was teaching me karate to fight to kill, not for self-improvement or sport but for war. We had no gi to wear after the war, but it didn't matter, we just trained very, very hard for real fighting. That is the way karate was taught in those days. Later on, I moved on to Master Kanken Toyama's dojo. Toyama shihan was a direct student of Yasutsune Itosu and Kanryo Higaonna.

Q: Do you think all those students from other styles come to you in order to overcome the flaws in their own systems?

A: I don't know. It is true that some styles have weak points and when the student reaches the black belt level he might see those so he decides to go out and train in a different style. Some styles are very strong but they are weak in defense. Other are very fast but lack stamina.

Q: What happened when you moved to Tokyo?

A: I began teaching karate a couple of years after I got to Tokyo. At that time I knew Mikami of the Japan Karate Association and also Fumio Demura of the shito-ryu style. We used to help each other and visit our respective dojos to teach and make technical exchanges. This was all a long time ago, maybe 30 years back!

Q: What style do you teach?

A: I teach gosoku-ryu karate. I like to say that it may not look too classy but it is very effective. I teach how to use power when power is the answer, how to use speed when speed is the answer, and how to use evasion when evasion has to be used. Neither one of those work all the time under all circumstances. You need to have all the physical elements but also intelligence in order to combine then efficiently.

Q: Do you teach karate in the traditional way or have you made some changes?
A: Of course I made changes. It is not that I have changed the basic techniques but since I have studied different styles I understand their strong and weak points. For instance, some karate styles are very good at offensive maneuvers but they lack an extensive repertoire in defensive actions. In gosoku-ryu I have incorporated many different methods.

"Since I have studied different styles I understand their strong and weak points. In gosoku-ryu I have incorporated many different methods."

Q: Your students are very successful in sport karate. Do you teach special techniques for competition?
A: Yes I do, but they are successful because they train hard and put a lot of time into it. What's funny is that a lot of them are very good at getting disqualified for attacking too hard. Competition techniques don't work in real life and in self-defense situations because the whole environment is different—but being a professional instructor means giving people what they want and need.

"Competition techniques don't work in real life and in self-defense situations because the whole environment is different."

Q: So you try to give each student what they are looking for?
A Yes. That's why in my dojo you can see movie stars, film directors, lawyers, undercover agents and even street fighters. I believe that a good

155

"You need different techniques because people are different—and you need to have tools to deal with different kinds of opponents."

instructor has to be able to teach every component of his art at every level. You can't teach a child the same way you teach an undercover FBI agent.

Q: Do you think that different karate styles competing against each other will lead karate to a modification of technique?
A: Eventually. They will have to analyze other styles and find about their own strong and weak points to try to overcome them. It also will affect kata performance, since shotokan people might be doing shito-ryu or goju-ryu kata if the kata their practitioners have selected for competition has its roots in other *ryu*. Little by little the styles will be modified.

"After seeing the weak points they expose during matches, we go back to the dojo and work on producing good competition fighters."

Q: How do you train students for competition?

A: I take them to as many competitions as possible to match them against different karate styles. I make them train harder discovering their weak points while they are under pressure and correct them. This is what I call "closing the gaps." Eventually, as they get smarter, all these mistakes will fade away, and they will become instinctive fighters. However, it is very different to be a fighter than a competitor. You have to watch the students in the artificial competition atmosphere. Then, after seeing the weak points they expose during matches, we go back to the dojo and work on producing good competition fighters.

Q: Do you have any favorite techniques?

A: I like sweeping and counter-punching a lot, but really I don't prefer any one technique. You need different techniques because people are different—and you need to have tools to deal with different kinds of opponents. This is

"I believe that in order to deliver or take a punch, the practitioner has to be strong. I've always trained like this but I don't push it on anyone else."

the reason why it is so important to spar against many different stylists.

Q: Do you have any objection to sport karate?
A: I don't think there's anything wrong with competition. What I really dislike is that it is very limiting as far as technique is concerned. And that is bad. I believe that there should be a lot more techniques and not only *gyaku tsuki* and *mae geri*. This is the reason for the poor attendance at karate competitions. What do the organizers expect when the techniques are so boring?

Q: Do you feel karate will go the same way as judo?
A: If we keep doing things this way, for sure. A long time ago they started to create rules for the judo until judo was not a martial art anymore. To prevent this from happening to karate we must have a widening of techniques, and not prohibit so many practical self-defense moves, like judo.

Q: You shocked everybody at Ed Parker's International Karate Championship in 1966 when you beat your own hand with a sledgehammer.
A: I believe that in order to deliver or take a punch, the practitioner has to be strong. I've always trained like this but I don't push it on anyone else. I will teach it if someone wants to learn, but a lot of it is mental training, too.

Q: How did you get involved with this kind of training?
A: My teacher told all the students that we must toughen our bodies and make them strong so we could attack anyone. I remember we had no makiwara at all, so we used rocks. I recall hitting one wrong and cutting my hand pretty badly. My teacher came and did what he thought would help me the most—he poured salt in the open cuts!

Q: So you believe in makiwara training?
A: If you are in a real fight with a big opponent you have to be strong, and you need a lot of power to be able to stop him properly. In the old karate tradition you had to kill him before he killed you. I like that kind of training. I teach two different styles of hitting the makiwara. First you must hit it relaxed and focus on the surface—I call this the "stopping style."

"You have to overcome the pain and the fear and go beyond the physical."

The next method is to carry the strike through. You must make the entire body a weapon—even your toes!

Q: What about your special hammer training?
A: I do special concrete training and hammer training—I have done this for a long time. I pound my hands, arms and shins with a two-pound hammer—this makes you very strong! Back in Tokyo I was good friends, in my younger days, with Mas Oyama and the famous pro-wrestler Rikadozan. We used to train a lot on the makiwara. In fact, when Master Oyama published his first book he decided to use my picture—but only my hand. He didn't want to use my face!

Q: It has a lot to do with mental training?
A: Yes. I believe it is the best way to train. It makes you tough and allows you to develop the true martial arts spirit. You have to overcome the pain and the fear and go beyond the physical. Of course, I use certain criteria to decide whether or not I will teach a student these special methods. They must toughen their bodies, and the best way is through these exercises.

With James Caan

"You can hit me anywhere you want, and it will probably hurt you more than it does me."

"Some people improve very fast while others need more time to learn the same material."

Q: How do you start students into the program?

A: He starts out slowly and gradually builds up. After a year, the student can punch the makiwara over 1,000 times without a problem. Of course, sometimes we have injures. People don't train like they should and make mistakes such as hitting the object improperly and breaking their bones. Unfortunately, it comes with the training. It happened to me many times.

Q: Do you think these programs are beneficial for the average practitioner?

A: I don't train so I can go to a tournament and do a show. I do it because I want to train my body so I will be prepared for any confrontation. That's the philosophy of my style. You can hit me anywhere you want, and it will probably hurt you more than it does me. The program prepares you to take on anything. At this point I can block a kendo stick with my forearm and sustain no injury.

Q: What is the most important factor in training students?

A: There's no simple answer to that. It depends on the student. Some people improve very fast while others need more time to learn the same material. There are guys that will never become good, but they really enjoy the training because it improves their health and therefore their lives. The bottom line is that they need a good teacher. But be careful, because a good karate man may be not a good karate teacher.

Q: How important is the length of time a person trains?

A: It is paramount. The student may have timing, speed, technique, et cetera, but after a few minutes against a good opponent technique goes out the window. It's only after at least ten years of training, when a student's body has absorbed the techniques, and the mind is free to work instinctively on fighting, rather than thinking about every move, that you can really be a karate fighter. It takes ten years to produce a mature karate student.

Q: What would be your message to all karate practitioners?
A: That they practice the art as a whole through kata, kumite and kihon. Today, many people train kata and kumite as if they were two different things. Actually, kumite starts with kata, and kata starts with kumite. This mindset would vastly improve any student's kumite. I don't mean the kind of kumite you see now, but the kumite using other techniques like *enpi* (elbow) and *hiza* (knee).

Q: But that's very dangerous.
A: Everything is dangerous if you can't control it. That's why you have to study kata for timing and control. Only if we do this will karate grow and avoid the same pitfalls and fate as judo.

"I do special concrete training and hammer training—I have done this for a long time. I pound my hands, arms and shins with a two pound hammer— this makes you very strong!"

Q: Do you like the way karate has developed in the West?
A: I really like the Japanese karate style, but I also understand that different cultures have different ways of approaching the same subject. It is impossible to regulate the whole karate world but it is not impossible to teach respect to the students—respect and etiquette. Unfortunately, many dojos in the West lack this. This should be preserved and passed down for future generations. Without respect and etiquette, karate is just common street brawling. O

Masters' Techniques

From an on-guard stance (1), the attacker
explodes with a right cross (2). Sensei Kubota
counters with an outward block (3), steps
in and pulls the attacker forward to a knee
strike (4), and executes shuto uchi to the
back of the neck (5)

From a ready stance (1), the attacker attempts a bear hug (2). Sensei Kubota grabs the left and right sides of the attacker's gi, and fires a knee to the side (3). He then elbows the attacker (4) and pulls him down (5).

Kenei Mabuni

A Balance of Heart and Body

AN AWESOME KARATE MASTER WITH A UNIQUE CHARISMATIC PERSONALITY, HE WAS BORN ON FEBRUARY 13, 1918 IN SHURI, OKINAWA. THE OLDEST SON OF SHITO-RYU FOUNDER KENWA MABUNI, HE STARTED TRAINING KARATE AT A VERY EARLY AGE AND OFTEN HELPED HIS FATHER GIVE DEMONSTRATIONS THROUGHOUT JAPAN DURING THE 1930S. WHEN THE DAI NIPPON BUTOKU KAI WAS FOUNDED, KENEI MABUNI HAD THE OPPORTUNITY TO TRAIN AND LEARN FROM THE NOTABLE VISITORS WHO CAME TO TRAIN AND LEARN FROM HIS FATHER. THIS INCLUDED SUCH LEGENDARY FIGURES AS KONISHI YASUHIRO, CHOKI MOTOBU, AND FUNAKOSHI GICHIN. SHORTLY AFTER THE DEATH OF HIS FATHER FROM A HEART ATTACK, KENEI MABUNI SUCCEEDED HIS FATHER AS THE SECOND SOKE OF THE STYLE AND ACCEPTED THE AWESOME RESPONSIBILITY OF MAINTAINING THE QUALITY OF SHITO-RYU KARATE WORLDWIDE. HIS TECHNIQUE AND KNOWLEDGE COMPLEMENT HIS EXCELLENT PEDIGREE. ON JANUARY 15, 1984, HE WAS PRESENTED THE DISTINGUISHED SERVICE MEDAL FOR HIS CONTRIBUTION TO THE MARTIAL ARTS BY THE JAPAN MARTIAL ARTS COUNCIL. KENEI MABUNI ALSO RECENTLY ESTABLISHED THE WORLD SHITO KAI KARATE-DO FEDERATION, OF WHICH HE WAS NAMED GOVERNOR. THE RESPONSIBILITY OF PERPETUATING HIS FATHER'S TRADITIONS COULD NOT BE ON BROADER OR STRONGER SHOULDERS.

Q: You were born in the dojo, so to speak, weren't you?
A: Yes. I began my karate training in Okinawa in 1925, when I was 7 years old. The dojo was part of the house my father owned so it was something very natural. He was a policeman at that time. My father, Kenwa Mabuni, trained extensively under two of the greatest karate teachers of that time—Anko Itosu of Shuri-te and Kanryo Higaonna of Naha-te. Later on, he develop his own method called "shito-ryu," a name that uses the ideograms from "Itosu" (shi) and "Higaonna" (to). It was his way of paying respect and giving credit to his teachers.

Q: What do you remember about training under your father?
A: Well, my father was a very strong man and very strict with me. He always gave me a sense of commitment in everything I did. As a boy I

*"I began my karate training in Okinawa in 1925,
when I was 7 years old. The dojo was part of the house
my father owned so it was something very natural."*

wanted to become stronger but later on I became fascinated with the philosophy and spirit of Budo. My father's teaching was based on the principles of *shin, gi,* and *tai.* "Shin" means heart, *"gi"* means technique, and *"tai"* means body. The practitioner should look for a perfect balance among these three aspects. Unfortunately, many of today's karateka fail to balance these elements properly. Technique-wise, the movements from Shuri-te are faster and they use a lot open hand techniques. Naha-te is based on the idea of power—the strength coming from the *hara* as the kata *sanchin* proves. The main idea is to keep your center of gravity low and use your hara along with the proper breathing patterns. At the time my father was teaching there was a rivalry between both schools of karate and, in fact, challenges weren't an uncommon thing. Don't forget that many other karateka came to train under my father and did not always easily accept my father as their teacher. He had to prove himself to them!

Q: Was your father ever concerned about the use and development of *ki?*
A: Of course! Not in a mystical sense, but in a very real and practical one. He was aware of the energy we all have and he knew how to properly use it for karate training. He studied the *Bubishi* and he knew how to attack the vital points.

Q: How important is bunkai for you?

A: Bunkai is a very important aspect if we are interested in learning the right form of karate-do. We have to notice though, that bunkai varies depending on the style that you practice and does not always indicate the skill level of the practitioner. For instance, shotokan styles favor more long-range techniques as compared to shito-ryu or goju-ryu. Therefore, the application of the physical techniques is based on a different conceptual approach. At short distance, you need to use your limbs and shoulders in a different way. One problem I have perceived in the understanding and development of bunkai is that many practitioners try to explain the kata techniques, or bunkai, and how they apply to a real situation, as they are performing the actual form. This is alright at a basic level but not for the advanced karateka. If you think about how kata techniques are applied to combat, then you're thinking that fighting and combat will give you a different mentality. If you understand this point you'll realize that your mind needs to be in a very different state,

"The classical or the traditional movement found in kata is one thing and the way you directly apply them in a real situation is another."

which gives a very different flavor to the kata technique. You can't try to put that into a real situation and squeeze the physical into the form of the kata. If you do that then you can come out with a very weird and unrealistic application of kata movements. The classical or traditional movement found in kata is one thing and the way you directly apply them in a real situation is another. The body mechanics may be the same but the flavor of the combat application is different because your state of mind is different. Only if you know what you're looking for will you find the karate behind a real confrontation. Curiously enough, bunkai doesn't make you a good karateka—kihon, kata practice, and kumite do. Don't be mistaken.

"Once the karateka has a kata with good technique and rhythm, the next stage is to introduce more advanced principles such as mental control and concentration."

Q: Is kata truly the essence of karate?

A: There is a very high number of practitioners all around the world who are interested in what we call "old" or "traditional" karate-do—and thus use kata as the center of their training. And this is good because it helps them to understand the roots of the art. Proper kata training is not as easy as it looks. Let's assume the practitioner has a good technical level in kihon, remember "No kihon, no karate." The first stage is to learn the pattern, to learn the actual form, and memorize the movement in the proper order. You have to make your body fit into the form. Then you start to add speed and power to each technique. Your body knows the movements so you can put more into it. The next step is to learn and develop the right timing and rhythm in the kata. This is a difficult part since now the practitioner controls the kata and the way the form is performed. Once the karateka has kata with good technique and rhythm, the next stage is to introduce more advanced principles such as mental control and concentration. His mind is the important point now. He can only focus on this once he has the physical control over the movements and rhythm of the sequences. Your mind has to be in control before, during, and after the execution of the form. This is a very difficult part of karate training, where kata becomes a kind of meditation. Reaching this level is extremely difficult and only then can you say "the kata is mine." Your mind takes control over everything else.

Q: What's your opinion on the evolution of kumite in competition?

A: Kumite is a misunderstood aspect these days. Kumite is not sport competition. Sport is one aspect of kumite. I would say that on the physical level, the most important principle in kumite is *ma* (distance). Interestingly enough, ma not only applies to kumite but also to kata training. Anyway, if a practitioner understands and is able to control ma he can control his opponent in a fight without delivering a single technique. Whoever controls the distance controls the fight. Other important aspects such as *mushin, sen no sen, go no sen*, et cetera, are only possible when the karateka has reached a certain level of technical profi-

"Kumite is a misunderstood aspect these days. Kumite is not sport competition. Sport is one aspect of kumite."

ciency and skill. He doesn't need to think about certain things so he can develop the higher principles of karate-do. He can feel his opponent's actions almost instinctively and is in perfect synchronization with every movement during the fight. His body is not in control, his mind is. He is able to read actions and react with no wasted movement or energy. This level of skill is very hard to reach and only comes after many years of intensive and dedicated practice and training. It's a kind of sixth sense.

Q: Do you see any differences between Western and Eastern practitioners?

A: It's hard to say, but I feel there are differences between an American or European practitioner and a Japanese karateka—and not only physically. The Japanese student will follow the sensei's instructions and try to think and figure out by himself why things are done the way they are done. The Westerner

"If you start training your mind from the very beginning, by the time you're old your mind will be strong and your body won't go down."

will ask "why" almost immediately, and even if he doesn't, his logical approach requires a reason why. Orientals more readily accept and understand the idea of training mind and body at the same time, whereas Westerners do not think about the mind that much but focus more on the body. Of course, there is a downside to this approach—the student will grow old like everybody else and then what? What happens when you cannot rely just on strength and physical abilities? That's the reason karate should be approached as a long-term goal. It's for the rest of your life, not just something you do while you are young. If you start training your mind from the very beginning, by the time you're old your mind will be strong and your body won't go down. If you're strong mentally and physically I believe you can face any problem in your life and come out victorious. In short, the instruction must be adapted to fit into the mentality and culture of the place where the instructor is sharing his knowledge. The teacher doesn't have to change the art, just adapt the way he's transmitting the information. But the information has to be correct.

Q: How does karate apply to the practitioner's life outside the training hall?

A: Alexander Pope said, "Some people will never learn anything because they understand everything too quickly." Karate can't be understood quickly. Karate training doesn't stop when you remove your karate gi. Karate is for life. It is true that there is a time for hard training and a time for soft training—but always the focus should be time for training. In fact, and in a traditional sense, the student has to know how to "steal" knowledge from the teacher. And in order to do this persistence is the keyword. Training alone won't make you a good karateka, but correct training and right attitude will. Keep training in the right way and in

"Karate is not about winning or losing but about character development. The character of the karateka is what is really important."

the right direction and the rewards will come. Some practitioners set unrealistic goals and they become disillusioned after a while. Karate is not about winning or losing but about character development. The character of the karateka is what is really important. Aim to develop the spirit and the higher self. It's important, through karate-do, to develop a philosophy of life that helps you.

Q: Is shito-kai in constant evolution?

A: My father never thought karate-do was perfect and finished. He knew the art was meant to grow and evolve, that's why at shito-kai we have studied and built-up the karate technique. Shito-kai contains a lot of techniques such as locking and throwing that are not so obvious at first sight. I'm constantly searching and learning. Karate is sometimes difficult to understand; you may train for a long time, day after day, and find nothing. All of a sudden, one day, you find out that you have truly improved not only in karate technique, but also in karate spirit. As a teacher, in order to improve yourself and teach properly, you must speak to people and have experiences in life. It seems that in

"Every style or ryu is a tradition, and the heritage of the different masters has to be preserved."

martial arts it is common to break with tradition—but there must be an understanding of what tradition really means to begin with.

Q: Do you think that the different styles of karate are important, or should the art should be unified like Kodokan judo?

A: I think each is definitely important. Every style or *ryu* is a tradition, and the heritage of the different masters has to be preserved. I agree that sometimes the technical differences are strictly based on a personal preference of doing things a certain way, but these personal preferences provide us with a very unique and different point of view. I truly believe that we should maintain the ryu—they bring different flavors. It is like painting—there are many schools of painting that were developed over the centuries, but all of them are art.

Q: Did you train in kobudo?

A: Yes, I studied kobudo. This art helps the karateka to understand certain karate principles on a different level. The use of *tai-sabaki*, *ashi-sabaki*, et cetera is very useful in both arts. Also, it is a great training tool to develop a keen sense of distance and focus. Don't forget that kime is different if you have a bo in your hands, than if you're punching with your empty hand. In the end, kime is kime, but your body feel and body mechanics are greatly improved if you practice kobudo. But I recommend to start training in karate-do first, so you develop an strong base for the weaponry aspect.

Q: Has your karate changed over the years?

A: Of course. I have less physical power and this affects the way I move and perform my karate. I tend to use more natural and circular motions in my technique. When you are young you can go straight all the time, but after a certain age you need to develop ways for your body to move fast naturally. You need more than simple basics. You cannot do karate as if you were 20 years old. You must train in the basics but use different and new training methods that help you to accomplish what you're looking for. There are always physical limitations and I try to find new ways to improve myself. Since karate-do has become a way of life for me, I sometimes question myself about the role of karate in my life, and about my existence—but that's part of my evolution as a human being. My advice for the younger practitioners is to not get scared because you'll question why you are doing it. It's OK, it's normal—everyone gets depressed with their own progression in training. What is important is to feel and spot these depressions and find a way to motivate yourself. Books, videos, and seminar with experts visiting your city or country are excellent methods of pushing through the bad patches.

Q: What is your opinion of combat sports such as kickboxing?
A: I think these modern disciplines have their place for people who have to go through a certain personal development. Unfortunately, kickboxing can be very unhealthy and detrimental in the long

"There are always physical limitations and I try to find new ways to improve myself."

run. Karate can be practiced for life but all these other combat sports cannot. They offer a certain amount of excitement until your body cannot take the punishment anymore. But to me they are sports—very effective and efficient sports—but sports nonetheless and not Budo.

"Tradition is not about technique, it is about ethics and morals. I believe in good etiquette and discipline in and out the dojo."

Q: Do you get tired of all the traveling you do?

A: Yes, I do get very tired but I also enjoy it. It is my responsibility to perpetuate the art my father Kenwa Mabuni developed. So I truly do it with joy. My actions speak for me. I judge myself and my own actions. I have to live with myself and as long as you're honest with yourself and the people around you, everything is alright. It's good to see the art of karate being practiced all around the world, but the real and true art of karate is very rare. It's important to be humble, to understand the simple things in life and training, to respect the senpai and your teachers. Even if they are old, they are still your teachers and respect should be paid to them. Tradition is not about technique, it is about ethics and morals. I don't believe in a soft approach to karate but in hard training, because for me karate-do is a martial art—it is Budo and not a sport. I believe in good etiquette and discipline in and out the dojo.

Q: How important is Zen training?

A: Zen is a big aspect of the Japanese culture and is deeply related to Budo. Zen is something that you cannot teach in a karate class. You can show a little bit but it's something the student has to pursue by himself in order to find its real meaning. I consider it a very important part because it is mental training, and the mental training will carry you when your body can't perform anymore. Zen training can greatly help your karate and in the end, help you in life. Real spiritual training is present in every moment of our lives. But don't forget that Zen training is not only done with your head, but also "with your flesh and bones," as the master said.

"Don't limit your training to only developing your body, but also develop your mind and heart as well. The path of karate-do is not an easy one, it is full of struggle and disappointments."

Q: How does one really understand karate?

A: Karate begins with the physical aspect, then is followed by the mental. But don't forget that to really understand, you must to forge your spirit through the physical. There is no other way. Karate training give us something special that cannot be found in other sports such as football or basketball. It doesn't make us different, but more aware of our inner selves. Karate-do is a way of life, and we shouldn't forget the "do" in our training. Don't limit your training to only developing your body, but also develop your mind and heart as well. Karate-do must be part of a person's life, not separate from it. The path of karate-do is not an easy one, it is full of struggle and disappointments. As in life, not everything always goes right—in fact it seldom does—but if we have the strength to pass these obstacles then we'll reach a higher level, not only as a martial artist but also as a human being. O

Kenzo Mabuni

Staying the Course

HE IS A CAPTIVATING AND COMPELLING MAN. BORN UNDER THE PRESSURE OF BEING THE SON OF ONE OF THE MOST IMPORTANT KARATE-DO TEACHERS OF ALL TIMES, HE HAS A RICH UNDERSTANDING OF THE MARTIAL ARTS. MASTER MABUNI TALKS IN ITALICS WITH EXCLAMATION POINTS TACKED ONTO THE END. HE IS PASSIONATE ABOUT THE IMPORTANCE OF KARATE-DO, BUT YET AT THE SAME TIME PATIENT AND UNDERSTANDING TO THOSE WHO PRACTICE IT.

HEAD OF THE SHITO-RYU NIPPON KARATE-DO KAI, THE ASSOCIATION FOUNDED BY HIS FATHER, KENWA MABUNI, KENZO MABUNI TEACHES THE STYLE OF SHITO-RYU ACCORDING TO THE ORIGINAL AND AUTHENTIC METHODS DEVELOPED BY THE FOUNDER. ALWAYS ON A VERY BUSY AND EXTREMELY TIGHT SCHEDULE, THIS REMARK-ABLE KARATE-DO TEACHER IS CONSIDERED AMONG THE MOST INFLUENTIAL AND BEST KNOWN KARATE MASTERS IN THE WORLD. IT IS WITH DEDICATION AND FORESIGHT THAT KENZO MABUNI—WITH A HIGH APPRECIATION FOR THE AESTHETIC, SPIRITUAL, AND PHYSICAL BEAUTY OF THE ART—HAS EMBRACED THE TASK OF PERPETUATING THE ORIGI-NAL METHODS OF SHITO-RYU KARATE-DO.

Q: What were your beginnings in martial arts?
A: I started karate training when I was 13 years old and have continued until today. This makes more than 60 years of training. I also trained in kendo and judo when I was young and my training in kobudo involved the bo and sai methods of the Tawada tradition. I don't think it is necessary for a karate practitioner to train in other arts such as judo or kobudo, but it defi-nitely helps you to get a better appreciation of other arts, and how your style or system can be used if you face an opponent who practices those other methods.

Q: What do you consider to be the heritage of the shito-ryu style?
A: My father devoted his life to the development of karate-do. This was unknown to the public and he received neither fame nor monetary rewards. The great inheritances of shito-ryu for the future generations are the tradi-tions my father learned from his two great masters—Yasutsune Itosu and

"My father knew over 90 different kata. He created some kata of his own but he didn't teach all of them in public."

Kanryo Higaonna. Of course, he received instruction from other people but these two traditions are the basis of his legacy. He left a great gift for us and I have a mission to teach it correctly to the next generation. Therefore, I must be steadfast, study further, and endeavor to clarify.

Q: What do you think are the most important qualities an instructor should possess?
A: An instructor has a big responsibility on his shoulders. It's important that the instructor study the way of karate-do together with his students. I think that an instructor should be *godan* (fifth degree black belt) and a certified *shihan* to fully instruct the students. He must possess a trustworthy character with strong will. I often find many instructors who falsify their ranks and create their qualifications by themselves. That has caused the chaos of today and misled innocent students. It's important the teacher know how to instruct with accuracy and correctness. The instructor should teach the art through current applicable ethics and the logic of their society. He has to accept the role of father to his students. In doing so he has a big responsibility to teach them the foundation of karate as well as the etiquette and morals. You must practice what you believe and believe what you practice.

Q: Shito-ryu has a very high number of kata; do you think is important to know all of them to master the style?
A: It's true that the shito-ryu style has a high number of kata that represent both the Itosu and Higaonna traditions. My father knew over 90 different kata. He created some kata of his own but he didn't teach all of them in public. This fact shows how important kata is in the shito-ryu tradition. It's

not necessary to learn all the kata, but each kata teaches something unique—that's why they are a precious treasure. *Kodansha* should know about 30 to 40 kata, and that can take somewhere between 15 to 25 years of continuous training and dedication to master. I don't consider any kata to be more important than another—all of them are important if you really want to have an understanding of the authentic shito-ryu legacy. Of course, each instructor and practitioner will have their own preferences and their favorite kata to perform—but it doesn't mean they won't learn, train, and develop the rest.

Q: From your point of view, what's the real problem with competition karate?

A: I believe the problem in modern competition has more to do with the judges than with the competition itself. The great hindrances to competitions ——————ied judges. Oftentimes, ————ople who only possess ——s by passing paper exam— ——ven though their own ——nowledge and back—

"I don't consider any kata to be more important than another—all of them are important if you really want to have an understanding of the authentic shito-ryu legacy."

nadequate to qualify them to even test for the position. In many —hat some person become a judge for certain political reasons or —ish motive to gain titles. Of course, if one is not even qualified to —en he is clearly not qualified to judge.

Q: What's you opinion of combat methods such as kickboxing and full contact karate?

A: I have seen kickboxing and similar disciplines but I consider them to be a sport, not a martial art which involves the aspects of Budo.

"Every karate-do practitioner should practice diligently within the dojo and should neither copy other people nor other styles."

Q: Has your personal training changed over the years?
A: Of course! My birthday is May 30, 1927 and I'm not 20 years old any-more. My daily training consists of kihon movements for one hour. I prac-tice bunkai for another 30 or 40 minutes more, and kumite-bunkai for half-an-hour. Usually I train by myself for another 30 minutes. There are changes and alterations to training methods according to the ages of practi-tioners and the instructor's applications. It's important to understand your own body so you can adapt your private training to that. Every karate-do practitioner should practice diligently within the dojo and should neither copy other people nor other styles. It is important that one must personally practice techniques through their own physical exercise and gain experi-ence through their own diligent efforts.

Q: Do you consider makiwara training essential for a karate-do practitioner?
A: The training with the makiwara post is to make the fist stronger by clinching the fist harder. This makes the technique more effective and the practitioner will learn the proper body dynamics of expansion and contrac-tion of the body as it relates to correct techniques and stances. Its use is not

just to toughen the knuckles, but it teaches and prepares the whole body to absorb the shock of landing punches. In the past, just about everybody had a makiwara to train with, but the times have changed. Nowadays, even the karate world champions don't use it. I think that part of the reason for this is that they concentrate too much on the sport contest aspect of karate where hard contact is not required—makiwara training seems to have no place. I don't agree with this point of view and I still believe that the makiwara should be used because it is another important tool that forges a strong spirit.

Q: Do you think that too much emphasis on kumite might prevent the student from reaching a full understanding of your father's teachings?
A: I think kumite practice is effective, but my father's teachings are steeped in tradition and it is up to us to retain those important aspects. If karate is to retain the elements of traditional martial arts, we cannot let it be reduced to a pure sport. Shito-ryu, from my experience in other martial arts and karate styles, is a very systematic training program devel-

"If karate is to retain the elements of traditional martial arts, we cannot let it be reduced to a pure sport."

oped by my father and style founder Kenwa Mabuni. The emphasis is on polishing the basics and this attitude is deeply related in the Japanese culture and the idea of paying attention and going very deep into every detail. It reflects the true Japanese view towards martial arts and life. This is the reason why kata practice has to be done with an emphasis on perfection and not just by going through the motions.

Q: Have your goals changed over years?
A: My goals have definitely changed. My body is not the same as it used to be. It happens to every martial artist in the world. The way you think

"The soft aspect is the other half of the equation. Power comes from a state of relaxation that allows you to bring the maximum kime in your technique."

changes, as does your training. When you get older the art is not about winning tournaments or similar things, it is about health and integration with yourself. Bringing your body and mind together becomes the main issue. What's the meaning of training? Why do I am doing this? What is my objective? As your body changes and your priorities change, the reason for your daily training changes. The objective changes as you do. We become more aware of what our body means to us and how to keep it in health and perfect condition. I think that karate is different for everybody and if your goal or objective is different, then your karate is different. The development of your mind and heart turns out to be the main goal. This is not only important as a martial artist but as a human being as well, and karate is a good vehicle and a powerful way to help you to understand yourself better. Karate is a very special experience.

Q: Karate is perceived as a 'hard" method. What's your opinion about using the concept of relaxation?

A: Relaxation is very important in the art. Until you really understand how it works, and how beneficial it is for your body and technique, your training will be limited. The soft aspect is the other half of the equation. Power comes from a state of relaxation that allows you to bring the maximum kime in your technique. It allows you to use a little bit more stretch for explosive power in the physical movement. Of course, your body structure has a lot to do with that, but a deep understanding of how the soft aspect of the physical techniques work will bring your karate to a higher level. I think many karate practitioners lack of this soft aspect. Please don't misunderstand me, hardness and strong muscles are not a problem but we need to develop a higher control of our bodies, and in order to achieve this the understanding of the concept of "softness" is paramount. By being relaxed you can have overall awareness and a deeper sense of body control. The idea of "*shizentai*" (natural body) becomes more important as we get older. Our karate should be natural. This kind of control of tension and relaxation is very important for kata training since it is the integration of the body and the imagination. Kata is good for your mind—it is moving Zen.

Q: What does kata mean to you?
A: For me, kata is an expression of daily human conduct and many of the principles are understood from studying many kata. For a authentic karate-do practitioner, kata must be the first priority. My personal feeling is that the karate professional must spend three years on a kata and three months in kumite as a proper ratio. Kata is not just a bunch of basic techniques organized in sequences. Kata, as I said before, is for the integration of the practitioner's mind and imagination. I don't have a preference for any specific kata in particular. My father studied and developed certain kata because he felt it was important for the shito-ryu practitioner to learn the complete syllabus of

"*Our karate should be natural. This kind of control of tension and relaxation is very important for kata training since it is the integration of the body and the imagination.*"

the styles practiced in Okinawa. It is a well-known fact the other karate masters came to my father to learn kata. For instance, Master Funakoshi and my father were great friends, they practiced together and exchanged ideas. In 1945, Master Funakoshi took his students Masatoshi Nakayama and Isao Obata to Osaka to study under my father, and later he introduced the shotokan version of *unshu (unsu)*, *niseshi (nijushiho)*, and *gojushiho*. The shito-ryu style contains beautiful kata, and yet I have found few instructors who teach the deeper meaning of the movements and the right appreciation of the more advanced aspects of training. It is important to understand that it is sometimes necessary to return to the most basic kata to correct one specific body motion used in an advanced kata, or to perfect a point in a particular technique. Unfortunately, in some styles, the study of the body

"Competition is not bad, it's a modern aspect of the art. When you are young you want to test your skills, and competition is good for that."

mechanics has replaced the traditional approach of actually learning how to apply the technique and this is not good. We must strike a balance. As old saying goes, "The person is the kata, and the kata is the person."

Q: Is competition or sport karate bad for karate?

A: Competition is not bad, it's a modern aspect of the art. When you are young you want to test your skills, and competition is good for that. When you enter competition you face fear, insecurities, and other emotional aspects. What is really important is how you deal with these circumstances—how you control these psychological elements. Anger and fear are the two emotions that can make you get into a fight. In competition you deal with one of them. So I think that as long as you know the right place for the competition aspect in your karate training and you know how to use it in order to become a more mature person and karateka, competition is good. The problem appears when you only train for competition or you perceive the art of karate only as a sport. To me this is a mistake and a diversion from the true origins and goals of traditional karate. The old argument of kumite verses kata is only a problem in sport karate. In Budo and traditional karate, kumite and kata go hand-in-hand.

There is no argument, no contradictions whatsoever. Sport karate and competition training not only takes its toll on the kumite aspects but on kata as well.

It's very common these days to see competitors who are more concerned about the look of the kata rather than the meaning of what they are doing. Kata competition, because of the sportive aspect, has become more of a gymnastic test due to the practitioner's attachment to the aesthetic values. The demands of kata competition have caused kata to evolve in ways opposed to the traditional criteria. In these contests, kata is purely performed for the visual effect of the movements, regardless of their meaning for application in a real situation, and things such as heavy breathing and unnecessary pauses have been introduced to impress the judges. Sometimes karate is not logical and the same is true with kata. If you take kata literally, and try to explain it, you're going to have some difficulty making it work. You have to look at kata with a deeper approach than just as simple external movements. Karate is greater than the parts and in order to fully appreciate kata we have to learn to look at it from the correct

"The demands of kata competition have caused kata to evolve in ways opposed to the traditional criteria. In these contests, kata is purely performed for the visual effect of the movements."

angle. We have to study bunkai because in the end kata is kumite, and it is only through a deep study of bunkai that the practitioner can learn and develop a knowledge of the close-quarter or grappling methods hidden in karate. The grappling, throwing, and arm locking techniques in karate are part of the self-defense aspects and not useful for sport competition. If you don't research bunkai you lose the most important side of the art. The right bunkai is dangerous and not beautiful to watch. Sport karate evolves as the development of the competitive aspects of karate-do evolves. However, the Budo essence of karate-do is the same as that represented by the *godoshin—shoshin, doryoku-shin, reisetsu-shin, jyo-shin,* and *wa-shin.*

"To really understand Budo you have to look at it from a variety of angles because it has many facets. Technique is not that important, but its history and philosophy are."

Q: Why is it so difficult to reach a middle point between sport and Budo?

A: Personally, I believe that we *can* find a middle point where sport competition helps karate and karate keeps the traditional values. For instance, let's take *shobu ippon* kumite—there is only one point and only one final action. The old samurai fought with swords and it was a matter of life or death. The loser died. In real fighting you could only make one mistake and if you did, you're dead. This is the same spirit we need in competition today. It requires not only physical and technical training but mental training as well. If the practitioner keeps in mind that he is "looking death straight in the face," that he is "at the edge of death," then his attitude will fit into the Budo precepts. The spirit that is facing death needs to possess a certain philosophy. He has to keep his mental and physical balance and not lose composure. In dealing with a life or death situation the technique is a very relative thing, not something absolute. This is what Budo is all about. But if the karateka thinks about the *shobu ippon* only as a game, then we lose all the important aspects of traditional training that goes far beyond the physical technique. To really understand Budo you have to look at it from a variety of angles because it has many facets. Technique is not that important but its history and philosophy are, and these transcend the physical technique. But don't fool yourself, transcending the techniques implies that there is technique in first place. It is possible to win a competition even though you don't have good basic karate technique, and this is not good. You may have good timing and sharp speed to score but lack good karate basics.

Q: Have you modified or changed any technique to suit modern times?

A: Execution will always improve. It doesn't mean we have to change the technique. These days, the instructors have a better understanding of physics and modern technologies so they use them to better perform and to explain the karate techniques. The technique doesn't change *per se*, but the way we move and understand the movement itself is at a higher level. We use modern technology to improve the art of karate—a more academic approach. A lot of the information we have at our fingertips today was inconceivable a few years ago. But as George Bernard Shaw wrote, "All progress depends on the unreasonable man."

Q: Your mother played a very important role in your father's life, didn't she?
A: Yes, definitely. She understood my father's goal and his dedication to karate-do. My father shared his views and thoughts about the development of the art with her. She was there all the time next to my father, supporting him and the family so my father could develop the art and pursue his training. She devoted her life to my father. She also had a very strong character and she used to help him with his training. For instance, my father used to hit the makiwara every day, rain or shine, early in the morning, pretty much the first thing after waking up. If it was rainy, my mother used to take an umbrella and hold it above the makiwara post so my father could punch it without getting soaked. A woman like that is very difficult to find and my father was fortunate. I truly think she deserves a lot of credit.

Q: Why do you think that most of your father's top students split off and developed their own styles after his death?
A: This question should be asked to all those who claim to be a shito-ryu stylist. Some people don't even have a real connection to the shito-ryu family. This upset me very much. All I have to say is that the Shito-Ryu Nippon Karate-Do Kai was founded at #2-5-32, Ikue, Asahi-Ku, Osaka, Japan. This site exists to this day as my residence. After my father's death my mother suggested that I preserve the continuity of my father's dojo through his traditions, technical lists, personal notes, and shito-ryu kata without any alterations. My mother appointed me the successor and the true heir of shito-ryu. Then my older brother Kenei Mabuni, who ceased training about twelve years prior to our father's death, founded shito-kai with many Osaka region and Toyo University college graduates. In 1955, Ryusho Sakagami of itosu-kai, Masaru Watanabe of seiki-kai, Kenjiro Tomoyori of kenyu-ryu and Chojiro Tani of shuko-kai separately claimed their independence by their own styles. As for as myself, I keep my father's traditions and teachings the way he taught them. It's my job to preserve his art and knowledge as purely as possible. O

Patrick McCarthy

Standing on the Shoulders of Giants

The true origins of karate are shrouded in myth, mysticism, and legend. Many say that karate was invented by Okinawan peasants to fight off well-armed foreign invaders, others claim it to be the warrior art of the upper-class nobility, still others suggest that it was invented by holy men to bring peace, harmony, and balance to its practitioners souls. While all of those explanations undoubtedly contain some kernel of truth, there is much more—and much less—to this rich and complex martial art. Patrick McCarthy has spent much of his life practicing, studying, researching, and writing about karate. A world traveler who has personally sought out the secret kata of karate's remaining "old" masters, McCarthy is also gifted academian who spent nine years translating "The Bible of Karate," the Bubishi, the most important historical karate discovery of our time, into English. Drawing from his wealth of personal and historical knowledge, McCarthy talks about the origins of kata, the differences between Japanese and Okinawan styles, and the practical and philosophical meaning of modern fighting systems.

Mastering the art of karate requires more than dedicated training and many get lost along its arduous path. McCarthy's diligent research serves as a reminder that karate, or any martial art for that matter, can never be mastered without the guidance of someone who knows the way. As Sir Isaac Newton said, "If I can see further, it is only because I stood on the shoulders of giants."

Q: You are well known in academic circles for your deep research into the traditions of classical karate. What is the most significant discovery you've made?
A: Discovering the timeless formula for unraveling the ambiguity which has long shrouded the original defensive intentions and application principles of orthodox kata. Described as the interrelated fabric from which all karate is woven, understanding this formula brings an entirely new appreciation to what has long been referred to by competitors as "worthless movements,"

189

"Adversarial-type training is an incredibly rewarding part of karate, especially when the athlete is fortunate enough to be guided by an experienced, intelligent, and caring sensei."

and by innovative fighters such Bruce Lee as "the classical mess." Regardless of the signature practice one embraces (ryuei, gojo, uechi, shotokan, et cetera) the defensive themes they address, or the fundamental tools they use (punches, kicks, blocks, stances, and strikes), and the common principles that support them always remain constant. This is important to recognize.

You see, "styles" (the way these fundamental teachings are used and imparted) represent little more than personal interpretations of common tools and principles. The signature delivery systems and training methods called "styles" have always evolved in accordance with the varying outcomes each pioneer sought to achieve. As a researcher, I was long challenged by this issue, but have now systematized this formula into simplistic learning modules which help to improve one's overall understanding of kata as an art. Teaching these modules in no way adversely affects the signature characteristics of traditional styles, it only enhances existing knowledge.

Q: After this research, and looking back to your earlier days, how do you perceive your personal career in karate competition?

A: It seems like a very long time ago, especially considering my present age and my sumo belly. In my opinion, adversarial-type training is an incredibly rewarding part of karate, especially when the athlete is fortunate enough to be guided by an experienced, intelligent, and caring sensei. The value of such training, irrespective of winning or losing, lies in how its benefits are personally applied to improving the quality of one's life. In my case, adversarial-type training and competition were my sanctuary and have been of immeasurable value.

Q: Your English translation of the *Bubishi,* which became a martial arts bestseller, earned you wide recognition as an expert researcher. Can you explain the story behind this once-secret manuscript?

A: Not in a couple of paragraphs. However, the nine-year collaborative labor-of-love translation effort would probably make an interesting book all on its own. Nicknamed "The Bible of Karate" by Uchinadi karate pioneer Miyagi Chojun, the *Bubishi* (*Wu Bei Zhi* in Chinese) is probably one of the most important historical karate discoveries of our time. It is the only remaining undisputed historical document that actually links karate to the original Chinese traditions from which it evolved. Additionally, it helps to identify the original defensive themes and application principles which kata (*hsing* in Chinese) addresses, while also outlining the holistic, moral, and introspective practices that balance physical training. Moreover, unlike other books, which talk all about *doing* karate, the *Bubishi* actually tells us how to embrace the art. For karate, the *Bubishi* is the original manual that brings physical, holistic, artistic, moral, and spiritual practices together. As I understand it, the *Bubishi* has also become Charles E. Tuttle's best selling martial arts title, so I presume that others feel the same way about it as I.

There is an ancient Chinese maxim which says, "*On ko chi shin.*" This means, "To study the old is to understand the new." In short, the *Bubishi* is *the* Bible of karate tradition—irrespective of modern interpretations—as all "styles" rest upon identical principles influenced only by various interpretations of common knowledge. Through studying the wisdom of the ancient masters we can better understand how and why karate is the way it is today. How many times have you re-read a passage in a book only to marvel over a newly found message? The *Bubishi* is the kind of book one gets more out of each time it's read.

Q: You've done wonderful research on the origins of goju-ryu karate, tracing its roots back to China. What are some of the most interesting facts you've discovered?

A: Well, I don't know if I'd call it "wonderful" research, but it was interesting for sure. I certainly think, if nothing else, I have helped clear up a lot of the ambiguity which has historically shrouded goju-ryu's evolution, practice, and purpose. Despite many tall tales which suggest an ancient Okinawa lineage, karate was never a cohesive or precise tradition during the old Ryukyu Kingdom (up to 1879 AD). The eclectic hybrids we now know as "karate" are a relatively new phenomenon that never existed in old Okinawa.

Old-school practices focused upon what little knowledge locals had of Fujian *quanfa*, which was not introduced and popularized until around the early-to-mid 1800s. Various signature delivery systems evolved based upon what little knowledge locals had, and varied from teacher to teacher depending entirely upon personal experience. In the old days it was more important who one learned from, rather than what one learned, because experience commanded respect. Locals who had studied and learned in China were revered second only to Chinese teachers. In an interview with 95-year-old local karate expert, Uehara Seikichi (a direct student of Motobu Choyu, the older brother of Choki,) I was told, "All old-school teachers taught the same thing. What made them different was the way in *which* they taught it, not *what* was taught." Learning what I have about martial arts history, culture, political manipulation, and human nature, it's my opinion that much of the oral testimony that cloaks karate is suspect and self-serving.

Be that as it may, I believe the following information to be true: Higashionna Kanryo (1853-1917, principal teacher of Miyagi Chojun) first began to learn *quanfa* when he was 14 years old. His interest stemmed from watching a public demonstration on March 10, 1867, at Ochayagoten, which featured Aragaki Seisho (1840-1920), and two of his students named Maeda and Tomura.

With Fujian monk fist and crane boxing being among the principal mid-19th century *quanfa* traditions introduced to Okinawa, Aragaki Pechin was recognized as one of the few stalwarts who vigorously embraced its practice. A court translator by profession, Aragaki was petitioned to travel over to Nanjing in 1870, but, before he left on his long voyage, he recommended young Kanryo to his colleague Kojo Taite (1837-1917) for further instruction. Kanryo not only studied Kojo's (pronounced "Cai" in Fujian Chinese) family style of Chinese boxing, he also received an invitation to personally study in Fuzhou at the Kojo dojo there.

I am not exactly certain why Kanryo ultimately decided to withdraw from the Kojo dojo in Fujian to seek instruction elsewhere; however, alternative testimony may provide some provocative insights. Nearly thirty years later Uechi Kanbun (1877-1948, uechi-ryu pioneer) also traveled to Fujian in search of instruction in *quanfa* and arrived at the Kojo dojo near the Ryukyukan. Allegedly, Uechi was continually ridiculed and made fun of in the dojo because of his nationality and a lingering speech impediment which effected his ability to speak Chinese well. Apparently he left in disgust and ultimately met up and learned under a powerful tiger-style boxer from Quangdong named Zhou Zihe.

How long Higashionna Kanryo remained at the Kojo dojo remains the subject of intense curiosity. Notwithstanding, he ultimately hooked up with an incredibly talented young boxer named Xie Zhongxiang (1852-1930, aka Ryu Ruko) under whom he spent considerable time learning from. It does not sit well with some people that Xie was only a year older than his Okinawan student, as oral tradition maintains that Ryu Ruko was much older. Nor does the fact that Xie was highly eclectic sit very well with those who would believe that Higashionna actually studied with God. No less interesting, however, is that Xie went on to found his own style (whooping crane) and actually became one of the most sought after martial arts teachers of his time.

Spending considerable time and effort evaluating those systemized personal interpretations carried on by the principal students of Higashionna Kanryo—Kiyoda Juhatsu (1886-1967) Toyama Kanken (1888-1966) Mabuni Kenwa (1889-1952) Gusukuma Shinpan

"Regardless of how one chooses to look at it, it has always been the human body which has ultimately dictated which seizing and impacting techniques best impede an opponent's motor function."

(1890-1954) and, of course, Miyagi Chojun (1888-1953)—I found significant differences and remarkable similarities. Moreover, after having met with Dr. Hayashi Shingo, the most senior kojo-ryu exponent on Japan's mainland, I clearly observed generic similarities between Aragaki's heritage, the legacy Higashionna's students carried on, and Fujian *quanfa*. As a researcher, this observation suggests a common source.

In the isolated case of goju-ryu, a name drawn from the *Bubishi* to describe the eclectic hybrid Miyagi Chojun pioneered, I found a plethora of influences that effected the development of his interpretation. In addition to learning under Higashionna Kanryo, Chojun was also tutored by Aragaki Seisho, white crane boxer Wu Xianhui (Go Kenki, 1886-1940), and tiger-fist boxer Tang Daiji (To Daiki, 1887-1937). Moreover, he actively partook in exchange training with many locals at the Ryukyu Toudijutsu Research

"As a researcher, I also realized how important traveling to Fujian was and so I made several journeys there."

Society (originally established by Motobu Choyu, 1864-1927), and also traveled all the way to Shanghai in 1936 to study under Shaolin monk Miao Xing (1881-1939) at the Chin Wu Association.

As a researcher, I also realized how important traveling to Fujian was and so I made several journeys there. In addition to other mandates, I sought out various teachers, schools, and styles that might share similarities that corresponded with what Miyagi Chojun pioneered as goju-ryu. My efforts were both insightful and rewarding. From one teacher to another, school-to-school and style-to-style, despite the plethora of different names, lack of uniforms, relaxed dojo atmosphere, and pliable but powerful physical characteristics, I was fascinated to discover a plethora of similarities in as many styles.

An issue which might be better explained in an entire dissertation is that all kata, regardless of the style from which they come, are comprised of short sets of composite movements set forth in geometrical configurations. Serving to address predetermined acts of physical violence, and knowing that its application principles focus on impeding motor function, it should come as no surprise to learn that all kata are based upon the same criteria, altered only in modern times by 1) modernization, 2) rule-bound competition, and 3) standardization. Much to my delight, I came to discover how each of the habitual acts of physical violence that had long plagued early Chinese society had been meticulously studied and brought together into ritualized practices by the pioneers of *quanfa*.

Through recreating the specific acts of violence, *quanfa* pioneers were able to bring their students into direct contact with each physical scenario. That way it could not only be addressed, but also played out to its end. This brilliant two-man format not only allowed learners to become proficient in negotiating turbulent self-defense encounters, it also provided them with a template from which solo exercises evolved.

As I came to understand it, 36 original acts of physical violence and 72 variations were divided into three categories: 1) mutual confrontation, 2) augmented confrontation, and 3) habitual acts of physical violence. This gave birth to 108 short, composite two-man drills imparted in 18 exercises, which linked defensive themes to application principles. It is from this original substructure that pioneers established various signature solo exercises (kata) which formed the foundation of karate and have been handed down to this day.

Not overlooking the overall anatomical, mental, and holistic impact that oscillating the limbs and stretching the torso has upon the human condition, pioneers spent generations forging signature delivery systems mimicking the fighting movements of birds, fish, insects, reptiles, and other animals both real and mythical. The length of a solo exercise, its geometrical configuration, varying physical idiosyncrasies, and order of composite skills identified signature practices while cleverly concealing defensive themes and application principles. Considering the fact that each spiritual recluse spent their entire lives within monastic sanctuaries embracing this entire art, it is not difficult to understand why, when taken out from within its venerable walls, its innermost teachings became lost.

Regardless of how one chooses to look at it, it has always been the human body—its unique form, function, and common anatomical weaknesses—which have ultimately dictated which seizing and impacting techniques best impede an opponent's motor function, which is the dispassionate aim of self-defense. These are the realities every learner has to understand.

Q: Although Okinawa is the birthplace of karate, it is mainly considered to be a Japanese art. What are the differences between Japanese and Okinawan karate?

A: Karate, as practiced in Okinawa's Ryukyu kingdom, was never a coherent, structured system, and training methods varied greatly from teacher to teacher. Japanese influence on Okinawan karate included: 1) the development of *ryuha* or *gi* (styles or schools) which reflected the Japanese martial art custom of direct lineage, 2) adopting the standard Japanese white training *do-gi* (uniform) designed by Kano Jigoro to be used in judo, 3) implementing the *obi* (belt), also borrowed from judo, 4) implementing the *dan/kyu* ranking standard used in kendo and judo, 5) adhering to Japanese dojo rituals and etiquette, and 6) establishing rule-bound competitive practices, based on kendo and judo's *ippon-shobu shiai* concept developed by Ohtsuka Hironori and Konishi Yasuhiro to test the technique and spirit of its participants.

Modern training protocols are based upon very recent rule-bound competitive outcomes. Such modern "standards" never existed in Okinawa where karate was practiced as a Chinese martial art.

Differences Between Japanese and Okinawan Karate	
Japanese Karate	**Okinawan Karate**
Reflects Japanese culture	Reflects Chinese-based Okinawan culture
Militaristic instruction	Less rigid with informal "sharing"
Inflexible system	Flexible system
Typical Japanese protocol	Typical local island etiquette
Non-application specific (kata-wise)	Application-based training
Competitive based	Non-competitive (originally)
Rule bound	Not rule bound (originally)
Limited two-man body conditioning drills	Emphasis on two-man conditioning drills
Japanese terminology	Okinawan terminology

Q: You have conducted extensive research into kata. What are your basic findings?

A: Well, without giving away my formula or my hard-earned secrets, let me give you some important insights.

Fact: Long ago, before written language, the ancient tribes of man passed their knowledge on through physical emulation—the very roots of kata. This living phenomenon not only served as an excellent vehicle to impart existing knowledge, but also provided the platform upon which more progressive learners could extrapolate and interpolate more improved methods of studying infinite principles.

Fact: The fundamental concept of kata is not the commodity of any one specific culture, but rather the product of humanity. As civilization evolved and language developed, the tribes of man took on individual characteristics—and his physical rituals also reflected these changes. Built upon ancient customs, profound spiritual conviction, and disciplined social ideology, the kata of karate-do is a microcosm of the austere culture it comes from.

Fact: Chinese spiritual recluses in monastic sanctuaries, dedicated to living in harmony with nature and their fellow man, believed that if and when the human condition (man's ego) could be harnessed, the need for physical violence could be reduced to pure chance.

Fact: These reclusive architects ultimately identified and catalogued no less than 36 different defensive themes in an effort to address each of these random, yet habitual, acts of physical violence that plagued the plebeian society in which they dwelt. With continued study, as many as 72 different variations were meticulously systematized. Ultimately, eighteen individual exercises (called *hsing* or *kata*) came to represent a total of 108 defensive themes and application principles. Historically, this phenomena represents the foundation upon which the kata of Okinawan karate unfolded.

Fact: It has always been the human body, its unique functions, and common anatomical weaknesses which have ultimately dictated how low-intensity seizing and high-kinetic impacts can best impede the motor functions of an aggressor: These bio-mechanics have always been the dispassionate aim of self-defense. Based upon this universal truth, the various races of man have continually pursued different ways to learn and improve these infinite principles of bio-mechanics.

Fact: In an attempt to establish teaching curriculums for the existing body of knowledge, various kata were brought together by many *Uchinanchu* (Okinawans) in an effort to produce personal force-delivery systems.

Fact: Kata are the time capsules of karate whose techniques, when properly understood, reveal practical responses to the habitual acts of physical violence which plagued early Chinese society.

Fact: Defensive knowledge and application culminate when composite techniques are brought together into two-man drills linking theory to practice. These drills are then ritualized in solo geometrical configurations called "kata."

Fact: Kata has traditionally served as the principal vehicle through which the "secrets" of karate have been handed down over the generations.

Fact: Katas are a geometrical collection of defensive and offensive techniques.

Fact: Katas are comprised of five principal sets of tools: 1) punches, 2) kicks, 3) blocks, 4) stances, and 5) strikes.

Fact: Historically, six kinds of composite exercises were used to facilitate the development of kata: 1) techniques of punching, 2) kicking methods and leg maneuvers, 3) postures and stances, 4) the use of the empty hand, 5) corresponding tools of impact, and 6) checking, trapping, and blocking.

Fact: The 12 fundamental defensive themes intertwined within kata include 1) seizing nerves, 2) attacking blood passages, 3) twisting bones and locking joints, 4) attacking connective tissue (tendons/ligaments/cartilage), 5) take-downs, 6) throws, 7) grappling, 8) chokes, 9) groundwork, 10) counterattacks, 11) impacting anatomically vulnerable zones, and 12) digging into the body cavities unprotected by the skeletal structure.

Fact: The four fundamental categories of application principles into which these defensive themes fall include 1) techniques of restraint, 2) neurological shutdown, 3) attacking the respiratory system, and 4) methods of stunning.

Fact: The fundamental principles upon which kata theory and application rest can be explained by both Western science and Eastern tradition.

Fact: Desired results must always be supported by corresponding training methods. If kata was forged to be used against a fighter in an arena, a warrior on the battlefield, or any other kind of *mutual* confrontation, its configuration and training methods would be diametrically different than they are. This does not preclude the use of application principles against said adversaries, it only suggests that they were originally developed, and constantly improved upon, for the express purpose of being used by average people against those who had little or no understanding of such application principles.

Fact: Kata is like a song in a foreign language—unless you understand the language of a song, its meaning will forever remain a mystery. If one does not understand the defensive themes present in the kata, the application principles will remain unknown! In today's segregated international karate community there are a plethora of "standards" and no end to indiscriminate learning. I wonder if French mathematician and philosopher Henri Poincare was talking about karate in 1905 when he wrote in his *Hypothesis of Mathematics* that "Science is built upon facts in the same way a house is built with stones; but a mere collection of facts is no more a science than a pile of stones is a house."

Fact: Karate-do cannot exist without a body of moral philosophy to govern the behavior of those who embrace its empowering practice. Learning kata without its corresponding philosophy creates a terrible imbalance, which is usually reflected in attitude, character, and behavior. Understanding kata is simply a matter of understanding facts.

*"Karate-do cannot exist without a body of moral philosophy
to govern the behavior of those who embrace its
empowering practice."*

Q: How did you manage to learn some of the rare "lost" kata?
A: I immigrated to Japan and spent nearly ten years researching karate and
kobudo there. Field research took me to Okinawa, Fujian, Shanghai, the
Shaolin Temple, India, Korea, Southeast Asia, Taiwan and the Philippines.
I was able to contact many of the most senior martial arts authorities of
our time.

"Learners need only look within to discover the brutally effective legacy handed down within these unique kata 'time capsules.'"

Q: Kata is described by many as a "classical mess." What do you feel kata really means to karate?

A: Historically, kata has always been the principal vehicle through which the art of karate has been taught. It was Bruce Lee who, in an effort to promote his eclectic training concepts, referred to ritualized practices such as *kata, hyung, hsing,* et cetera as the "classical mess." Irrespective of physical violence being the nature and nucleus of karate, its training methods and moral philosophy actually prepares a defender to avoid fighting. Up to, during, and even now, kata, for many, was and continues to be a misunderstood practice. Make no mistake about it, however, if kata was meant for actually combating warriors of the battlefield or confronting prizefighters in an arena, its training methods would be diametrically opposite to what has been classically handed down. I think the misunderstanding evolves from the fact that too many were under the impression that karate kata was some omnipotent fighting discipline. The fact is that it is not. My comments are not meant to be derogatory or preclude the fact that such techniques can be reinterpreted to negotiate varying scenarios of physical confrontation. It is merely to explain the differences. The techniques which comprise kata are composite in nature and meant to be used for self-defense only. Those who do not understand this cannot recognize its value. Today, young people are very interested in the "best" fighting system. It is perfectly plausible and highly acceptable to want to improve one's fighting skills by borrowing and modifying techniques. For whatever it's worth, I highly condone such practices. However, this is not kata or karate and there's no need to reinvent the wheel for this art. Learners need only look within to discover the brutally effective legacy handed down within these unique kata "time capsules." I am passionately dedicated to imparting this timeless message.

Q: I'm going to mention some names; please describe what you consider their best qualities as martial artists and their place and influence in the history of karate-do. Let's start with Bushi Matsumura.

A: In my opinion, Bushi Matsumura Sokon Chikudon Pechin (1809-1901) epitomized what a *bujin* (martial artist) should be: strong, healthy, and a man who had to fight for everything he ever achieved. He was confident, but a little shy around people; honest, but not naïve; charitable to the point where he often did not have a lot left over for himself. He was a man who stood up for what he believed in and supported others regardless of the cost. Matsumura was an innovator who helped combine embryonic practices and eclecticism into a tradition called karate. I admire him because he was not a man who just practiced martial arts in the dojo—it permeated his entire character and he walked the walk until the day he went to the big dojo in the sky.

Q: Itosu Ankoh.

A: A student of Matsumura, Itosu Ankoh (1832-1915) was, in my opinion, the greatest innovator in the history of the modern tradition. Gaining the support of the entire local community, he was able to successfully bring together many of the leading authorities of his era to organize the tradition into a new practice called karate-jutsu. Thanks to his efforts, a new and open era was ushered in which help redefined the practice and purpose of karate. Karate-do was established upon the foundation he built.

Q: Higashionna Kanryo.

A: Bushi Higashionna (1853-1917) sometimes referred to as the "great restorer of *quanfa*," is widely recognized as the principal force behind establishing a systemized method through which *quanfa* could be imparted in and around the Chinese district of Naha. One of the reasons why he never made a bigger impact upon the evolution of karate was because he allegedly fell victim to depression and alcoholism after returning to Okinawa from Fujian. Notwithstanding, the two principal streams of karate handed down in modern Okinawa come from him and his colleague Itosu. Sadly, many of the two-man drills, acupuncture practices, herbal medicines, and weapon traditions Higashionna brought back from Fujian are no longer connected to the legacy he handed down.

Q: Motobu Choki.

A: Motobu Choki (1871-1941) enjoyed a hard-earned reputation as the toughest pound-for-pound *bujin* of them all. The bastard son of a wealthy

Okinawan businessman, Choki was brought up in the red-light district of Tsuji by his mother, a professional woman. Without strong paternal guidance during his formative years, Choki quickly established alternative role models like Miyamoto Musashi, whom he sought to emulate. Growing up on the streets of Tsuji, trouble became his companion. This contributed to his aggressive behavior and practical fighting experience. Although his welcome was always short-lived, Choki gained valuable tutelage under experts like his older brother Choyu, Bushi Matsumura, Itosu Ankoh, Matsumora Kosaku, and Sakuma Okina. He is least remembered for being the first to introduce karate on a full-time basis to the mainland of Japan in 1921 when he migrated to Kansai. He is best remembered for having quickly dispatched a foreign pugilist at the Butokuden in 1922. As a karateka, he began to recognize the importance between the defensive themes and application principles intertwined within kata. Many of the two-man *tegumi* training drills he used, which linked the two, are now being restored and finding their way back into the mainstream.

Q: Funakoshi Gichin.
A: Funakoshi Gichin (1867-1957), has been erroneously described as being "the father of modern karate," a definition which belongs undisputedly to Itosu Ankoh. Funakoshi was among the first wave of Okinawan pioneers to introduce modern defensive practices to mainland Japan. Having almost single-handedly introduced and developed karate in the Tokyo area during the early '20s. His contributions were paramount to the evolution of modern karate and he laid the groundwork for what became JKA shotokan. Probably best remembered for his demonstration at Japan's first athletic exhibition in Tokyo in 1922, his literary contributions and his first generation of students (Ohtsuka, Konishi, and Nakayama), who virtually revolutionized the purpose and practice of karate through the introduction of rule-bound competition.

Q: Miyagi Chojun.
A: So much has already been written on Miyagi Chojun that it's hard to say more. However, I'd certainly like to add that Miyagi spent the better part of his adult life seeking ways to better understand and improve karate. With this being said, though, why are so many people so adamant about not continuing his mission? His message was clear: karate is a living experience for the people it serves. Something he wrote which had a big impact upon me when translating his 1934 *Outline of Toudido*, was his comment, "I realized that the need for self-defense must have unfolded with prehis-

toric man due to the animosity inherent in human nature."

Q: Mabuni Kenwa.
A: In my opinion, probably the most brilliant of the first generation Okinawan pioneers to introduce karate to the mainland of Japan was Mabuni Kenwa (1888-1952). In my opinion, the magnitude of his research, even to this day, has yet to be accurately measured or completely understood. There were absolutely no limits this man would not go to in order to better understand and improve karate as an art. Everybody went to this man to learn, including Funakoshi. He was a big inspiration to me during my many years of field research in Japan. Among his

"Irrespective of physical violence being the nature and nucleus of karate, its training methods and moral philosophy actually prepares a defender to avoid fighting."

most admirable traits was his integrity. Everyone respected him and, when no one else could or would, Mabuni was able to bring many leaders together to help improve the art whom, otherwise, could not stand to be in the same room with each other.

Q: Nagamine Shoshin.
A: Having had the distinct honor to personally know and train with this important icon of karate, the late Nagamine Shoshin (1907-1998) was of enormous assistance and inspiration to me. I simply cannot say enough nice things about this wonderful human being, the last of the old-time *bushi* in my opinion.

Q: Miyazato Eichi.
A: Miyazato sensei was a virtual legend in karate and a man with whom I also enjoyed the pleasure of befriending and training under. Miyazato was a wonderful human being in person, and a walking encyclopedia of information. His dojo, the Jundokan, is probably the most famous in all of Okinawa and has produced incredible masters like Morio Higaonna and Teruo Chinen.

Q: Can you define the meaning of *shuhari* and how it applies to karate and other martial arts?

A: "And in the end," like T.S. Eliot wrote, "we arrive back at the place we first started and know it for the first time." Simply put, *"shuhari"* describes the transitory process from infancy to proficiency but should not be limited to just physical prowess or technique. It applies to learning in general, and reaches beyond the physical to the philosophical and spiritual, and back again. The process knows no time limits or political boundaries and is an excellent yardstick to accurately measure the level of one's own position in the privacy of one's own thoughts.

The term *"shu"* literally means to protect or maintain and represents "learning from tradition." This is the way the chain of tradition is perpetuated and passed on. This initial stage of training is an indispensable step on

Shuhari: The Circle of Learning		
Shu	**Ha**	**Ri**
To learn from tradition	To break the chains of tradition	To transcend the tradition
Youth	Adulthood	Maturity
Physical	Philosophical	Spiritual
Obedience	Separation	Divergence
The egg	The hatching	The flight

the infinite ladder of growth and development in karate-do. There are no time limits for each of the three stages, and transition from one level to the next is neither simple nor immediate. Rather, levels tend to overlap each other in the transition phase, which allows for a gradual withdrawal from one level and a subtle entry into to next plane.

Secondary conditioning takes one beyond the boundaries of physical training and away from the tyranny of worldly delusion, the preoccupation of materialism and other ego-related distractions. *"Ha"* literally means "to detach" and refers to breaking free the chains of tradition. However, often misunderstood, it does not mean to depart from that which has given us strength. Rather, *"ha"* represents a transitional phase from which a person emerges strengthened through the power of introspection. Described as exploring the "world within," the kata and protracted meditation become the focal points through which the supreme power of one's mind is first

realized. Having a pro-
found affect upon every
aspect of one's life, the
understanding of karate-
do, daily training, and
life itself, takes on a
completely new mean-
ing as one continues a
relentless pursuit to the
next phase of mastery.

"*Ri*" is the final stage
of transition and literally
means to go beyond or
transcend. This is what is
commonly referred to as
enlightenment or spiritual
emancipation. Provoked
by relentless austere conditioning, philosophical
assimilation, and pro-

"Karate is a microcosm of the austere culture from which it comes. Karate-do reflects ancient rituals, inflexible social ideology, and profound spiritual conviction."

tracted introspection, the intermittent flashes of penetrating wisdom become
more frequent as one becomes absorbed into the inner-abyss, and emerges
reborn. Those who fail to enter remain forever unfamiliar with the true
essence of karate-do.

**Q: Is it necessary to be Japanese or Okinawan in order to reach the higher
levels of karate?**
A: No, it is not necessary to be to be any particular race to achieve the
higher levels or deeper understandings of karate. However, in the same
breath, let me also say that when a learner cannot understand the historical,
linguistic, or anthropological context from whence karate evolved, the art
loses its cultural identity; hence, the inner-workings of its ritualized trans-
missions. Karate is a microcosm of the austere culture from which it comes.
Irrespective of its Chinese origins and early Okinawan cultivation, karate is
a miniature representation of Japanese society. Karate-do reflects ancient rituals, inflexible social ideology, and profound spiritual conviction. Hence, if
a learner cannot perceive and fully understand this phenomena then their
understanding is destined to remain superficial. There's a wonderful passage
written by the late Zen prelate, D.T. Suzuki, in Eugene Herrigel's publication entitled *Zen and the Art of Archery*, which illustrates an important, but

"Learned correctly, karate grants us the inner-fortitude to deal with personal issues that need to be changed and the dignity to accept those which cannot."

little understood message. Suzuki wrote, "One of the most significant features of Budo, as it is studied in Japan, is that it is not intended for utilitarian purposes only or for purely aesthetic enjoyments, but is meant to train the mind; indeed, to bring one into contact with the ultimate reality."

Q: Do you think that karate can be both sport and Budo at the same time?
A: Karate can be no less than five things: 1) A sport which is governed by rules whose outcomes dictate the training methods used to achieve them; 2) A form of physical fitness, which forms the seat of mental well being that people of any age can benefit from; 3) Embraced at different levels it is also a way of life punctuated with Eastern holistic philosophy and highlighted by ancient introspective practices; 4) A business which, like other businesses that market intangible products and conform to specific ethical guidelines and practices, contributes in a positive way to society; and 5) A form of self-defense which learners can use to make intelligent defensive decisions, providing the user has forged the physical prowess necessary to respond effectively, fully understands its varying parameters, and has developed the fortitude necessary to face one's fears. Ironic as it may sound, the essence of karate is learning how to *not* fight.

Q: You have collected a great amount of testimony from great masters. What are the major differences and similarities you have found between all of them?
A: In retrospect, that's an easy question to answer. In my opinion, it's teaching methods! Irrespective of the different cultures, languages, costumes, terminologies, and nationalities, those teachers who made the most profound

impact upon me had an indescribable inner-strength and calm about them which commanded my full attention. Despite a plethora of different teaching methods and personalities, I discovered their fundamental defensive themes and application principles to be virtually identical.

Philosophically, one common message that had a big impact on me was self-esteem, integrity, and building bridges between people. In many

"Despite a plethora of different teaching methods and person-alities, I discovered their fundamental defensive themes and application principles to be virtually identical."

ways their message came across like one of the twelve steps of Alcoholics Anonymous: Learned correctly, karate grants us the inner-fortitude to deal with personal issues that need to be changed and the dignity to accept those which cannot.

Q: Funakoshi Gichin is considered the father of modern karate. However, he was junior to many other lesser-known karate teachers who received much less credit. What's your opinion about this matter?
A: Well, taking nothing away from Funakoshi's brilliant efforts, I'll just say that history is always written by the powers-that-be.

Q: Lately, the martial-arts world seems to be very busy and occupied with the often-stated ideas of being effective in real combat, absorbing what is useful, rejecting the useless, and transcending the traditional arts. What do you think about this modern approach to martial arts?
A: Well, the only thing absolutely certain in life is change, isn't it? The late American anthropologist, Joseph Campbell, told us, "Every generation produces innovators who, in an effort to keep man's traditions a living experience for the people they serve, reinterpret the common principles upon which it rests." In doing so, each generation is guaranteed a more innovative method of doing the same thing. For those who are able to unravel the mysteries of history and understand the precepts and ideas present in ritual-

"Understanding that the source of weakness lies within each of us reveals the true location in which all of our battles must be first fought."

ized tradition (Budo) there is no need for the reinterpretation process. Human beings have not changed much anatomically since prehistoric times. Hence, the defensive themes and application principles always remain the same. Why reinvent the wheel?

However, if the term "real combat" has a military connotation to it, then I would have to admit that I am not qualified to speak on the subject. The training methodologies for battlefield engagement, like street fighting, are completely different and require a totally different mindset and training methods than what karate, as a defensive tradition, offers. However, if I were asked to offer any advice to someone looking to improve their safety on the streets I'd say, "Common sense and fast feet."

Q: How has karate has changed your life?
A: It has taught me to look inward to face my own fears, better understand the pitfalls of ignorance and misunderstanding, and helped me overcome my own weaknesses in order to find out how to become the person I want to be.

Q: Do you think martial arts can make you a better person?
A: Well, "better" is a relative term, but yes I do. I believe that as long as there is a need to overcome weaknesses, stay healthy and fit, combat the high levels of stress in life, understand who we are, why we're here, where we're going, and find a method to overcome the obstacles we'll most certainly encounter in life, there will always be the need for a tradition that has the answers: karate-do is one such tradition. It teaches those willing to learn that the source of human weakness is internal not external. Hence, our journey must ultimately be inward not outward. Understanding that the source of weakness lies within each of us reveals the true location in which all of

our battles must be first fought and won before this tradition can ever serve to improve our daily life. Training in Budo (of which karate is an integral part) strengthens the body, cultivates the mind and nurtures the spirit so that a budoka can contribute to the welfare of humanity. All the ancient and modern masters have supported this belief.

Q: You have also made a study of Zen. How did this interest evolve?
A: From my own ignorance and misunderstanding.

Q: Do you teach this Zen philosophy to your students?
A: No. However I do, probably too often, insist that they get in touch with their inner-self to listen to their soul and spirit to overcome ignorance and misunderstanding. As foolish as I am, I have come to believe that confusion is completely inward and can only be overcome by pounding a footpath paved by physical conditioning, moral philosophy, and methodical intro-spection. Most of them think I am getting too old! Notwithstanding, knowl-edge is wisdom; integrity, the glue that holds the fabric of our character together; egotism the wind that blows out the lamp of knowledge; and wis-dom the final frontier.

Q: Does your organization help in this search for truth?
A: The International Ryukyu Karate Research Society is dedicated to improv-ing and promoting the "old-ways." Represented in twenty-four countries, our movement was built upon cooperation rather than confrontation. Established in Japan in 1989, we take pride in bringing together and men-toring young researchers, teachers, students and other like-minded people in support of common goals. We welcome group or individual member-ships and encourage all martial artists to consider becoming part of our growing movement. O

Chuck Merriman

Wisdom of the Ages

CHUCK MERRIMAN'S KARATE CAREER BEGAN IN 1960 AND WITHIN A FEW YEARS HE HAD BECOME ONE OF THE LEADING FIGURES IN AMERICAN KARATE AND THE PERSONAL BODYGUARD FOR STARS SUCH AS DIANA ROSS AND THE ROCK GROUP KISS. HE ALSO MANAGED THE FIRST PROFESSIONAL, CORPORATE-SPONSORED KARATE TEAM, WHICH COMPETED ACROSS THE GLOBE IN THE 1980S. MERRIMAN HAS COACHED THE BEST COMPETITORS IN THE UNITED STATES AND WILL SHARE HIS 40 PLUS YEARS OF KARATE EXPERIENCE AND TRAINING SECRETS ONLY WITH THOSE WHO ARE TRULY SERIOUS ABOUT LEARNING THE ART.

HIS EVOLUTION AS MARTIAL ARTIST LED HIM TO TRAIN WITH SENSEI MIYAZATO EIICHI FROM OKINAWA, IN THE TRADITIONAL GOJU-RYU STYLE. MERRIMAN'S GOAL IS NOT ONLY TO PRODUCE GOOD KARATEKA, BUT ALSO BETTER HUMAN BEINGS IN THE PROCESS. SENSEI MERRIMAN IS ONE OF THE ICONS OF AMERICAN KARATE AND AN ORACLE OF KNOWLEDGE FOR THE YOUNGER GENERATIONS.

Q: How did you get started in martial arts?
A: I started judo in 1960 in Norwich, Connecticut. I then moved to New York in 1961 to continue my training in karate under Sensei Chris DeBaise. At that time I was living in the dojo of Bernie and Bob Lepkofker, the so-called "Judo Twins," who were 6-foot-4 and weighed 225 pounds. Living at the dojo was not all that different from the hard, disciplined training in Japan. Anyway, the judo classes were held on the fifth floor and on the third floor Sensei Chris DeBaise was teaching shito-ryu karate. The karate studio had a shower in it and I was allowed to use it. After observing the classes for a long time I went to DeBaise and naively asked if he could teach me kata. He agreed, and so I found myself practicing judo and karate seven days a week! I used to compete and for a long time I was one of the top kata competitors in the country.

Q: What sparked your interest in martial arts?
A: Martial arts always appealed to me because it was an individual effort and accomplishment. In school I was always too short for basketball, too

"I used to go train in Okinawa at the Jundokan, where Miyazato Eiichi Sensei used to teach. At the time of his passing, he was a 10th dan hanshi and successor to the founder of goju-ryu, Sensei Chojun."

skinny for football, and too slow for track. But martial arts just seemed to fit me naturally—it clicked for me.

Q: Did you receive instruction from Peter Urban?

A: Yes. But only after DeBaise decided not to teach anymore and gave me a recommendation. Urban's policy was that even the black belts from other schools had to wear white belts and line up in the back of the class. It was interesting because if you wanted the right to sit with the black belts you had to earn it. One day I decided to take a spot with the *shodan,* and that meant I had to justify it. After the warm up, Sensei Urban lined up all 15 black belts and I had to go through them all! It was not a matter of winning or losing but a case of survival. I have good memories of Sensei Urban. Some people criticize him but he was very truthful and ahead of his time. He was not cut out of a mold. There was only one of him. Some of the things he said at that time nobody understood, not even me—but with today's perspective he was terribly right.

Q: What happened next?

A: I amicably left Urban in 1967, and I never had a feeling of belonging to goju-kai since. After I disassociated myself from Urban, I always felt outside of it. It is true that Yamaguchi Gosei was a great man and a great karate teacher but I couldn't relate to him much. So when Gonnoyoe Yamamoto, who was another of my teachers, started his organization and broke away from Yamaguchi Gosei, I moved with him. This was from the mid-'60s to the early '70s. The last time I trained under Yamamoto was in 1972. For many years I was pretty much on my own. By this I mean I didn't belong to any organization. I did not change anything but I had to adjust certain things to being by myself. I was teaching my students exactly what I was taught by my teachers. I never created, invented or developed a new style.

Q: Did you enjoy your experiences under Sensei Higaonna and the International Okinawa Goju-Ryu Karate Federation?

A: I knew Sensei Higaonna since 1975 and he always gave me a lot of advice even though I didn't belong to his organization. He never put me off or had a bad attitude because I wasn't his student. Because of this I enjoyed being around him. So after some years I decided to join with him. I gathered all my students and told them what I was planning to do. I don't like to tell people what to do because I don't like to make decisions for anybody. This way I don't have to pay for a wrong decision. Anyway, everybody agreed and we went full force with IOGKF. It was a great time. The atmosphere, the people, the training—everything. No chips on the shoulders or wrong attitudes by anyone. This was a reflection of Higaonna's behavior and personality. Budo is a "warrior way" and in Okinawa the word *"bushi"* means a "gentleman warrior." Gentleman is the important word here. It means the character of the person. You are a guide and example to follow and you do what you say. People judge you more by what you do than by what you say. In karate, with rank comes responsibility. This is what *"do"* means.

"You are a guide and example to follow and you do what you say. People judge you more by what you do than by what you say. In karate, with rank comes responsibility. This is what 'do' means."

Q: Did you train and study in Japan?

A: In Tokyo I trained under Sensie Yonemoto (Okinawan goju-ryu) and I used to go train in Okinawa at the Jundokan, where Miyazato Eiichi Sensei used to teach. At the time of his passing, he was a 10th dan hanshi and successor to the founder of goju-ryu, Sensei Chojun. It is interesting you mentioned two different words: "training," and "study," because they are completely different. Studying is much more than showing up for practice, just like studying in college is not just showing at the school and then sitting

"At this point in my life I prefer kata, but in order to be a complete karateka you need to strike a balance between both, since one doesn't exist without the other."

there. Study is a learning process which entails research about philosophy, technical aspects, physiology, and other related matters. It is much deeper than just training.

Q: So you had different teachers all these years, right?

A: Yes. I must say that during all my years of practice I have been extremely fortunate to have such a great teachers as Sensei DeBaise, Sensei Peter Urban, Sensei Yamamoyo Gonnoyoe Sensei (goju-kai), Sensei Higaonna Morio, and Sensei Miyazato Eiichi of the Jundokan in Okinawa. My judo teachers were Bernie Lepkofker, Nakabayashi Sadaki and In Soo Hwang.

Q: Do you prefer kata or kumite?

A: At this point in my life I prefer kata, but in order to be a complete karateka you need to strike a balance between both, since one doesn't exist without the other.

Q: How important is the sport aspect of karate in your teaching and coaching?

A: I don't stress any aspect of how students should apply the knowledge and ability that they've gained through their training. It's up to them to apply all this information in as many beneficial ways as possible. As far as coaching, the first important thing is to know the rules. As a coach, you must know the rules because those apply to everybody and they might be decisive in sport competition. On other hand, a coach doesn't need to teach technique to the competitors since they already know it. The whole thing is more about bringing out their talents, and knowing what buttons to push to make them believe in themselves—in short, to make them do what they do best. A coach is a motivator, a helper, an advisor—and not just a technical teacher. You must treat every member of your team equally, no favorites. Never lower your standards to treat someone special. Set an example to the players with your attitude and behavior because you have to find a common ground to

bring everyone together. Compared to other sports, in karate everybody competes individually—they are a team but it's not like basketball or football where they play all together. So the psychology and the approach has to be a little bit different. Just remember that karate was never designed to be a sport.

Q: You coached a professional karate team, right?
A: Yes, I did. The object was to upgrade the level of professionalism in karate and to try to make karate a regular professional sport. But martial arts people are very different than athletes in other sports. Getting paid is a residual benefit of being a professional. Professionalism is an attitude, a way of behaving and relating to the people around you—and some of them didn't have a clue. Few people understood that their role had changed and they had to conduct themselves in a different way. Therefore, certain attitudes were a major factor in disbanding the team. But it was a very educational experience anyway.

"Just remember that karate was never designed to be a sport."

Q: What are the good and bad sides of competition?
A: A desirable aspect of competition is that it is an area where a student can place themselves in a stressful situation with an unknown quality and quantity of opposition. Then they can evaluate themselves in light of the final outcome. An undesirable aspect is that competition is strictly subjective in judgement and is someone's opinion of your performance, not necessarily what actually took place. Many people confuse tournaments and competitions with reality and by doing so gain a false impression of their true ability and knowledge.

"An undesirable aspect is that competition is strictly subjective in judgement."

Q: If karate becomes an Olympic sport, could it lose part of its purity and spirit?
A: I don't think the Olympics did much to preserve the purity and spirit of judo! In my opinion, it did exactly the opposite. In my logical mind, why would the outcome for karate be any different? And don't

215

"Authentic, traditional karate hasn't changed—just the people in it and their perception of what karate really is!"

forget that the Olympic Organizing Committee is experiencing it's own purity, spirit, and ethics problems at present.

Q: What styles have you studied other than goju-ryu?
A: Originally Sensei DeBaise taught shito-ryu, but it was for a very short period. I did attain *sandan* in kodokan judo and shodan in hakkoryu jiu-jitsu.

Q: Do you recommend that your students study other styles?
A: Not really. Okinawa goju-ryu is an extremely deep style of karate which requires a great deal of time and effort. I don't think it is necessary to study another style of karate if the karate style you choose provides the proper self-defense structure within its framework of teaching. The old phrase "jack of all trades, master of none" immediately leaps to mind.

Q: What is the ideal relationship between student and instructor?
A: An ideal student/teacher relationship should contain the same qualities as any other successful relationship—mutual respect, concern for each others welfare, consideration, patience, honesty, integrity, and openness.

Q: How has karate changed in the last 30 years?
A: Authentic, traditional karate hasn't changed—just the people in it and their perception of what karate really is!

Q: What is the importance of kata?
A: Kata, and its components of kihon bunkai and oyo bunkai, is the very essence of traditional, authentic karate. You can practice kata alone, in a small area without the need of training aids. Kata affords a serious student an opportunity to analyze—kihon bunkai–and put to use—oyo bunkai—the training, knowledge, and experience that the student has gained through

years of training. Oyo bunkai—to apply what you have analyzed—allows the student to develop the kata (pattern or form) and the kihon bunkai (basic or standard analysis) on a more personal level without restrictions.

Q: What do you think about full contact karate and kickboxing?

A: In my opinion, full contact karate and kickboxing are essentially the same sport, with some rule variations. I have a great respect for the courage and commitment to the rigorous physical training that these athletes exhibit. I think it is an exciting spectator sport. I have coached and trained real world champions in every category of sport karate, including WUKO/WKF, Pan American Games, AAU, Open Circuit, PKA, PKC and WAKO. My son, Chad, is a national and international competitor and champion in all aspects of sport karate and is also a silver and gold medallist in Golden Gloves boxing. He is also an excellent judo player.

"If you look at the professional players in any sport they don't play a game every day, they do drills. Many people in karate were sparring constantly and I realized that drilling was the key."

Q: How did you coach karate?

A: I analyzed everything and found that there are three things that a competitor needs to score a point: distance, timing and target. If you look at the professional players in any sport they don't play a game every day, they do drills. Many people in karate were sparring constantly and I realized that drilling was the key. I believe in drills, therefore I devised drills to develop coordination, lateral movement, and timing. These drills helped to instill muscle memory in the fighter to react in a certain way. They instill programming into your muscles to react before you think. If you have to think, you've been already hit. I used drills to develop stamina, awareness, and kime. Later on, you put all the elements together to make them work in kumite. On a mental level, I always stressed that every fighter should find

"It is very important to understand that you retain what you practice frequently, not what you practice intensely."

their exclusive routine or ritual in order to build up their energy and spirit. This is something very personal. Something similar to what actors do.

Q: What is your personal training like now?
A: My personal training at present is centered on developing a better understanding of the kata of goju-ryu. *Oyo bunaki* is my main point of study presently. I have also started Zen training at Kozenji Zendo in Shuri, Okinawa under the watchful eye of Zen Master Sakiyama Sogen Roshi. In his years as a young man, Sakiyama Roshi was also a student of Sensei Miyagi. It is very important to understand that you retain what you practice

frequently, not what you practice intensely. I try to stick to a well-rounded program since it's the key to well-rounded development.

Q: Do you think the art of karate has to change accordingly to the practitioner's age?

A: Absolutely! Karate doesn't change, we do. I don't think it's a case of "has to change," but being aware of the natural process of physical and mental changes normally associated with aging. In you want longevity in your karate life, then the training in your younger years should be geared toward enhancing your ability to train in your later years.

Q: What's your opinion on the qualities and rank an instructor should have before starting to teach?

A: The standards for rank in karate are nationally and internationally different and vary from style to style, dojo to dojo, and teacher to teacher. Because of this, I don't think rank, as such, should necessarily be a factor

"I think a primary talent a teacher of any kind should possess is the ability to communicate knowledge and experience."

in determining teaching ability. Qualities of a good teacher, on the other hand, are more easily outlined. I think a primary talent a teacher of any kind should possess is the ability to communicate knowledge and experience to each individual student on their level of understanding. The coach needs patience to allow each student to develop at their own pace, but with the encouragement to develop to their fullest potential. Mutual respect, courtesy, consideration, mutual welfare, honesty, integrity and openness are all desirable qualities for a good teacher. It is essential to develop these qualities and not just pay lip service to them.

"As far as the dojo philosophy is concerned, I would say that I use a benevolent dictatorship. I know it may sound a bit harsh but that is the way to do it."

Q: What is your philosophy in the dojo?

A: That's a hard question to answer. Westerners don't understand Japanese or Okinawan culture so it's kind of difficult to import it to the United States. But I do believe that traditional karate and traditional martial arts are good for society because they're based on respect—which is what our society needs. In traditional martial arts you learn these values. As far as the dojo philosophy is concerned, I would say that I use a benevolent dictatorship. I know it may sound a bit harsh but that is the way to do it. Everybody has a lot of opinions about everything but in my dojo you train under my circumstances or not at all. Too many young people are making their own decision when they don't have the ability to make good decisions yet!

Q: And your philosophy in life?

A: Karate is something a person is, and not so much what they do. You can't cut all the different aspects into pieces since they are all one thing. You learn from your teachers and your coaches, but in the very end it is all about you. You have to try to be the best you can be and take responsibility for your success or failure. Karate is a tool that we use to train our mind, spirit, and bodies.

Q: What do you feel is wrong with karate today?

A: Nothing is wrong with karate! But maybe those of us who profess to practice and teach karate should examine ourselves more closely as to what our perception of karate is, and if our intentions and motives are correct within the context of that perception.

"The proper study of karate-do should be for the purpose of developing yourself to your highest potential—mentally, spiritually, and physically."

Q: Do you use meditation on a regular basis as part of your training?

A: No, I don't use meditation as a part of my training or my teaching. I am presently pursuing a study of Zen but I don't consider Zen a meditation in the strictest sense. Roshi said, "Zen and karate are not the same, but can complement each other."

Q: Is there a particular message you want to share with the karateka and martial artist in general?

A: The proper study of karate-do should be for the purpose of developing yourself to your highest potential—mentally, spiritually, and physically. It's essence is to learn how to live correctly and to be a positive and beneficial influence on those who rely on your guidance. O

Sensei Merriman faces his opponent (1). Grabbed by the wrist (2), he traps the wrist (3), and pressures the joint upwards as in saifa kata (4). When the aggressor throws with a reverse punch, Merriman blocks with the palm of his left hand (5), and delivers an uraken *to the temple (6-7).*

Facing his opponent (1) Sensei Merriman blocks the gyaku tsuki chudan with his left hand (2), and the left hook with his right hand (3). He then uses his left hand (4), to position himself on the outside of his opponent (5), where he grabs the wrist of the extended arm (6), and strikes the aggressor's elbow joint (7).

Takayuki Mikami

The Essence of Perseverance

BORN ON DECEMBER 10, 1933, TAKAYUKI MIKAMI HAD NO INTEREST IN THE MARTIAL ARTS BEYOND THE REQUIRED PHYSICAL EDUCATION PROGRAMS OF JUDO AND KENDO. WHEN MIKAMI FINISHED HIGH SCHOOL IN 1952, HE WENT TO TOKYO TO ATTEND HOSEI UNIVERSITY AND IT WAS THERE HE STARTED KARATE TRAINING.

IN 1958, AT THE SECOND ALL-JAPAN CHAMPIONSHIPS HELD BY THE JKA, THE COMMUNITY OF KARATE GOT THE ULTIMATE LESSON IN SPIRIT, POWER, AND COMBAT PSYCHOLOGY. TAKAYUKI MIKAMI AND HIROKAZU KANAZAWA HAD WHAT WAS DESCRIBED AS THE MOST STIRRING AND IMPORTANT MOMENT IN THE HISTORY OF THE JAPAN KARATE ASSOCIATION. THAT MATCH WENT DOWN AS LEGEND.

IN 1963 HE TRAVELED TO THE UNITED STATES, PLANNING TO STAY ONLY A YEAR, BUT DESTINY HAD DIFFERENT PLANS FOR HIM. A FIRM BELIEVER OF KARATE BEING A BRIDGE BETWEEN CULTURES, AND AN EFFECTIVE TOOL FOR SELF-IMPROVEMENT AND UNDERSTANDING, MIKAMI SENSEI IS ONE OF THE FEW SENIOR INSTRUCTORS WHO HELD TECHNICAL POSITIONS WITH BOTH THE JKA AND THE WUKO.

WITH THE 21ST CENTURY BEGINNING, TAKAYUKI MIKAMI IS STILL CONSIDERED ONE OF THE TOP KARATEKA AND INSTRUCTORS THE JKA EVER PRODUCED. ALTHOUGH HE NEVER TRAINED DIRECTLY UNDER FUNAKOSHI, MIKAMI REPRESENTS EVERYTHING THE SHOTOKAN FOUNDER ORIGINALLY CONCEIVED WHEN HE CREATED THE ART.

Q: Can you tell us about your beginnings in the art of karate?
A: I joined the karate club as soon as I entered Hosei University. I was a little boy from a farm, and Tokyo was a very tough city. I guess since I felt the need to build my confidence and improve my physical strength I decided to join the karate club. The first instructor I had was Mr. Saiki and then Mr. Kimio Ito. The training was very hard and there was a high level of dropouts, particularly during the first year. Once I started karate training I lost interest in everything else, so unfortunately my thesis for my major in Japanese Literature was four years late.

225

"The old training was very samurai-like. We used to drill, and drill, and drill without the instructors explaining anything."

Q: So you didn't start your training in the JKA?

A: No. When I was in my fourth year at the university, Ito Sensei told me about entering the JKA to become an instructor. At the time they didn't have their own dojo or instructor program—everything was under construction. This special training began in the Spring of 1956. There were a lot of good karateka. Students from other universities joined the course, which helped to raise the training level. It is true that many dropped out, mainly due to political problems, and in the end very few of us remained training at the new JKA dojo where Masatoshi Nakayama sensei was the Chief Instructor. We used to do a lot of kihon—thousands of repetitions of each technique. Master Nakayama was a very tough instructor. The old training was very samurai-like. We used to drill, and drill, and drill without the instructors explaining anything. If you didn't understand the technique, you did it 100 more times. You had to find it out by yourself. In Japan this way of teaching is called "teaching through the body."

Q: What are your memories about early days in the Instructor Training Program?

A: As everybody knows it was very hard, but let me explain this carefully. When I say "hard," I mean really hard and not just concerning physical training. It was comprised of two different parts; we, the students had to do all the work—I mean from cleaning the dojo to preparing the food, et cetera. We were doing practically everything to keep the whole thing going. Of course, we were being watched all the time, 24-hours a day, by our *sempai*. Nakayama Sensei kept an eye on us and when he couldn't, then Mr. Ito and Mr. Tagaki would watch over us. We couldn't be found chatting or things like that. In the training aspect, don't forget that karateka from all over were anxious to check us out since we were receiving special training. I remember that teachers from Kansai area, which was very strong at that time, used to send up to ten students to test the three of us. The Takushoku University coach used to do the same—send a bunch of people to train with the three JKA instructors—and we three had to fight the whole line! Also some other groups and styles came to the JKA to challenge us. The sparring classes were very tough. It was free-sparring with no referee whatsoever.

Q: Who were the other two?
A: Sensei Kanazawa and Sensei Takaura. Everybody knows Kanazawa sensei but Mr. Takaura is not so well-known because he stopped training karate.

Q: Did you ever train under Master Funakoshi
A: No, never. He was very old at that time but I saw him many times at the JKA headquarters. He was always present at the belt test watching what you were doing. He was so old that he looked like a god to me.

"It was like a mission to us. We were ready to give everything we had in training."

Q: Why was that particular generation of practitioners so special?
A: I guess we were happy to have the chance to leave the country to spread karate around the world. It was like a mission to us. We were ready to give everything we had in training. We worked extremely hard in a very difficult time for Japan, just after the war. We never looked for the easy life; our motivation for training was very, very different from the practitioners today. Also, it was a very important that we were allowed to constantly train—and

227

"A good instructor is not only a good technician."

this intensified our practice sessions. The JKA was well-regarded for its high technical level. For instance, after the instructor's program I kept training full time for another seven years! That's the reason why the JKA had such a great technical level compared to other schools and styles.

Q: Do you think it is not the same in the present?

A: Of course not. To begin with, the people training in Japan have no plans to leave the country whatsoever. They don't need to go through the hard times and difficulties. This will definitely affect the future of the art. Technique-wise I believe it will be the same but the spirit, attitude, and philosophy will not be.

Q: Is it true that you designed the Instructor Program for the JKA?

A: Yes, it is. The course was composed of two parts; one was strictly physical technique and the other consisted of a series of reports that the students had to submit. These essays touched different subjects. A good instructor is not only a good technician; he must know how to teach a class, how to instill karate values, and how to deal with his student's psychology. Not all the people taking this course were interested in getting an instructor's certificate. Some of them just wanted to improve their technique and knowledge.

Q: Why did you decide to come to America?

A: Well, the JKA sent me to teach. I was sent to Philippines in 1957 to teach an introductory course in Manila. This three-month period was extended to one year. After returning to Japan I remained as a JKA instructor until moving to America in 1963. I began teaching in Kansas City but after having some problems with my sponsor I talked to Mr. Hidetaka Nishiyama and he

said it was OK to leave Missouri and move to New Orleans where somebody had requested a Japanese instructor. But not everything was as easy as it sounds. When I arrived there I thought I was going to live in an apartment, not sleep on the dojo floor; and that my food was going to be provided—but none of that happened. Everything was very different from what I had expected. Let alone the legal problems.

You see, I was in America on invitation, with a flight ticket paid by my hosts. The Immigration Department wanted me to go back to Japan and apply for a permanent residence visa. Once I had to travel back to Kansas City to teach for another karate group. But the person who initially sponsored me got mad and reported me to the authorities. Fortunately enough, I had already applied for a resident visa, but my passport was with my lawyer. They came to check me out during the weekend and, of course, my lawyer's office was closed. Since they didn't believe me, I had to spend a couple of days in jail.

Q: What was your first impression of American karate?
A: To be honest, I had a very bad impression. I attended what was supposed to be a karate tournament, but saw no karate that I recognized. That day I realized how great of a misunderstanding the Americans had about real karate. I felt I had to stay and teach the art properly.

Q: What's your opinion of karate as sport?
A: People come to martial arts for several reasons and sport training is only around 10 percent. What we are seeing is a new karate born of a blend of Japanese tradition and Western customs and culture. Even in Japan many karateka call their teacher "coach" not "sensei." They conceive it more as sport. These days, karate has an sportive aspect, even the so-called traditional exponents go to tournaments and enjoy the sport. Let me tell you that I don't think this is bad as long as we keep it in the proper perspective. Today, even the most traditional Japanese arts engage in contests. Unfortunately, in order to win, many competitors do wrong things such as cheating, acting, et cetera. And, of course, this is completely opposed to the spirit of martial arts. I don't think competition has to interfere with the traditional principles of the art. Winning or losing is not the most important thing in competition. The sport competition teaches us a lot of things that can't be learned in the dojo such as pressure in front of people, mental control in an strange environment, et cetera. But like I said you have to keep the right perspective.

Q: Don't you think that mixing two cultures is kind of confusing?

A: It might be, and honestly I think it is. The Japanese philosophy and the Western philosophy are different. Maybe the goal is the same but the approach definitely is not. The Western practitioner in a final match will jump and celebrate after scoring a point. In the true spirit of Budo, however, you must concentrate and stay calm and focused, keeping all your emotions under control. This allows you to develop energy while exerting control over the ego. In the West, the karateka build their energy using their ego. Doing it this way is a very easy method to get a big head. And once you lose your spirit it is very difficult to get it under control again.

Q: What does karate means to you?

A: This is a very difficult question to answer. I can tell you, though, that I'm proud I never changed my direction in karate. I don't care about all the difficulties and hard times I went through, I always got self-satisfaction and spiritual development by keeping the same path throughout my life. Sometimes when I got bored I kept doing the same basic things over and over again until I reached a new level. I always tried to communicate with everybody, although the old JKA policy was not to. I believe that communication can help you to find your own way. I also believe the one must be honest and sincere, putting 100 percent into everything you do because without effort nothing is gained. Karate is about effort and sacrifices. It is true that sometimes we make mistakes but we must always make a real effort.

Q: How do you perceive the correlation between kata and kumite?

A: They are two parts of the same whole. I know some people think they don't need kata in their quest to be great fighters but they are wrong. This is an incorrect approach to karate. The student has to dedicate the same amount of time to both aspects but keep in mind that kata needs a very in-depth study. The analysis of one single kata may take years; by this I mean the different uses of the same technique, and its application in kumite and self-defense. I recommend to study one or two kata deeply, although you can get a lot of knowledge and inspiration by learning others as well. Kata teaches the correct body positioning, the proper execution of the techniques, focus, balance, et cetera. One gains powerful techniques from correctly using the body. Why do you think the best kata people are the best fighters? Unfortunately, practitioners today rely too much on their own physical power instead of learning proper form and technique.

"That was the hardest match I ever fought in my life! Kanazawa sensei and I knew each other very well since we sparred in the dojo all the time."

Q: Why do some change the kata?
A: Well, Funakoshi sensei changed all the Okinawa kata to better fit into his conception of shotokan karate. Originally, the stances were narrower and higher, but JKA changed to deeper and lower positions in order to increase the difficulty and improve the training methods to achieve better physical development. The original stances were made for fighting but since the purpose no longer holds they adapted karate to the present day, looking for a better overall physical development.

Q: Your fight against Kanazawa sensei is considered a classic in karate circles. How difficult was it?
A: That was the hardest match I ever fought in my life! Kanazawa sensei and I knew each other very well since we sparred in the dojo all the time. I was aware of his longer reach so I had to be very careful while trying to

"In real traditional karate if you had to fight, you would kill and you can't do that today. Traditional karate is not about technique, like the people like to describe, it is about attitude."

break through his guard. He was cautious about my speed so he didn't want to close the distance improperly. After a while we were very tired, both physical and mentally. Concentration was a key factor. A lot of people from my hometown of Nigata where watching, including my family. Kanazawa sensei had support from his family as well. Neither one of us wanted to disgrace or disappoint our families. I realized that Kanazawa was thinking the same way. So I said, "Why should I give up?" I knew that I had to use all my speed to score on Kanazawa since he is a strong fighter. We faced each other for four overtime periods, stalking each other and seeking that decisive psychological moment to launch the final attack. But that attack never came. There was nothing left in our bodies. Only our spirits kept us fighting. Finally, we both were declared champions. It is the only time this has ever occurred. The next year I won both the kumite and the kata titles. But I have to tell you that without all that support coming from the people there I would have quit or even lost the match!

Q: What's your definition of traditional karate?

A: Let me tell you that all dojo do some kind of sport competition, at least a little. In real traditional karate if you had to fight, you would kill and you can't do that today. So what do people mean by traditional? Traditional karate is not about technique like the people like to describe, it is about attitude. It's about life or death and not about doing *hikite* when you punch *gyaku-tsuki*. I guess karate has lost some of its essence. It was originally for self-defense but the demands changed with the times. We were trained based on the fact one was a warrior.

Q: Do you think karate must change with the practitioner's age?
A: Of course! Your body changes so the way you do things has to change. Not the inner principles behind the motion, but certain aspects of it. I started to modify some things according to my body when I was 50. Shotokan is a great style but it is very difficult for older people. It is important to find ways of adapting the methods without losing the principles. Unfortunately, power and speed in techniques is over-emphasized and a lot of karate techniques do not need that much power or speed. As your joints start to hurt, you need more effective, practical techniques. It is very important for the practitioner to be aware of the *sho-ha-ri* principle which is the normal way of the martial arts in Japan. First you strictly train under your teacher and you imitate without questioning—*sho*. Then comes *ha*, where you master the physical techniques and gain your own insight into the nature of the art, spirit, and techniques and incorporate these insights into your daily practice. Finally, after many years comes *ri*, where you separate from your instructor and go out on your own.

Q: Have you ever studied other arts?
A: Yes. I studied iaido. I'm also very attracted to some circular motions of tai chi, aikido, and jiu-jitsu. Weaponry training is very good as a supplementary aspect. It must be extra, not the central part of your training.

Q: Would you give any advice to karate practitioners in general?
A: Sometimes karate is boring and I understand. Everything is boring if you do it everyday for 30 years! The secret lies in not giving up, but in training the simple things until you feel better. That's the real test of Budo. The hardest thing to teach in martial arts is spirit, but it is the most important aspect the art of karate can offer to its practitioners. The mental and spiritual aspects of the martial arts can help one to overcome any kind of difficulties. That's the key—learning how to keep going day-by-day. O

Minobu Miki

Karate's Modern Traditionalist

ONE OF THE WORLD'S HIGHEST RANKING SHITO-RYU STYLISTS, SAN DIEGO-BASED MINOBU MIKI IS FROM A JAPANESE FAMILY STEEPED IN THE TRADITIONAL ASPECTS OF THE MARTIAL ARTS. KNOWN FOR HIS VERY TECHNICAL AND PRECISE KATA, MIKI HAS A DIRECT TRAINING LINEAGE TO SHITO-RYU FOUNDER KENWA MABUNI THROUGH KENWA'S SON KENZO. RECOGNIZING THE NEED TO MODERNIZE KARATE'S TRADITION-ALLY HARSH TRAINING METHODS, MIKI HAS NEVERTHELESS REMAINED TRUE TO THE ART'S HIGH SPIRITUAL AND MORAL PRINCIPLES. WITH ONE FOOT PLANTED IN THE PAST AND THE OTHER ROOTED IN THE PRESENT, MINOBU MIKI IS A LIVING EXAMPLE OF HOW KARATE'S HONORABLE TRADITIONS CAN SURVIVE THE MODERN WORLD'S QUESTIONABLE VALUES.

Q: How did you get started in martial arts?
A: The era was only a decade after WWII ended, when I was a child. I saw many injured war veterans who had lost legs and arms. I also witnessed many shelters and saw many playgrounds that had holes from the bombings. So as a child, I developed a subtle insecurity and feeling of danger around me. I was raised in a martial arts environment. My father was a judo black belt and my family was associated with iaido master Masayoshi Shinoda. Mr. Shinoda later received the Medal of Honor from the Japanese emperor, Hirohito. My aunt had a degree as a dance master and my whole family was involved with Japanese cultural arts. Both of my sisters trained extensively in Japanese dance. Additionally, the iaido master, Mr. Shinoda, and my family had a very close relationship which supported both arts.

I began my martial arts training in Japanese swordsmanship, or kendo, at the age of 8 while in elementary school. I also trained at a dojo located in a nearby police station. Then in junior high I began training in judo at school and a neighbor's judo dojo. I started karate-do at the age of 16. My friend and I commuted to a dojo a few towns away by train. There were only a few karate dojos then and there were no children involved like today. As a matter of fact, many high schools forbid their students from tak-ing karate-do. They thought the training was too damaging to proper growth

"The beginners were taken outside where the makiwara posts were standing. We had to hit them until the skin on our knuckles came off."

and too violent for students. My first teacher was Mr. Koshi Yamada. I hardly saw my master since we had many high-ranking instructors who came to teach us.

The entire dojo was made of wood, including floor and surrounding walls. But the school was not well-kept and many of the windows were without glass. When it rained, the students close to the windows would get wet. In the summertime, the instructor often had to halt our class to kill mosquitoes himself since if we moved even a little, he would shout at us or hit us with a *shinai* stick. In the wintertime, there was no heating. On snowy days, the instructor told us to run outside in only bare feet. In the wintertime, the dojo floor had frost around the perimeter. So, everyone would try to arrive first in order to stay in the center part of dojo that had no frost. When I joined the dojo in late spring, my sensei told me, "If you can bear us for three days then you can make it." Of course this was after I paid the initiation fees and monthly dues. There was no dressing room, we simply had to change clothes in the corner of the dojo.

After a few years, the dojo moved to a location that I could no longer commute to. So I was forced to change schools to seido-ryu. The master there was Seido Mizuno whose style was one of the generic shito-ryu styles. This dojo had more people in the classes and was not as intense as the Koshi Kan dojo where you were taught how to knock down the opponent. But at this dojo too, the workouts were very hard. At the first class, the beginners were taken outside where the makiwara posts were standing. We had to hit them until the skin on our knuckles came off. Then the instructor said, "Okay, it looks good. You must hit the makiwara post everyday to toughen up your fists. Do you understand?" While we were standing in front of the makiwara, a few other students were pulling carts full of roof tiles. The instructor picked one of the tiles up and suddenly broke it on his forehead. It shattered with a loud sound. We were all stunned by this demonstration. The instructor said, "These roof tile are good," as if he were tasting some fine food. After such an act, we did not want to argue with him.

Q: In our modern society where empty-hand fighting is not an issue anymore, is the art of karate-do still beneficial?
A: Karate offers a way of self-defense, firstly by technique and then by mental attitude. Through the practice of the art, an awareness of the self develops along with an understanding of how to avoid conflict. We end up looking more for "human harmony." Karate-do is an education, a lifetime study, and if we study the origin of the art we'll learn correct values and many good lessons. That's why I believe that deeply studying the original methods will bring us a

"Karate offers a way of self-defense, first by technique and then by mental attitude."

greater insight into the way of the empty hand. This is one of the reasons why I think 14 is a good age to start training karate. The mind is a very important tool in the development of yourself as karateka. Under this age, the mind is not sufficiently developed and the training is just play. Personally, karate has allowed me to develop mentally and physically in a manner I never would have been able to without it. The amount of control that regular karate training gives you is easily explained, but the overall feeling of being "in control" that one gets, is not so easily defined. In fact, I think it's impossible to explain to someone who doesn't train.

The ultimate goal of karate-do training is to make a better person, one who contributes to society as a whole. This is accomplished through disciplined physical and mental training. It creates a disciplined person who will

"Freestyle fighting is good for the sport but there is the danger of digressing from other important aspects of the martial arts."

develop self-esteem and confidence from this training. You should not look only at the physical aspect of karate-do and the development of effective techniques that can be harmful to others, you must develop the correct judgement that will allow you to abide by the law, humanity and common sense. How and when to use devastating techniques on others is important. It is like gun control, if a firearm is used to break the law, it is a crime. But if it used in the correct way it is a very powerful and effective tool to keep one's safety and peace. It is best if you never have to use it in your life. Karate-do practitioners should know the consequences of using their force.

Q: How do you think sport affects the Budo of karate-do?
A: A simple sportive conception of the art is the responsible factor in losing many effective techniques found in the kata *bunkai*. They can't be used within the competition framework so practically nobody practices them anymore. Sporting kumite is good but this point should be kept in mind. Freestyle fighting is good for the sport but there is the danger of digressing from other important aspects of the martial arts. In Japan, our Budo of the past was something extremely bloody and vicious as to what methods one could resort to. In looking forward to a peaceful future, the conversion to a competitive sport is the best way to spread the outstanding points and benefits of Budo to the world—if it is done properly, that is. On other hand, the sportive science has evolved greatly and this allows practitioners to be more prepared and in better condition to absorb and perform the physical techniques.

Karate-do is a part of Budo, and karate competition is a part of karate-do as a whole. It is true that karate-do has developed and spread rapidly due to competitions and sporting events. This has led to many practitioners believing that winning techniques and certain kata performances are the ultimate karate techniques. Sport karate is limited in the type of techniques allowed, for the safety of the competitors. On the other hand, Budo is a way of killing an opponent. The sport aspects of karate encourages and develops athletes with goals that are different than the ultimate goal of Budo.

Q: What order of importance do you give to kihon, kata, and kumite?

A: Kata is the instrument or material used to teach students. This inheritance from the masters contains their ideology and methodology that is called the style or *ryu-ha*. Kumite is the physical application of movements from a particular style. Today, there are no obvious differences between the styles at sports competitions. It used to be that you could tell what style they practiced by their first *kamae* or stance. Also, techniques have become international and universal at world com-

"If sports competition continues to diverge from the Budo aspects, then the realistic and original ideologies of karate-do techniques will be lost."

petitions. If one contestant is very successful at scoring or winning, immediately those movements and tactics are copied. Even in kata competition, if a certain kata wins in world competition, immediately that kata becomes popular and many other competitors begin performing it. This is another bad aspect of sports karate—only winners are praised in competition scenes. There are many inferior international judges who do not really know the kata's original methodology and content. Instead, they tend to look for and give higher scores to the kata that was performed using only strong physical movements. If sports competition continues to diverge from the Budo aspects, then the realistic and original ideologies of karate-do techniques will be lost. Kihon is the basis for correct execution and the method to develop the physical and ideological characteristic of each style. The kihon of the style must used in both kumite and kata.

If the students want to develop a good understanding of kata, they need the kihon and the kumite aspects to be properly balanced. One without the

"The basic requirement for a good karate is kata. Kata cannot be just remembered in the mind only."

others is no good. The basic requirement for good karate is kata. Kata cannot be just remembered in the mind only. Many physical repetitions are necessary to add it to the memory as well as perfecting each movement within the form.

Q: What are the real differences between shito-kai, itosu-kai, tani-ha, shito-ryu, hayashi-ha, and shito-ryu?
A: After the founder of shito-ryu, Kenwa Mabuni, passed away, shito-kai was created by mostly Toyo University graduates with Mr. Kenei Mabuni and late Mr. Manzo Iwata as their leaders. However, there was problem within the organization. Osaka area instructors had learned directly from Kenwa Mabuni whereas the Tokyo area instructors learned mainly at Toyo University. These two groups are technically different even in their kata. Only recently after many meetings have they been able to come to an agreement and produce some videotapes. Their curriculum was changed recently by a majority vote of their senior members. If karate-do is Budo, it is not correct to decide the curriculum by the will of the majority. They created many new terminologies, movements and altered kata from the founder's shito-ryu versions. The eastern Japan (Tokyo) group had more voting rights than western Japan which was the home base of shito-ryu. The name was changed to shito-kai in 1968. They collaborate with the national karate organization of Japan, the Japan Karate-Do Federation.

The late Ryusho Sakagami created itosu-kai after Kenwa Mabuni died in 1952. He claimed that was Kenwa Mabuni's last wish and that the itosu inheritance and traditions were to pass on to him. Obviously, Sakagami altered many of the kata to his version of shito-ryu, and therefore created his own itosu traditions. Since Sakagami was the senior student of Kenwa Mabuni, his methodology has influenced many generic shito-ryu practitioners—especially the eastern Japan karate-do practitioners including the eastern shito-kai group under the late Manzo Iwata. Even shotokan practitioners have been influenced by Sakagami's methodology, as evidenced by the fact that they have learned many shito-ryu kata and then altered them to their own style. Tani-ha shito-ryu was created by the late Chojiro Tani who also created the shuko-kai branch of shito-ryu. He was famous for his creative new methods and kata. When he performed some kata, he wore a mask and kimono while demonstrating. The style of shuko-kai is very unique and most shito-ryu stylists do not consider it a part of shito-ryu. Teruo Hayashi separated from seishin-kai to create his own version known as Hayashi-ha shito-ryu in 1970. Kosei Kuniba, who founded keishin-kai,

"If the students want to develop a good understanding of kata, they need the kihon and the kumite aspects to be properly balanced."

was the landlord of that dojo. The dojo was originally one of Kenwa Mabuni's branch dojos in the southern part of Osaka City where the late Kenyu Tomoyori, who founded Kenyu-ryu, mainly taught. When Kuniba started an independent dojo listed as a shito-ryu dojo, senior shito-ryu instructors refused to recognize it. He then went to Okinawa and received a certificate of authenticity from the late Shoshin Nagamine of shorin-ryu, who called Kuniba's school motobu-ha shito-ryu. They also affiliated the Nippon Karate-Do *rengokai* (organization) with Sakagami, and learned many kata from itosu-kai traditions. Hayashi-ha shito-ryu is from seishin-kai. However, according to the heir of shito-ryu, Kenzo Mabuni, it was not directly affiliated with shito-ryu or Kenwa Mabuni. Most of the high ranking shito-ryu practitioners say that Kenwa Mabuni wished to have Soke Kenzo Mabuni inherit his style. In fact, Kenzo Mabuni inherited his father's organization, Shito-Ryu Nippon Karate-Do Kai. More importantly, he inherited his

"Kata is the instructional material and inheritance within the style or school. The unique strategy and tactics for that school or style are taught through kata."

father's entire curriculum, including personal notes and especially kata that were not published. Mr. Mabuni continued his father's guidelines and methodology. The most important aspect is that he never altered his father's kata or curriculum.

Q: Do you have any favorite kata in the shito-ryu system?

A: I do not have a favorite kata, but I have learned a few kata directly from the heir of shito-ryu, Soke Kenzo Mabuni, which were left unpublished by his father and founder, Kenwa Mabuni. These unpublicized kata including *kenosha, quench,* and others. By learning authentic shito-ryu kata, I have learned much history and many of the reasons why kata has evolved to today's competition. I also have a lot of interest in other styles' kata that stem from original shito-ryu kata. Kenwa Mabuni really influenced all of major styles' kata. Many unpublished kata that Kenwa Mabuni left behind are very interesting. I am proud to be one of the only people in the world who knows these kata.

Q: Do you prefer kata or kumite?

A: Kata is the instructional material or textbook of each style and thus is essential to that style. Kumite on the other hand is the application of the techniques—kumite for fun, kata for learning. I do not have a preference. Kata is the instructional material and inheritance within the style or school. The unique strategy and tactics for that school or style are taught through kata. It is most important to understand kata through *furyu monji.* In the Zen sect, these words can be translated as, "One must learn through one's own physical experiences that which one cannot express by written form." Even many traditional instructors do not know the correct bunkai or *oyo,* much less the meaning and purpose of *kakushi-waza* or the hidden techniques.

Q: What do you think about the unification of kata in the World Karate Federation?

A: This has been on the agenda many times at the WKF Technical Committee meetings. But the committee has never come to an agreement to have kata from all styles conform to only one certain form. There must be many different stages in the development of kata which reflect the major styles of the four founders: Kenwa Mabuni, Chojun Miyagi, Gichin Funakoshi and Hironori Otsuka. There are many controversial differences even within the same style. Each senior instructor will tell the student, "This is the way I learned." But there is no consistency. With strong influences from the International Olympic Committee, there is pressure to allow kata events to permit new free-form or open kata.

"The student must understand the way his body works, because this is crucial in order to execute the physical techniques properly."

The agenda of making new free-forms was proposed by many European countries to our WKF Technical Committee meetings when I was a WKF World Technical Committee member. Their idea was that only a few kata have been winning in the last two decades and if the Olympic event is to see the highest possible individual performance, then it must create a form to give a more objective scale to measure the performances, rather than depend on the judges' subjective and personal experiences. The kata judges often do not have enough knowledge of all the kata of all the styles. Most of them are only knowledgeable in one style; some of them do not even know all of their own styles' kata well, and what they do know is often from only one instruction that they have received. Kata competition has many aspects of individual

"The modern derivations of the old kata are more concerned with the external appearance rather than with the meaning behind it."

timing and personal movements. If the timing of kata changes, then the meaning of the movements changes; but the judges usually give higher scores to the demonstrator's looks rather than technical performance aspects, and ignores certain styles' traditions and methodology. The judges tend to give higher scores to the performers who demonstrate power and focus even though the original kata requires no excess power or focus. The competition kata judges will give the scores to the competitors by the genetic ideas of competitions and the rules, not necessary to the tradition or methodology of the style.

Q: What do you think about the kata competition compared to the traditional way of doing the forms?
A: Well, first we have to understand that there are limitations on what the judges can or cannot judge. These days, in sport kata competition, there are other factors more important that the meaning of the technique. A real kata doesn't have to be appealing or attractive, but a competition kata has to be. In sport, there is too much emphasis on beauty at the expense of power. And power is important to perform a kata well. There is a trend to over-emphasize the form, as there is no need for power. The general style is softer, the breathing rhythm sometimes has nothing to do with the meaning of the technique. The timing of the movement has been altered to allow the judges and the audience to better perceive the physical action. A kata must be neither too quick, nor too slow. Some parts must be fast and some slow, according to the demands of the movements and application. The judges must look for a fighter as well as an artist. The modern derivations of the old kata are more concerned with the external appearance rather than with the meaning behind it. The interpretation of the kata is a personal matter, but kata is good for the mind; it is moving Zen and can be learned and understood on many levels.

*"We must stick to the traditional way but if we stay 'too traditional,'
then this might stop the development of karate."*

On other hand, I'm a strong believer that you should incorporate techniques from kata at a very early stage. I also understand some of the criticism
of classical applications in kata since I have seen some impossible bunkai
which any man in the street would undoubtedly question. But if you truly
understand the art of karate, then kata is kumite. I believe that the person
who looks seriously at the kata of karate, can be said to be studying the art.

Q: How important is the students' ability to think during the bunkai phase?
A: It is very important. The mental aspect or attitude is paramount in this
aspect of karate-do. However, the physical side is more important in the
beginning. You must push the physical side first using your mental power,
then both start to interrelate. The student must understand the way his body
works, because this is crucial in order to execute the physical techniques
properly. The practice of bunkai should be carried out slowly for a better
understanding—at least at first. Once the bunkai is understood, then it must
be practiced at full speed. Otherwise, there is no reason for doing bunkai—
it's pointless. Kata without the element of realism is a waste of time.

Unfortunately, these days we are not aware enough of these important elements in training, and even the simplest physical task becomes a chore. We depend too much on devices that do work for us!

Q: Is it correct to say that you're a mold and that many karateka are trying to copy you? Do you think students should try to copy their teacher?
A: It is normal for a student to try to emulate his sensei. There's nothing wrong with that. The problem lies when the students don't understand the basic principles within that particular technique and try to directly copy the sensei. Likewise it is wrong for a teacher to insist his students copy him. His work is to improve the student's technique as best suits their physique. Also, the student has to understand that quality is more important than quantity. We must stick to the traditional way but if we stay too traditional, then this might stop the development of karate. I always emphasize the traditional side of karate and when one is an instructor, one should always do your best. When I see students do some movement the wrong way, I sometimes think that the way I explained the technique wasn't all that good. The teacher has to learn how to communicate with students of different levels in order to assure they understand properly what is being transmitted. It is wise to have various approaches to teach the same movement or technique.

Q: You are very close to your students, how have they affected your own progress?
A: Sometimes I have the opportunity to train with my peers. When I practice with them I must be better than them because they are equal and above me. Therefore when I train with my students, I must also practice my best and give them the proper role model, which involves the best technique, attitude and mental alertness. I think of my student as my teacher. Another interesting factor is that when you train with your peers, the techniques are direct and correct. There are many factors that make everything difficult such as his mental alertness, the respect not to attack or counter without reason, et cetera. A lower grade student will present a series of untimed and uncoordinated random movements which are very hard to deal with. So as a teacher, I must learn to deal with the unexpected. If you try to do the same things, they won't work because the teacher has progressed above this level. Then he has to adapt.

Q: How important is physical conditioning to you?

A: During the early days, the training methods were very primitive. We all carry wounded bodies because of that! Personally, I don't want my students to suffer the same injuries I had in my youth. This is my responsibility to them. The karate practitioner must treat his body with utmost respect. It is very important for the modern teacher to study anatomy and physiology in order to understand how the body works. Then he can eventually develop teaching and training methods that help the student to improve their technical skills without getting injured. Some of the old conditioning methods are not so good for you in the short or long term. These days, karate-do is not just for self-defense but also to live a longer, healthier, and happier life. I believe that training must be as natural as possible. Of course, you can use weights. I don't really think there is a need to increase muscle size but it's better to improve your speed with maximum kime. Lots of techniques can be practiced this way and I find this is an excellent way to get better in the art.

"During the early days, the training methods were very primitive. We all carry wounded bodies because of that!"

Q: What do you think of makiwara training?

A: I use it. It's a very useful tool to develop focus. It also helps to forge a strong spirit, but pain is part of the process. If you don't know how to do it, it's easy to damage your hands irreparably. I think traditional training is the best. It builds stamina and technique. But it is very important to know the right way of doing it. Most people think that makiwara training only had meaning in the past because the hands and feet had to be deadly weapons, and with sport competitions taking over there is no need for that. Well, this is just one part of the whole equation. The makiwara is not only good for your conditioning but it also teaches you a lot about the proper kime and the right positioning when delivering the technique. Unfortunately, people think that the bigger your calluses are, the better you are at the art. Calluses are just a by-product of the training. As I said, it develops your wrists, elbows, hips, knees, et cetera. My advice is to find a true master that can

*"The teacher must educate the students about the real art,
the real karate-do, not simply about the sport."*

teach you how to properly use this piece of equipment. The concept of kime has recently changed to a much lighter physical definition. It looks like fewer practitioners are using makiwara training than in previous generations. The idea of *ichigeki hissatsu* from Japanese Budo, that was inherited from Japanese sword methodology, seems lost in modern competition techniques. The concept of *ma* should not be translated only as "distance" but should also include many other essences involved with controlled distance or effectiveness. On the bad side, competition creates conceited individuals who are contradictory to the idea of Budo.

Q: Do you think people's perception of what karate-do is all about has changed in the last decade?
A: Definitely. The level of awareness in the practitioners is higher than ten years ago. A great responsibility lies on the instructor's shoulders. The teacher must educate the students about the real art, the real karate-do, not

simply about the sport. High technical standards must be kept in order to assure future generations the quality of the art. This is the only way to grow in a positive direction. We must sacrifice and train toward the goal of achieving high levels of technical and spiritual mastery and settle for no less. Keep high standards is the best way to preserve good karate. The body is like iron—the harder you beat it, the harder it becomes. By the same token, we have introduced important changes in the way the art is being taught these days; there are some exercises that are not used anymore. As you know, a lot of long-term karateka have hip, knee, or foot problems since the training was brought in line with a need to be "tough." I agree that it was a bit barbaric and now we are finding that there was no need, that we created more problems than we solved. Today, we have a better knowledge of physiology and biomechanics and there is a better understanding of the legal and insurance aspects. Teachers are more inclined to look after their student's welfare and this is very good for everyone.

Q: What do you see as being the most important attribute of a student?
A: Attitude. A good student is one who is willing to listen and learn. Attitude is the most important aspect. If the student is brought up the correct way they will understand that winning tournaments is not the most important thing, but that loyalty and having an open mind are far more desirable attributes. For me, always persevering and trying to do your best throughout your life are the most important things that karate training has taught me.

Q: What about the non-technical aspects of the instructor. What kind of characteristics should they have?
A: They may soon need to have a four-year college degree just as public school teachers must have now. This is in addition to their skill in karate-do. Today, we see so many fake degrees being touted just because that person likes to use the title of a Ph.D. This, even though they bought it through a mail-order correspondence course. Further, stricter health codes should be enforced. Since this is a physical sport, instructors and students come into regular contact with each another. Health safety should be one of the primary goals of instructors.

Q: What are the most important points in your teaching?
A: I am like a translator in that I digest the knowledge of the East and hand it down to the West. I try to be the karate-do instructor that will teach students the correct, authentic traditional shito-ryu ideology and philosophy. I wish to have students who will inherit this virtue through my instructions. O

Masters' Techniques

Sensei Miki squares off with his opponent (1), and takes the initiative by moving in with a oi tsuki jodan (2), followed by a gyaku tsuki chudan (3), which opens the high area (4), for a mae mawashi geri jodan (5).

Facing his opponent (1), Sensei Miki closes the distance with a gyaku tsuki chu-dan (2), and recovers immediately, angling his body (3), to score with a jodan tsuki (4). He then positions himself (5), and finishes with a mae mawashi geri jodan technique (6).

Sensei Miki and his opponent square off (1). Miki closes the gap, covering a possible attack by the opponent's lead hand (2), and positions himself at the proper angle (3), to execute a inside sweep (4), which sends the opponent down and opens him up to a finishing punch (5), allowing Miki to gain final control (6).

Sensei Miki faces his opponent in a kamae *position (1). The opponent attacks with* a mae geri chudan *which is blocked by Miki (2), who counterattacks (3), using* haito uchi jodan *(4).*

Masatoshi Nakayama

A Legacy of Excellence

ONE OF GICHIN FUNAKOSHI'S TOP STUDENTS, NAKAYAMA WAS BORN IN 1913 INTO A FAMILY OF KENJUTSU INSTRUCTORS OF THE SAMURAI TRADITION. HE STUDIED KENDO UNTIL HE ENTERED TAKUSHOKU UNIVERSITY WHERE, BY MISTAKENLY READING THE CLASS SCHEDULE, HE BEGAN KARATE-DO TRAINING UNDER THE LEGENDARY FUNAKOSHI. UPON THE DEATH OF MASTER FUNAKOSHI IN 1957, NAKAYAMA WAS APPOINTED CHIEF INSTRUCTOR OF THE JAPAN KARATE ASSOCIATION, AND WAS PUT IN CHARGE OF DEVELOPING THE STANDARDS FOR THE NEW ORGANIZATION.

IN 1971, NAKAYAMA, WHO WAS ALSO AN ACCOMPLISHED SKIING INSTRUCTOR, HAD A TERRIBLE ACCIDENT WHEN HE WAS STRUCK BY AN AVALANCHE. THE DOCTORS GAVE HIM ONLY FEW DAYS TO LIVE AND HIS FAMILY WAS CALLED TO HIS BEDSIDE FOR HIS FINAL MOMENTS. BUT SENSEI NAKAYAMA NEVER GAVE UP AND, AGAINST ALL ODDS, PROVED THE DOCTORS WRONG AND LEFT THE HOSPITAL FOUR MONTHS LATER AND RESUMED HIS TRAINING.

WHEN HE PASSED AWAY IN APRIL OF 1987, DUE TO A STROKE, HE HAD SET NEW STANDARDS FOR THE ART OF KARATE-DO AND INFLUENCED THOUSAND OF PRACTITIONERS WORLDWIDE. MASTER NAKAYAMA WAS A GREAT TEACHER IN THE TRUE BUDO TRADITION, AND IS CONSIDERED TO BE AMONG THE MOST INFLUENTIAL KARATE MASTERS OF ALL TIME. HIS LEGACY OF EXCELLENCE, DEDICATION, AND TRUE BUDO MAKES HIM AN EXAMPLE TO ALL KARATEKA REGARDLESS OF STYLE, AND ENSURES THAT THE WILL LIVE ON FOREVER IN THE HEARTS AND MINDS OF THOSE HE SO DEEPLY AND PROFOUNDLY TOUCHED.

Q: How did you start in martial arts?
A: Budo was part of my family. My grandfather belonged to the Sanada clan of Samurai. Budo was always present in my education. My father was a disciplinarian since he was a military man. As far as my training, I did kendo before entering Takushoku University.

Q: Is it true you entered Takushoku without your father's permission?
A: Yes! I always wanted to visit China and Takushoku was the best university for getting training and education to work and teach overseas. So I

"Karate in its early days had no match rules, although there was a gentlemen's agreement to avoid attacking vital organs."

secretly took and passed the entrance examination.

Q: How did you start practicing karate-do?

A: I already had kendo training so I looked for a kendo class at Takushoku. I checked the training schedule and I misread the timetable and showed up at a class where everybody was wearing white uniforms! I had read a little bit about karate and all those movements were kind of amusing so I decided to sit there and watch. Suddenly, one of the men approached me and challenged me to try it and I did. Very soon I realized that it was not as simple as I thought. That day I had my first challenge of trying to perfect the karate movements—and I still have that feeling of wanting to perfect karate inside of me. Up to this day, I still wonder what the schedule for the kendo classes was!

Q: What was Sensei Funakoshi like in and out of the dojo?

A: Sensei Funakoshi always kept very strict discipline inside and outside the dojo. Karate-do was a way of life for him, not something to be left behind when you left the dojo. The training under him was very hard and demanding; the classes consisted of long hours of performing each technique hundred of times. Kata was repeated 50 or 60 times and makiwara training was done until our hands bled. Master Funakoshi used to join us for makiwara training and hit the post with his elbow thousands of times. He seemed to enjoy that particular aspect of training.

Training and traveling with him allowed me to see the man he was from many perspectives. For instance, he always seemed to be in a constant state of vigilance, no matter where he was. This made a big impression on me. Many times he did things to teach me that I was still young and immature and that I needed more self-discipline and self-restraint because those aspects are where true courage lies. He showed me that it takes more courage to walk away from a fight than to get into one. He was a visionary

"Sensei Funakoshi always kept very strict discipline inside and outside the dojo."

who was able to see that the students—who mainly came from kendo and judo, where sparring was a usual aspect of training—needed sparring in karate-do training. He devised sets of five-step sparring sequences the students could practice in a more combative environment than the techniques of kata. Don't forget at that time we only had kata and kihon as methods of training. Of course some of the students were hot-blooded, and if you failed to counter-attack at the right time they would hit you right away without waiting for you! As I said, the training was very hard and from the original group of 50 or 60 students, only five of six were left after a couple of months of practice.

Q: Few people know you trained in Chinese martial arts.
A: I trained in 1937 when I was sent as an exchange student to study Chinese language and history. To be totally honest, I was not impressed by the Chinese methods of fighting because they emphasized circular movements and at first sight they seemed to lack focus. But after training with several teachers my opinion started to change. I studied mainly under an old teacher called Sifu Pai, of a northern style. He was really good with his legs and his defensive actions were marvelous. Since the northern styles emphasize the use of the legs, I developed two new kicks. One was the pressing block with the sole of the foot *taisoku uke*, or with the lower shin, *haisoku uke*, and the other was the reverse roundhouse kick, *ura mawashi geri*. These techniques were added to shotokan later in 1946 when I

"Our Japanese students never asked these kind of questions. I guess it has to do with the culture and education of the people."

returned to Japan and, of course, with the permission of Sensei Funakoshi.

Q: What else did you do in China?

A: During my stay at Takushoku University I majored in Mandarin Language and Chinese History so it was natural for me to go there. I planned a trip and in 1935 traveled on foot across the Greater Khingan Mountains of Outer Mongolia. In 1937 I returned as a exchanged student, as I mentioned before, and that was when I studied the Chinese martial arts.

Q: Did you have time to practice karate-do in China?

A: Of course! I practiced every day. When you find yourself in a strange country you feel lonely, afraid, and insecure. But because of those struggles I became aware of important things such as self-reliance and self-confidence which helped me to overcome my loneliness and fear. Those situations are when the values of Budo have to be used in real life.

Q: What happened upon your return from China?

A: I had the intention of teaching the Chinese language, but I soon realized that was impossible. There was no way I could get a teaching post after the war ended. The economic and social chaos were huge. So I end up making a living selling underwear!

Q: Did you get in touch with your karate colleagues?

A: Yes I did, but it was hard. Many of them had died and even Gichin Funakoshi's son, Yoshitaka—who was going to be the heir and leader of the shotokan—had died of tuberculosis in 1945. On the top of that, martial arts were banned after the occupation authorities issued an edict. The situation was really bad in all aspects.

Q: You were one of the top instructors for the Strategic Air Command when the U.S. incorporated unarmed training, right?

A: Correct. It was very interesting because all of the students were young men in their early 20s who were in Japan for only six months. I was traveling around Japan teaching the soldiers who were stationed there. It was rewarding to meet some people today who come up to me and tell me that I trained them at that time! It's a great and enjoyable feeling. Teaching

"I was traveling around Japan teaching the soldiers who were stationed there."

these American students allowed me to realize that we needed more detailed explanations of "why" we were doing the techniques in the way we practiced them. The American students required explanations of the movements, so we started to analyze the movements and come up with theoretical explanations based on the laws of physics. Our Japanese students never asked these kind of questions. I guess it has to do with the culture and education of the people.

Q: How did the Japan Karate Association start?

A: A friend of mine had a great relationship with the head of the Japanese Ministry of Education. The ban of karate was not lifted until 1948, and in 1949 Sensei Funakoshi had a meeting to discuss the martial arts and the future of karate after the war. It was in that meeting that the nucleus of the JKA was formed and I was put in charge of the technical standards for the new organization. In 1955 the JKA was incorporated as an educational body under the Ministry of Education. We had to come up with the technical and grading standards to be registered with the Ministry of Education. Under the total supervision of Sensei Funakoshi I began to formulate the instructor program. I received great help from other karateka such as Teruyuki Okazaki, Hidetaka Nishiyama and Motokuni Sugiura. In 1957, after the death of Sensei Funakoshi, I was elected the Chief Instructor of the Japan Karate Association. In 1958 the JKA was declared an official body by the Japanese

"Training and traveling with him allowed me to see the man he was from many perspectives."

government and we made a great effort to unify many of the other shotokan karate schools in Japan.

Q: You were one of the students Sensei Funakoshi took to visit Kenwa Mabuni of shito-ryu. What can you tell us about that meeting?
A: Sensei Mabuni was a very respected karate-do master and Gichin Funakoshi had high respect for him. He was a living encyclopedia of kata from many different sources. Sensei Funakoshi took me with him to visit Sensei Mabuni and he told me to learn two kata from him—*ninjushijo* and *gojushijo*—so we could study them later on in detail and more carefully. Eventually, we changed the format to specifically suit the structure of the shotokan method, conforming the movements that are not practiced by our members. Gichin Funakoshi wanted to grasp the essence of the different karate-do styles and incorporate them into his method. It's important to remember that these kata were added to the basic 15 kata that Funakoshi taught. For instance, his son Yoshikata, went to Okinawa and returned with *sochin*. All these additions definitely improved the art and never in any way changed the basic concept of the karate taught by Sensei Funakoshi.

Q: Everybody speaks about the confrontations and the brutal sparring between schools in the old karate days. Was that true?
A: In the early days of karate-do, for some years after 1935, college karate clubs all over Japan held inter-school matches. They were called

"kokangeiko," which translates as "exchange of courteous practice." The participants freely attacked each other with all the karate techniques at their disposal, and the original purpose was to promote friendship between clubs, not to beat anybody up. For instance, one person attacked only once. Then his opponent counterattacked, again just once. They continued in strictly controlled alternation. But sometimes the young blood of the students ran too hot to be satisfied with such tameness. They could

"They could not resist the temptation to use to the fullest the techniques they had learned and the powers they had gained through daily training at the dojo."

not resist the temptation to use to the fullest the techniques they had learned and the powers they had gained through daily training at the dojo. There would be five or six contestants from each university in these freestyle matches. If something happened or went out of control, it was the responsibility of the judges to step in and part them. The truth is, the judges rarely had time to exercise their responsibility. Some of the contestants had broken teeth or twisted noses. Others had earlobes nearly ripped off or were paralyzed from a kick to the belly—the injured crouching here and there around the dojo—it was a bloody scene. It was tough.

Q: There weren't any kind of rules at that time, right?
A: Not at all! Karate in its early days had no match rules, although there was a gentlemen's agreement to avoid attacking vital organs. Despite the wounded, the custom of holding such matches remained popular for some time. I was a student in a karate club in those days. If the custom were to continue, I feared karate would degenerate into a barbarous and dangerous art. Yet, defeating an opponent is the common aim of all the martial arts in Budo. Don't forget that karate was developed in Okinawa, where the people were strictly forbidden to own weapons. Practitioners used train themselves through practice centering on kata. They held no matches. Although

"Without practice against an opponent we cannot have the chance to work at our greatest capacity. Fighting is dangerous, but fighting is indispensable."

we can maintain our technique through practice without an opponent, we cannot improve our mental and physical conditioning in preparation for actual battle if we adhere to the kata method all the time.

Q: How do you think a practitioner can develop that particular aspect without crossing the line?
A: Well, the practitioner needs to learn how to overcome anxiety and how far he should stand from an opponent. Without practice against an opponent we cannot have the chance to work at our greatest capacity. Fighting is dangerous, but fighting is indispensable. Only through it can we maintain the essential skills of karate. Even after graduating from college, I still kept hoping to see the development of a true match that would make karate a modern martial art. Once I organized a match with the contestants wearing protective gear, but the special clothing was an obstacle and turned out to be itself the cause of unexpected injuries. I had to keep looking for a solution. That was just before the beginning of World War II.

Q: What happened then?
A: After the war, even though Japan abandoned the militarism of the past and made a fresh start as a nation based on pacifism, the college karate clubs kept holding their wild fighting contests, and the number of injured kept mounting. In the new climate of peace, violence in any form was a hateful thing and not accepted in the society. If karate remains as it was, I thought, it will be regarded as the embodiment of violence and will eventually fade away. Yet judo and kendo were developing as sports. The glorious contests of swimmers and baseball players were brightening the postwar gloom. Young karate practitioners began to hope that karate would become a sport, and in order to do that it would have to have rules for matches.

Q: Was that the reason why you developed match rules?

A: I thought it was the right time for us to make a sport of karate. I studied the rules of many sports and observed matches. Finally, I developed rules that allowed contestants to use karate techniques to the fullest without injuring each other. However, if we put too much emphasis on fighting we become loose in our technique. To prevent that I made a kata competition, too.

"I developed rules that allowed contestants to use karate techniques to the fullest without injuring each other."

The kumite matches I had worked out were first performed in Tokyo at the All-Japan Grand Karate Tournament in October 1957, under the auspices of the Japan Karate Association. They were most impressive— attacks and counterattacks with rapid, powerful, well-controlled techniques. Not one contestant was injured in the freestyle fighting and they were a great success. That was the beginning of the freestyle fighting matches performed today in karate tournaments around the world. Finally a match form close to actual fighting had come to the public.

Q: So you finally succeeded?

A: I think I did, but I'm still afraid of one thing, however. As karate matches become popular, and they are these days, the karate practitioners become too absorbed in winning. It is easy to think that gaining a point matters most, and matches are likely to lose the very essence of karate. Karate matches are degenerating into mere exchanges of blows. Moreover, I cannot say whether the idea of free-fighting matches the soul of karate as taught by Master Funakoshi, the founder of karate-do. The soul of his karate requires quite a high standard of ethics. And we can't ever forget that.

"I practiced every day. When you find yourself in a strange country you feel lonely, afraid, and insecure."

Q: Do you think Master Funakoshi would be against these type of matches?

A: Let me tell you this, Master Funakoshi often recited an old Okinawan saying: "Karate is the art of virtuous men." Needless to say, for students of karate to thoughtlessly boast of their power or to display their technique in scuffles goes against the soul of karate-do. The meaning of karate-do goes beyond victory in a contest of mastery or self-defense techniques. Unlike common sports, karate-do has a soul of its own. To be a true master is to understand the soul of karate-do as a martial Way. Karate-do has grown popular these days, and its soul is apt to pass from our minds. We must strive to strike a balance and I believe that if the practitioner trains with the right spirit, then the balance can be reached. Don't forget that in karate there is no initial movement.

Q: What exactly does that mean?

A: It is said that karate has no initial move or *sente*. That is an admonition to practitioners not to launch the initial attack and a strict prohibition against thoughtlessly using the techniques of karate. The masters of karate, especially Master Funakoshi, strictly admonished their pupils with those words again and again. In fact, it is not going too far to say that they represent the soul of karate-do. The idea of no initial attack in karate is embodied in the kata. As far as I know, there are 40 or 50 kinds of kata and each begins with defense or *uke*. You may argue that since karate was born as an art of self-defense, it is natural that it has no initial move. That is certainly true, but if you immediately conclude from the words, "There is no initial move in karate," that you can freely counterattack, you have not yet fully grasped the soul of karate-do. The underlying meaning of those words is much deeper. In addition to refraining from attacking first, practitioners of karate are required not to create an atmosphere that will lead to trouble. They also must not visit places where trouble is likely to happen. To observe those prohibitions, the practitioner must cultivate a gentle attitude toward others and a modest heart. That is the spirit underlying the words, "There is no initial move in karate," and "Spirit is the soul of karate-do." One master says, "Karate is based on attempts to avoid any trouble, so as not to be hit by others and not to hit others."

"One master says, 'Karate is based on attempts to avoid any trouble, so as not to be hit by others and not to hit others.'"

Q: Is that when karate-do becomes more than a fighting art?

A: The soul of karate-do is the wish for harmony among people. Such harmony is based on courtesy, and it is said that the Japanese martial ways begin with courtesy and end with courtesy. Such is the case with karate-do. Master Funakoshi collected the kata of his forerunners and then systematized them into 15 kinds of kata for practice. One, called *kanku*, symbolizes the wish for harmony, the soul of karate-do. Unlike any other pattern, it begins with an action unrelated to defense and attack. The hands are put together, palms outward, and the practitioner looks at the sky through the triangular hole formed by his thumbs and fingers. It expresses self-identification with nature, tranquility, and the wish for harmony. The practitioner of karate must always have a modest heart, a gentle attitude, and a wish for harmony. Karate is truly the art of virtuous men.

Q: What about the saying, "There is no posture in karate?"

A: This concept summarizes the proper attitude in training or actual fighting. Together with the previous one it is an integral element of the soul of karate-do. When we say, "There is no posture in karate," we basically mean that you should not stiffen your body—you should always relax to be ready for any attack from any direction. When the gale blows, the stiff oak resists and breaks, the flexible willow bends and survives.

But even if there is no physical posture, you may think a certain mental posture is necessary. You cannot relax your attention. That is why in karate-

"At the highest stage, practitioners of karate should in actual fighting have posture of neither body nor mind. Herein lies the deep meaning of 'There is no posture in karate.'"

do, there is posture but no posture. Practitioners assume a mental posture but not a physical posture. Actually, that is not the highest stage of the art. At the highest stage, practitioners of karate should in actual fighting have posture of neither body nor mind. Herein lies the deep meaning of "There is no posture in karate." It is this highest stage which shows the essence common to the art of Budo.

Q: Has this something to do with the idea of "no mind?"

A: Definitely! In the 17th century, the Zen priest Takuan gave Yagyu Munenori a treatise which had a great influence on the ideological side of the martial ways of Japan. It is popularly called *Fudochi Shinmyo Floku* and in it, Takuan wrote, "If you place your mind on the movements of your opponent, your mind is absorbed by the movements of your opponent. If your mind is on the sword of your opponent, your mind is absorbed by the sword of your opponent. If your mind is on cutting your opponent, your mind is absorbed by cutting your opponent. If your mind is on your sword, your mind is absorbed by your sword. If your mind is on not being cut, your mind is absorbed by not being cut."

Where, then, should the mind be! You should put your mind nowhere. Then your mind is diffused throughout your body, stretched out, totally unfettered. If your arms are important, it serves your arms. If your legs are important, it serves your legs. If your eyes are important, it serves your eyes. It works freely in the body wherever necessary.

Takuan further said, "If you concentrate on one place, your mind, absorbed by that place, is useless. If you are worried about where to place your mind, your mind is absorbed by that worry. You should throw off worry and reason. Let your mind go over your entire body, and never fix your mind on a certain place. Then your mind must accurately serve in response to the needs of each part of your body." In short, the Zen priest says that the mind, if placed nowhere, is everywhere.

Q: Does this mental state affect the physical performance of the practitioner?

A: It sure does! I'll give you an example; when we first learn how to drive a car, we find it very difficult and take every precaution. But once we have thoroughly mastered driving, we can be quite at ease while we drive and still not break the rules. We aren't very conscious of our driving technique.

This is the highest stage of actual fighting in karate-do, where we do not have posture of mind. In the martial arts, when we have attained the highest stage after long years of training, we return to the first stage. In the first stage, where we do not know any posture or technique, we do not fix our minds anywhere. When attacked, we simply respond unconsciously, without strategy. But as we come to understand posture, the use of technique, and fighting tactics through our study of technique, we occupy our minds with all sorts of things. The mind is divided into attack or counterattack and loses its freedom. After a long period of further practice, we can move unconsciously, freely, and properly.

"Let your mind go over your entire body, and never fix your mind on a certain place."

That is the highest stage of karate-do, the true meaning of, "There is no posture of mind." That stage can be reached only after hard and painstaking training, but it has nothing to do with physical strength. In the West, physical strength counts for much in the martial arts. Men of a certain age must quit. Karate-do, however, emphasizes technique based on the practice of kata. We can continue to practice this martial art for a lifetime, no matter how much our physical strength declines. The more we practice, the more gracefully we can move.

"Karate-do emphasizes technique based on the practice of kata. We can continue to practice this martial art for a lifetime, no matter how much our physical strength declines."

Q: Do you think there is a danger if karate-do becomes a simple sport?

A: That danger exits, but everything is in the instructor's hands. Karate, if practiced properly, can be used as self-defense and a sport without losing its essence. If the principles are taught properly it won't matter what the practitioner is doing—he will be doing "karate-do." The art has to be used to develop the person and it's when the student trains only for competition when the direction is wrong. The secret is to train "in the art," not "in the sport." We must train with a balance in our minds. Competition karate has to maintain the idea of *ikken hisatsu*, which will keep the seriousness of true Budo and not simply allow the sportive scoring of points. If we do this, karate-do will keep its essence as an art and will be practiced by people of all ages, because is not simply a sport but a complete art used to develop the whole individual. The art of karate-do is about daily practice and if you follow this, the real truth will come to you because life is the same as karate training—a daily and constant practice.

Q: What do you think of those who train in different systems at the same time?

A: Everybody can do what they please, and I respect any position. For me, as a *budoka*, the idea of Budo is to train, study, and develop one art so using this as a vehicle we'll improve as human beings. The important aspect is not to learn more and more systems but to go deep into one art so you can develop the correct spirit of Budo, which goes deeply into life. If you use logic, in a lifetime it is impossible to develop true mastery in many styles and methods; maybe you'll reach a level of simple physical skill but not true mastery. The correct idea of Budo is to concentrate on something

and master it. I always compare this to a doctor. There are many branches of medicine but doctors become specialist in their fields. They know more than any other average doctor in that specific field. In short, the idea is to go deep into one art since after many years of training you'll be able to understand any other system and grasp the essence of it. Once again, I want to emphasize that this is the Budo attitude and approach.

"The idea is to go deep into one art since after many years of training you'll be able to understand any other system and grasp the essence of it. This is the Budo attitude and approach."

Q: You had a terrible accident when skiing. What happened?

A: I was a ski instructor in 1971 and I took some students to the Japanese Alps. The conditions were so bad that I ordered the students to take off the skis and walk. The snow mass suddenly started to break and after I put the last of the students in a safe place the avalanche struck me. I was sent to the hospital where the doctors said that I had only just a few days to live. My family was at my bedside ready for me to die. Fortunately, I didn't! That accident happened when I was 58 and I truly believe my karate training saved my life. I was in a very good physical condition for a man of my age, and my body could take the stress of everything it had to go through. The doctors said that it was a miracle that I recovered the way I did. I think it was simpler than that—the art of karate-do saved my life.

Q: Any fear or regrets after all these years?

A: No, not really—no regrets. Maybe a few things could have been done in a different way but I always tried my best to promote and expand the art of karate-do all over the world. And fears? I hope when I die and meet Sensei Funakoshi that he's not angry with me for introducing the sportive aspect into the art. After all, he wanted to see his art practiced and recognized all around the world and the sportive aspects did just that. O

Hidetaka Nishiyama

Karate's Driving Force

ONE OF THE TRULY GREAT MASTERS AND PIONEERS OF JAPANESE KARATE, HIS CLASSIC WORK, KARATE: THE ART OF EMPTY-HAND FIGHTING, WAS PUBLISHED IN 1960 AND IS STILL CONSIDERED THE DEFINITIVE TEXTBOOK ON THE SUBJECT. A DIRECT STUDENT OF GICHIN FUNAKOSHI, SENSEI NISHIYAMA BEGAN HIS STUDY OF KARATE AT THE AGE OF 15. IN 1961, SENSEI NISHIYAMA MOVED TO THE UNITED STATES AND FOUNDED THE AMERICAN AMATEUR KARATE FEDERATION. BEFORE LEAVING JAPAN, HE WAS ONE OF THE FOUNDERS AND LEADING EXPONENTS OF THE JAPAN KARATE ASSOCIATION, IN CHARGE OF THE FAMOUS INSTRUCTORS SCHOOL WHERE MASTERS LIKE KANAZAWA, ENOEDA, MIKAMI AND SHIRAI CAME FROM.

FEW PEOPLE KNOW THAT THE LEGENDARY BRUCE LEE WAS HIGHLY IMPRESSED WITH SENSEI NISHIYAMA'S KICKING TECHNIQUES AND LEG CONTROL, AND THAT AFTER WITNESSING A DEMONSTRATION GIVEN BY HIDETAKA NISHIYAMA, DECIDED TO CHANGE HIS TRAINING METHODS FOR KICKING. ALTHOUGH MASTER NISHIYAMA LIVES IN LOS ANGELES, HE IS ONE OF THE FOREMOST AMBASSADORS FOR KARATE IN THE ENTIRE WORLD. WITHOUT A DOUBT, HIS ZANCHIN STILL EXPRESSES THE DECADES OF GRUELING TRAINING FORGED UNDER THE SAMURAI SPIRIT.

Q: Sensei Nakayama was a father figure for many JKA instructors. How did you feel when he passed away?

A: Really sad. I felt tremendously sorry that we lost him. I always felt that karate needs people like him to reach higher stages of development. He worked very hard until the last day of his life giving seminars, lectures, coaching at the university, giving demonstrations, et cetera. During the war he went to China to research karate's roots. What is more, he took his wife and two children along! He was a big influence in my life, along with my kendo teacher, Morio Mochida. I can only say that Sensei Nakayama devoted his life to the promotion of karate-do.

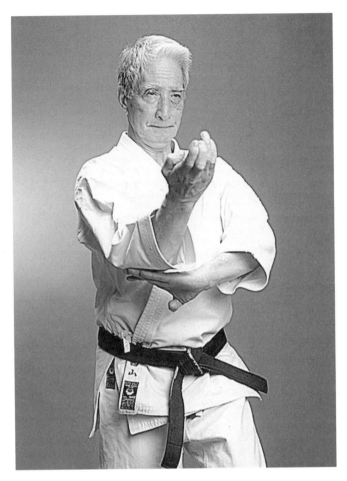

"Competition is good but only while keeping the real values of traditional karate. Don't forget that karate-do is based on the art of self-defense."

Q: You wrote a great book about karate many years ago. Any plans for a new one?

A: Several different publishers have been asking me to write a new one. I guess that when I get time I want to produce a new book specifically for instructors—not for students—a pure textbook for instructors that would require a program on how to use the book. To me it's sad to see how many good karate-do practitioners ignore how to coach or instruct in a professional way. It is not enough for the teacher to demonstrate the technique and for the students to repeat it in the old way. We must advance more in order to progress.

Q: Why did you found the International Traditional Karate Federation?

A: There were just too many kicking and punching courses being called "karate." Basketball, soccer, and handball are "ball games," but yet are not the same. The ITKF is based on the original idea of karate-do, not "new" or "sport" karate. To avoid confusion, and therefore to clarify what real and traditional karate is, I founded the ITKF.

Q: Are you against sport karate?

A: Not at all, but I'm against a conception of karate as simply a sport. Competition is good but only while keeping the real values of traditional karate. Don't forget that karate-do is based on the art of self-defense. In karate there is something called "*todome*" or "finishing blow." It is very similar to the idea in the old fencing schools of killing the opponent with only one action. Of course, the final idea of any martial art is to win without fighting.

"He was a big influence in my life. I can only say that Sensei Nakayama devoted his life to the promotion of karate-do."

Q: When did you start training in martial arts?
A: It was a very long time ago. I think it was about 1943. Karate was not popular at that time, but judo and kendo were. I did them because martial arts training was incorporated into the school system. But I liked them very much, so it was not a problem for me. I heard about karate and I got interested. Unfortunately, I had to look all over Tokyo but finally found Mr. Toyama's dojo. I began my training there and a lot of people began telling me that I should go to Mr. Funakoshi's dojo. I stayed with Mr. Toyama for over a year-and-a-half and then I went to Master Funakoshi's school.

Q: Was Gichin Funakoshi your actual instructor?
A: Yes, he was. Sensei Funakoshi instructed me at that time. Remember that it was wartime—all the senior instructors were away at the war. So mostly at the university we saw only Master Funakoshi and Master Kuriyama. I did train sometimes with Master Funakoshi's son, Yoshitaka. He was young and very strong. I remember that all the young students were trying to copy him. Master Funakoshi's techniques were in principle the same as Yoshitaka's, but the external form was different. I guess some of the youngest students didn't understand that, since they were only looking at the external form.

Q: Why did you drop judo and kendo for karate?
A: It is not that I didn't like kendo or judo, but having a small body I was not well-suited for judo practice. In karate, small size is not a drawback.

273

"The number of karate practitioners was very small because the war created a big blank in the instructor's ranks. Karate was an almost unknown martial art."

Q: So when you started to train, karate wasn't popular?

A: That's right. The number of karate practitioners was very small because the war created a big blank in the instructor's ranks. Karate was an almost unknown martial art. That's why it was so difficult to find a dojo—only in three or four universities could you find one.

Q: You mean that the best instructors were serving in the war?

A: Yes. All the top instructors were at war, so the senior people were those from the university. It wasn't until 1949 or 1950, when these instructors returned to Japan, that things started getting back into order.

Q: I guess the post-war period was not the best time for karate reconstructions.

A: It was not, but they had to do it. I was the captain of the university team and we started a rotation training in different university dojo because almost everybody had forgotten their kata. People who had studied for a long time couldn't remember, so we all had to get together, pool our information, old reading materials, and our personal experiences. We also used to gather to train under Master Funakoshi.

"The student had to pick up things for themselves and to do so they had to study their master's daily life."

Q: I've heard that there was a difference of opinion between the seniors and the people at the universities.

A: I think it was more a matter of loyalties and not so much a difference of opinion. The older ones felt they were more traditional, and in the university there was a little bit of class distinction, so some egos came out. Then we decided to start the Japan Karate Association. I recall that we had no dojo so we still rotated around the universities. Without a central dojo, things were no as smooth as they should have been. Master Hironishi was very good in bringing people together but later on he decided, along with some other shotokan schools, to form the shotokai.

Q: How was the training at this time?

A: Well, we didn't practice many techniques or combinations. No variety at all. One hour *kiba dachi* (horse stance), 1,000 punches, 1,000 kicks, and pretty much that was it! Sometimes we would repeat the same kata a hun-

"They never liked coaching or teaching scientifically. You had to find out for yourself the right way, just by feeling the technique."

dred times in a row. We had this kind of training all the time. The first day I went to class, my teacher showed me the kiba dachi stance and left me there for an hour! I was so mad, I don't know why I went back the next day. The instructors did not teach with a lot of explanations. This was not the way during those days. The student had to pick up things for themselves and to do so they had to study their master's daily life—how he worked, how he lived, how he expressed himself in different circumstances. After three or four years, the master would decide to start teaching techniques, but without much detail—maybe just a few special points. They never liked coaching or teaching scientifically. You had to find out for yourself the right way, just by feeling the technique. And of course, you were never supposed to ask questions.

Fortunately, for many, these days there is more teaching, more explanations, and more help on the instructor's part. Curiously, the principles are the same, they haven't changed. We have new ideas and training methods but the fundamental principles are the same. Sometimes I wonder how the old masters knew about the right physics and dynamics of the human body.

Q: Do you think the same principles apply to all different karate styles?
A: Yes, of course! The principles are the same. Goju-ryu, shito-ryu, shotokan, wado-ryu, et cetera, all share the same basic principles. It just happens that the explanations are a little bit different and the form looks different. For instance, goju-ryu uses short movements since it was devised for short distance fighting. They look for developing strong muscle power for close range techniques. Shotokan put more emphasis on wider movements

and dynamic body actions—getting the power more from rotation and body shifting.

What it is true in any style is the fact that regardless of the style, every karateka needs to know how to develop power in short range and long range using strong muscle actions and contractions. We must think how to make power in different ways. All the actions must start from the floor for external force. This is the very basic principle of momentum and as Newton mentioned in his first, second, and third laws, without an external force you never increase energy and momentum. It has to be remembered that all the actions in karate are from the floor. I practice shotokan, but shotokan is not the only karate. We must never think shotokan is complete or that shotokan is the best.

"We must think how to make power in different ways. All the actions must start from the floor for external force."

Q: Who do you remember from the old days who is still active in karate?

A: Sensei Kase, Sensei Kanazawa, and Sensei Mikami—I can't remember anymore! Taiji Kase was a student of Sensei Hironishi and Hirokazu Kanazawa and Sensei Mikami were among the first people to graduate from the Instructor's School. That was around 1957 or 1958. I remember that I met Sensei Kase and Sensei Sugiura just after I graduated from Takushoku University. Mr. Sugiura is a very nice person and very serious about everything he does. I recall that Mr. Kase was working for a company at that time but that we always found time to get together for training.

"You have to keep studying and training for self-development in the art if you really want to reach a very high level."

Q: You mentioned very important names in karate history. How do you think they reached such a high level?

A: They continued training and studying—they never stopped. They always looked for their own personal development. That's the reason they are so good. Look at instructors such as Enoeda, Shirai, and Kanazawa. They were very young men when I first met them as the chief of the JKA instruction department. I have to tell you that there were many instructors who were at the same level as them, even better than them, and with more and better understanding of the principles. At that time they were not so special. But these other instructors did not continue their development and quit. Conversely Enoeda, Kanazawa, and Shirai dedicated their life to the art of karate. You have to keep studying and training for self-development in the art if you really want to reach a very high level.

Q: Why was the art of karate being taught at the universities?

A: Sensei Funakoshi was responsible for this. In the beginning he brought karate to the universities. But after the war, General MacArthur passed a law that no martial arts could be practiced at the universities. So we kept training by going to Mr. Yoshida's backyard after finishing classes at school. After a while we returned to the university because the law was relaxed.

Q: It is true that you used to put on a white belt and go into the Instructors School classes?

A: Yes! It was during the beginnings of the Instructors Course at the *honbu* dojo. I did it to see if I could learn *gyaku tsuki* or *kiba dachi*. I tried to think just like a beginner and I took notes about the instructor's performance and teaching ability—then I brought it up in the course. I know it was very difficult for the new instructors but it was also for me. I knew that I had to do it so I could find out by personal experience if the beginners were receiving their instruction properly. After all, that's what karate-do is all about—personal experience.

Q: It is said that at this time there were a lot of challenge fights.
A: No, that's not correct. There was great rivalry and the kumite matches had no rules and no control, so it was very hard. This used to happen during *kokan geiko* or exchange training. But no challenge fights happened. In fact, we developed a great friendship through these special training sessions.

Q: Was *kokan geiko* only for shotokan members?
A: No, other styles were invited also. It was not restricted to shotokan schools only.

"I'm not against sport, but the problem with modern competition is that you don't need to feel Budo. In real karate, if you miss your block you are going to get hurt."

Q: Do you think karate competition with rules is better than the way you used to fight—with no rules, no control, et cetera?
A: I'm not against sport, but the problem with modern competition is that you don't need to feel Budo. In real karate, if you miss your block you are going to get hurt. There's no second chance. This state of mind changes your whole conception of what you're doing in kumite. You must pay much more attention to your training. If there's no contact in sport karate, why train the kihon? You don't need power! The punch might make contact and the fighter score the point, but in a real situation, there is no damage! For

me, this is not karate and I believe that the sport side is growing a lot and the spiritual and Budo side is going down. Of course, it is better to have a set of good competition rules, but I guess it's very hard to please everybody. I support the traditional conception of karate-do.

Q: What's your personal opinion of kata?
A: Kata is karate. All karate techniques are taken from kata. Let me put it this way: if you look at the history of karate, all the old masters developed certain kata based on their perception of combat. Original kata is very valuable. What some people don't understand is that while they were going through this research, they found out the very essence of movement in the body. What they did was to understand the principles behind the physical motion and its relationship with the body, and use it in the application of the technique. In the old days, we never referred to kata as form, as we understand it today. Kata used to mean "symbol," although it was written in the same way. The physical movement was just a vehicle to understand and identify the internal principle. Only after that did they began to apply the technique. It is very important to teach these aspects in the right way, with the complete spiritual dimension that is called in Japanese *"fudoshin."*

Q: How do you think a student should approach their kata training?
A: The practitioner must first study the kata at the outside form, but seek the principles. Kata is like saying "for example." Later on the student must connect the principle to the application. The old masters experienced these applications. Therefore, the practitioner has to study the outside form first, then understand the principle, and later on connect the principle to the actual application. Unfortunately, many teachers and students have decided to change the outside form right away. You must study and understand—not just look at the outside form which is just an example. The old masters would first study the outside actions of the kata then digest it. They would make the kata their own, but not by changing the techniques and movements, but making it match their own body. For instance, I visited Master Kenwa Mabuni's shito-ryu dojo for several days to learn kata from him. His kata was very beautiful. He had a very skillful body. Some people have very strong kata but are not beautiful. This is because they have not made the kata match their body. This is something very important to remember for every karate-do practitioner. Unfortunately, once you have trained the wrong way it is very difficult to change, because your body structure is set and bad habits are almost impossible to change.

Q: What it is karate-do for you?

A: As a physical art I could say that it provides an excellent all-around exercise to develop coordination and agility by using all body muscles in a very balanced way. As a self-defense method, and through the training and use of the principles and knowledge of the art, the student is prepared to both physically and mentally defend himself against any attack. Of course, the sport is important but only if we follow the precepts of the art and we don't forget the very essence of it. On other hand, karate is art not science. It is an art that uses scientific principles. Science doesn't make karate. Personally—and because I learned my karate from the feel of the techniques—I think no science can explain this feeling. It can only explain the way the movements are done and the physical science behind the movements.

"Karate is art not science. It is an art that uses scientific principles. Science doesn't make karate."

Q: What is your idea of perfect training?

A: It depends very much on the instructor. The first thing a good teacher has to do is to make the student understand how to develop internal energy. It is very important to assimilate and develop the energy coming from the ground. You only have to look at golf players and the kind of shoes they use; their shoes have cleats in order to better adhere to the ground. If you apply the same concept to karate training, it is easy to understand why rooting to the ground is so important. The energy goes from the ground to your feet, all the way up to your legs and hips, to be exerted from the limb doing the punch or the kick. In karate, this kind of energy is explosive if you focus it right at the moment of impact.

"If a junior can fight different seniors after five or six hours of hard training, and still have the spirit to face them, then he has overcome great psychological barriers."

Q: Is there a way to get a student to actually use this power?
A: In a way. I have gone through this kind of training myself. The idea is to give the junior student the right spirit. If a junior can fight different seniors after five or six hours of hard training, and still have the spirit to face them, then he has overcome great psychological barriers. The junior is always afraid of his senior, this is the first barrier. It is not physical, it is mental. So the senior hits him and pushes him by yelling, "Kick! Punch! Get up!" He doesn't beat him badly but pushes and forces him to fight back.

Q: Did you ever met the founder of aikido, O'Sensei Ueshiba?
A: Yes, I had the opportunity of talking with him on a private basis. I was very close to Sensei Gozo Shioda since we were at the same university. I remember the three of us talking about the *tai-sabaki* principle. Of course, you can find this principle in other arts but I always tried to use valuable knowledge and apply it to the art of karate.

Q: Is it true that you have been studying Chinese chi gong?
A: The real masters of chi gong have great mental power. As a young practitioner, I remember trying to find a gap in my kendo master's defense, but I

could never perceive any flaw. After all these years of training, I came to realize it is the mental part that is decisive in real combat.

Q: In every karate style there are different interpretations for each kata. Do you think this is correct?
A: Like I said before, kata is the symbol of karate so it never changes. Unfortunately, 95 percent of the people don't understand kata—only the outside movements which are irrelevant without understanding. Each kata evolved out of the experience of the masters. Through it, they embody the principles of karate. The good student has to learn through careful imitation and endless practice. This is the traditional way, not only for karate but even for other things like flower arranging, for instance. The student must copy the designs for a long time and, in the end, once he has picked up the principles, develop his own way.

I always say that you have to develop you own way, but this is where scientific explanations of each movement come in. Every karate practitioner has a different body. Through training and understanding kata in the right way, they seek their final form—they become their own masters for expressing karate. The principles are there and they come out naturally. The good karate master teaches his students to find their own way, not to follow his. Students that venture out on their own too soon, or without the right amount of knowledge and understanding, will never know what they're doing. In martial arts there is not a set logic, everything is a matter of experience.

Q: What is your final advice for all karateka around the world?
A: All traditional karate is one—karate-do. Traditional karate is Budo. We must keep this philosophy. We must continue developing new teaching methods to give the next generation the best possible karate. This is our responsibility as leaders. O

Teruyuki Okazaki

The Ultimate Development of Character

MASTER OKAZAKI WAS BORN IN JUNE OF 1931 IN FUKUOKA, JAPAN. IN 1947 HE
STARTED HIS KARATE TRAINING WITH MASTER FUNAKOSHI AT TAKUSHOKU UNIVERSITY.
IN 1961 HE WAS SENT TO THE UNITED STATES TO TEACH THE ART OF THE EMPTY HAND
WITHOUT KNOWING A SINGLE WORD OF THE ENGLISH LANGUAGE.

HIS PHILOSOPHY, CHARISMA, AND VITALITY IS SECOND ONLY TO HIS HUMILITY. HE
IS A MAN DEVOTED TO THE PRINCIPLES OF GICHIN FUNAKOSHI AND A FIRM BELIEVER
THAT THE OLD VALUES TRANSCEND TIME AND CHANGE. HIS MOTIVATION LED HIM TO
MEET DR. MILORAD STRICEVIC, A RESEARCHER IN THE FIELD OF SPORTS MEDICINE.
TOGETHER THEY WROTE A BOOK, KARATE DO: A MODERN TEXTBOOK, THAT IS PROBA-
BLY THE BEST BOOK EVER WRITTEN ON KARATE. HE IS THE CHIEF INSTRUCTOR OF THE
INTERNATIONAL SHOTOKAN KARATE FEDERATION AND THE CHAIRMAN OF THE JAPAN
KARATE ASSOCIATION WORLD FEDERATION.

HIS GOAL IS TO EDUCATE STUDENTS ON THE MEANING AND VALUE OF KARATE AS A
WAY OF LIFE, NOT AS A SPORT. SENSEI OKAZAKI SPENDS ALMOST THE WHOLE YEAR
TRAVELING TO INSTRUCT HIS STUDENTS ALL OVER THE WORLD. HIS GOAL IS VERY SIM-
PLE—PRESERVE HIS TEACHER'S ART AND PRECEPTS AND "KEEP TRAINING."

Q: You studied directly under Gichin Funakoshi. How was the training?
A: Usually, Master Nakayama led the classes. Master Funakoshi would sit
down and tell Nakayama sensei what to do. He was always there observing.
Master Funakoshi always stressed five important points in his teachings: the
mental aspects, the physical aspects, staying calm, being exact, and being
natural. He liked to explain how the human body works and how important
it was to use the corrent techniques to attack the right body parts.

Q: Was it the way you expected?
A: No way! The training was very hard, very difficult. I recall that for the
first three or four months all we did was punching techniques—straight
punches. The training sessions were up to six hours each day, six days a
week. Master Funakoshi never said that we should copy his form because
he understood that his body weight and his body-type made the stances and

"It's important that the instructor knows how to communicate and give something to the student so we create a better society."

the form of the techniques that way. He was a very scientifically-minded person—don't forget that he was a school teacher. He developed the physical techniques in a certain way but he used to say, "Don't copy. Judge it by your body type." It is very difficult to explain his movements. They looked almost without power, and more like a beautiful ballet.

He was very open-minded. For instance, he never taught us kobudo but he introduced it to us. For him karate was empty-hand, but I remember him saying, "If you ever have to use a weapon, use the best one to fight with!"

Q: How many people left?
A: Many of them. A lot of people left. We would stand in *kiba dachi* and punch for two hours in the morning. Then the same for another two hours in the afternoon and for another two hours in the evening. Most people just gave up. The next three months were dedicated to kicking—just kicking techniques. After six or seven months of this kind of training, they started to combine both aspects and kata training was incorporated into the classes and became the focal point.

Q: What was the purpose of this training?
A: We were like machines. This kind of training built up our muscles to an extraordinary degree. Our arms and legs were really powerful. But I didn't understand that back then. It took me over a year to see that the more hard work I put into my training the more benefits I got from it. If I missed one training session I didn't feel good at all—not my body, not my mind. But it wasn't like this in the very beginning.

Q: What do you mean?

A: Well, in the very beginning I was training in kendo because kendo and judo were the common arts. I didn't enjoy judo very much, mainly because it had been thrust upon me from my early days in grammar school, so I was kind of rebellious against it. Anyway, at Takushoku University the captains from each martial art came and gave demonstrations to introduce the arts.

Q: So you were impressed with karate?

A: Yes, but also with aikido. I really liked them both. So I signed up for both classes.

Q: Who was the aikido teacher?

A: Morihei Ueshiba himself! I was very fortunate. My karate teacher was Gichin Funakoshi and my aikido teacher was Morihei Ueshiba!

"The training was very hard, very difficult. The training sessions were up to six hours each day, six days a week."

Q: Was the term "shotokan" used to describe Funakoshi's style of karate?

A: No, not at all. There was no style. Master Funakoshi just called it karate-do because he wanted it to be called karate-do. But out of respect his students started calling it "shoto" which it was Master Funakoshi's pen name. At that time, we did not have any style. We were practicing karate-do. Of course, Master Nakayama wanted us to train under other karate masters, that's why he used to invite Gogen Yamaguchi from goju-kai and Hinori Otshuka from wado-ryu to teach us a different approach to the art. All these instructors gave lectures on their methods of karate and taught us various kata. I really think this was an excellent approach to help us better understand the complete art of karate-do.

Q: Did Master Funakoshi get together with other top teachers like Master Kano or O'Sensei Ueshiba?

A: Yes, of course! Master Funakoshi enjoyed very much being with Master Mifune of judo, Master Morihei Ueshiba of aikido, and Master Nakayama of kendo. They used to give demonstrations together. He always said to us that he respected very much Master Jigoro Kano's thinking of the martial arts. I know Master Kano helped Master Funakoshi when he started to teach the art of karate in Japan. He always felt that judo had to study some karate techniques. They were very close friends and they had a lot of respect for each other. I remember that every time we passed in front of the Kodokan, Master Funakoshi always took off his hat and bowed. "He's my teacher," he used to say. "Of course," we all answered, "but he's judo." And Master Funakoshi replied, "It doesn't matter, a martial art is a martial art and I must respect it!"

Q: How did you decide to concentrate on karate-do?
A: It's a funny story. The training in karate classes for the first three weeks was only *usaki tobi* or rabbit hops. Thousands of them everyday, for hours and hours. Non-stop. We would get so tired we would literally fall over on our faces, but there was Nakayama Sensei and other *senpai* to push us until we got up and kept going. I wasn't happy with that and I decided to quit. I told my roommates, their names were Irie and Onoue, that I was going to quit and concentrate on aikido training. They were my very good friends, we had been together for a long time. Pretty soon, they started to make fun of me, calling me "sissy," and saying that they would never give up. This made me so mad that I promised myself that if they could do it, I could too. So when I was going to be accepted by O Sensei as a regular student, I stopped aikido and concentrated on karate, only to keep face with my two roommates!

Q: So what happened to them?
A: Well, we were going to test for black belt under Master Funakoshi, so I was very serious about it. My roommates decided they wanted to quit. But I had made a promise and was pushing them to their limits in the training sessions in the early morning and in the afternoon. I insisted that they train for their test. Well, they passed the test but I flunked! Master Funakoshi said I was not good enough. My attitude was bad, very bad. I flunked many times because of it. I was a young guy thinking in the wrong direction. Master Funakoshi picked up on this right away. It was not my techniques which made me fail the test, since it was equal to the other students who passed, but my attitude. Finally I got really depressed so I went to ask Master Funakoshi why I failed the test. Of course, everybody was shocked that I actually went to speak to him. That never happens in Japanese traditional culture.

Q: What did Master Funakoshi say?
A: He said that he really understood my problem and that he was going to tell me the essence of karate-do—but that I should be very prudent with it's

use. Then he sat down, and I did the same with great ceremony. I was so excited, and Master Funakoshi seemed to be really concentrating. I was nervous, and after a while he leaned over and said, "You know Okazaki, the true essence of karate-do is keep training—keep training everyday."

Q: Was that what you expected?
A: I don't think so, but I haven't stopped training since. After that, my attitude changed and finally I got my black belt. There is an interesting story about myself right after I passed the test. I was really proud of it and Nakayama sensei was the person in charge of teaching the beginners. One day he said, "I want you to assist me today!" Of course, I was more than pleased. All of a sudden, Master Funakoshi came in and started to look around. He remembered my name because I'd been

"My generation was very fortunate to have trained under Funakoshi sensei and to have been led by Nakayama sensei."

there for a long time and he asked me: "When did you pass the black belt test?" Right there I thought, "Master Funakoshi is getting old; he's getting forgetful." "Sensei, you took me for the test," I answered. Then he said, "If you are a real black belt you have to prove it. I'm sure you will be able to knock me down. Punch me or kick me. Go ahead!" I was really scared and thought, 'No way. If I touch him, my seniors will kill me right here!' The problem was that I was a very short-tempered guy and I said to myself, "OK. I might die but I have pride and I'm a black belt!" So, I attacked him in front of the whole class, with all the students and Nakayama sensei looking on. I charged and punched at him. I thought that he was on the floor when I felt somebody tapping me on the shoulder. "You need more practice Okazaki!" I don't know how he did it. My classmates said that I did a good job, but it looked as though I went through Master Funakoshi's body. Definitely, he was something special. Nakayama sensei told me that Master Funakoshi knew how to absorb and use the attacker's energy against him.

"The most important thing is do your best. Not only in karate but in everything you do in your life."

Q: Do you ever feel a great responsibility at being one of Master Funakoshi's students?

A: Yes, all the time. My generation was very fortunate to have trained under Funakoshi sensei and to have been led by Nakayama sensei, but I guess that no one considers themselves good enough to do the job we have to do. We were educated to believe in high quality karate-do, both technically and spiritually. This is the only way karate can be passed down to future generations.

Q: Why did you decide to come to the United States?

A: Master Funakoshi's last years were taken up with instruction and preparation to send instructors all over the world. In 1953 we did a nationwide U.S. tour for judo and karate. After that tour, Master Funakoshi received a lot of letters asking for instructors, so they sent me over in 1961. But there was a big problem. I couldn't speak a word of English. It was terrible for me. They sent me to Philadelphia because they thought it was a more convenient location. Anyway, the major problem with that plan was my English! You know, in the beginning I couldn´t read the menus at the restaurants so I used to point at something. It could be soup or chicken, or steak. I had a very hard time. Like karate training! But my English improved thanks to my wife. The most important thing is do your best. Not only in karate but in everything you do in your life. We are all human beings, there no way we can be perfect. But the idea of getting better and better everyday is what's important. Just do your best.

Q: Have you found that your teaching has changed over the last thirty years?

A: Before I came to this country Mr. Kosaka, who was the president of the Japan Karate Association and the Japan Foreign Minister, hosted a farewell party for all the senior instructors. He came to me and said, "Okazaki, the first thing you have to do is to have some friends who are lawyers and doctors." At that moment, I didn't understand what he meant. Now I do. When I came to this country I tried my best to make people understand karate-do, I had to be strict—but have control at the same time. You cannot be physically abusive. I always used a *shinai* stick but it depends how you use it. If you hit hard it is not good, but sometimes it is good to make a loud sound so the students wake up. Think about it as an instructional method. Times and society have changed both here and in Japan. The basics are the same because we are human beings but the mental attitude has changed. Students think that if they pay this much, they must get that much. That's what they believe and we can't blame them because they are like part of a machine. The youth don't practice how to think. Karate-do or other physical disciplines teaches them that if you don't sweat and work really hard for something, you'll never get anything. But if I used the same teaching methods that I did forty years ago, I wouldn't have any students!

"Karate-do or other physical discipline teaches them that if you don't sweat and work really hard for something, you'll never get anything."

Q: Did you finish your studies in the Takushoku University?
A: Yes, I did.

Q: When did you become an official JKA instructor?
A: I guess the Japan Karate Association was officially organized around 1955. So I was hired as an assistant instructor and quit the job I had. I became the first coach at the instructor's course. Master Nakayama had plans to make official instructors and I became a kind of guinea pig, because he used to give me several projects to study, practice and report on. He analyzed everything I gave him and later on he started the official instructors program. Like I said, I became a coach to the instructor trainees. The first graduate was Mr. Mikami, and then Mr. Kanazawa, and Mr. Takakura. The idea was that becoming a karate instructor was to be the equal of studying the curriculum in a university to become a teacher. We had courses on how to teach the techniques, how to practice by yourself, and on subjects like physics, scien-

"The real meaning of Budo is to go into life more deeply and improve physical and spiritual qualities through hard training."

tific aspects, et cetera. One of the prerequisites was a degree from a four-year college. So this course became sort of a Master's degree.

Q: You consider karate to be a sport?
A: No. Karate-do is Budo and Budo is not a sport. The real meaning of Budo is to go into life more deeply and improve physical and spiritual qualities through hard training. The essence or concept of sport is to get away with the toils of life and have some fun. Master Funakoshi was against tournaments but I remember Nakayama sensei telling him that it was a good way to promote the art and introduce it to the public. Nakayama Sensei stressed that it is not about trophies and medals but to bring the art into the public eye. Master Jigoro Kano also recommended that Master Funakoshi have a ranking system as a motivational tool. These old masters were training for personal development and didn't need these kind of external rewards. But the times changed and people think and train for different reasons. The environment and the economic situations are all very different. But these masters reached a very high level with the old methods. That's why I keep training—to reach their level of excellence. That's the real challenge for the modern martial artists.

Q: So you are against karate being accepted in the Olympics?
A: I would like to see what Nakayama sensei suggested before passing away—the Budo Olympics. All Budo arts together, exchanging techniques and training methods where there are no winners or losers. This would return us to the original concept of Budo and we could educate people about the art and the true meaning of the Way of the Warrior. Nakayama sensei said to me, "We must make people understand the true martial arts way." And this is what I'm trying to do, and the very reason why even after a tournament we still do the dojo *kun*.

Q: Did Funakoshi ever get involved in grappling or throwing techniques at all?
A: Yes, he did. In fact he explained that many of the kata applications, the *bunkai,* were throwing techniques. But he always stressed that before you

throw your opponent to the floor you must punch or kick first in order to finish them. He liked to throw the opponent in front of the next attacker, using him as a kind of protective shield.

Q: Do you try to preserve Master Funakoshi's and Sensei Nakayama's teachings and philosophy?
A: Of course. That's my goal and purpose. Nakayama sensei was like a father to me—sometimes like an older brother who was always there helping me and guiding me. Master Funakoshi was like a grandfather. I must fulfill my obligation to my original teachers. Karate-do was taught by Master Funakoshi and Master Nakayama as a way of life. He gave us, his proteges, the *Shoto Ni Ju Kun* or "20 Precepts To Live By." The idea of those is that karate-do is Budo and its goal is to develop character in human beings and to avoid conflicts.

Q: Is getting a black belt the ultimate goal of karate-do?
A: Not at all. A black belt is just the beginning of a journey. It is a degree of skill but not of the ability or understanding of the teaching methods. These are two very different things. I strongly emphasize to my instructors to be patient, to understand.

Q: Do you have any plans to go back to Japan?
A: My teacher sent me here in 1961, so here I am. I was ready to go back anytime they decided, but it didn't happen. Unfortunately, both of them have passed away. Compared to them, I am nothing. I hope they feel proud of me wherever they are now.

Q: Do you think karate-do keeps you young?
A: Daily training gives you vitality, energy, and health. Keep training! keep training! We can never reach perfection, but we must keep training. That's my challenge and responsibility as Master Funakoshi's student and a teacher of his philosophy.

Q: What would you like your last will to be?
A: I would tell my students the same thing I always have and encourage them to follow Master Funakoshi's philosophy and seek perfection of character, respect others, always endeavor to avoid violent behavior, and be sincere. Those are the final goals we are all aiming for. O

Osamu Ozawa

Tempered by Fire

BORN IN KOBE, JAPAN, OSAMU OZAWA BECAME, AT A YOUNG AGE, ENTRANCED WITH NOT JUST THE MARTIAL ARTS BUT ALSO WITH THE LIFE OF THE WARRIOR. AT AGE 17, HAVING ALREADY STUDIED WADO-RYU KARATE-DO, HE LEFT KOBE FOR HOSEI UNIVERSITY WHERE HE BEGAN TRAINING UNDER GICHIN FUNAKOSHI. IN 1944, OZAWA WAS CALLED UP TO SERVE IN THE JAPANESE IMPERIAL NAVY AIR FLEET BUT HIS MILITARY CAREER ENDED IN A FLIGHT ACCIDENT THAT PUNCTURED ONE LUNG. UNTIL HIS DEATH ON APRIL 14TH, 1998, OZAWA SENSEI WAS THE HIGHEST-RANKED SHOTOKAN KARATE MASTER IN THE WESTERN HEMISPHERE. HE WAS AN EXTRAORDINARY MAN WHOSE LIFE WAS IN THE HANDS OF THE GODS FROM BEGINNING TO END.

Q: What was your family situation during your youth?
A: My family was not rich but we were well off.

Q: Did you live up to your parents expectations?
A: I don't think so. I guess my parents had a lot of dreams for me—I would grow and mature, attend the university, and enter the family firm. But I guess that was a dream destined not to be.

Q: How was life during pre-war times?
A: Life at that time was very disciplined. Life, pre-war, was very, very strict. It was a time of rising Japanese militancy in people minds. I remember that both judo and kendo were part of the educational system for imparting the ways of the warrior to the young.

Q: What was your goal as a teenager?
A: I wanted to be a professional military man but my mother was disgusted with the idea. I went to a junior military school and applied. I took the test but I failed. It was very demanding physically and mentally. Out of every 100 applicants, one was selected.

"Life at that time was very disciplined. Life, pre-war, was very, very strict. It was a time of rising Japanese militancy in people minds."

Q: Because of your disappointment, did you give up?

A: Not at all! I remained undeterred in my goal and again, when I was 15, I tried to apply to a junior military academy sponsored by the Navy.

Q: Were your parents happy with that idea?

A: Of course not! My family was very disappointed with me. My mother was unhappy and my father didn't understand because he wanted me to attend the university to study business.

Q: How were people selected for karate classes at the university?

A: I remember that nearly 80 people signed up for the university karate team. Mr. Ito gave a short lecture on the history and traditions of karate and then an explanation of the art. He made us try the makiwara. I had trained before, and I had struck makiwara to toughen my hands. But many there had never seen the striking pole—then it was wound with tough rope. Mr. Ito commanded me to hit the makiwara 50 times with each hand. It didn't bother me but those who had never struck it were a different matter! Their hands were split and bleeding—some even cried.

Q: What did the seniors say?

A: Not too much. "Today is your day to decide—stay or go," they said. About 30 stayed. Over half indicated that they wanted to go. For those who stayed they announced that the training "was going to be different from then on; six days a week, six hours a day." The training became more severe than military discipline. In the military, superiors could beat subordinates with a bo, or order troop punishment but in karate we would be left sitting in *seiza* for hours, forbidden to move. Being struck in the face was common punishment. The training was hard, terrible hard. It was about spiritual training...but technically...I don't know now. I have to confess that I was frightened: I didn't want to stay, but I was scared to quit.

Q: Why?

A: Because there was a formal ritual to say goodbye to all the members training in the dojo. It was a very formal occasion. The members were lined up according to seniority, from junior to senior. Then you approached them one by one. You said, "Goodbye," then the person would strike you in the face. I was really scared to quit!

Q: What's your opinion of Master Funakoshi?

A: Sensei was a very strong, very wise man. I don't think a day goes by that I do not think of him. I meditate in my dojo sitting before his photograph in the *kamiza,* and burn incense in his memory. Before the war, I don't really think we believed he was a great man. Sensei was very soft spoken; he would observe as seniors Obata, Hironishi and Tagaki supervised the training. Master Funakoshi would walk up and down the lines and stop and talk with every student and

"The training was hard, terrible hard. It was about spiritual training. I didn't want to stay, but I was scared to quit."

correct this or that. Sometimes at night I would go to the dojo and practice my kata singing a poem written by Sensei Funakoshi that begins; "There is an island to the south, where there is a beautiful art. This is karate."

Q: How did the war affect Sensei Funakoshi's students?

A: It was a big change. A lot of classmates were being called up for military service and faces began to disappear from the dojo. Whenever anyone left, we had a farewell party. We would gather in a restaurant and wish farewell to our comrade. We would toast their fortunes. I remember that the training in the second year was not so unbearable as the first.

"We believed in our minds, in our hearts and souls, that we were to lay down our lives for the nation."

Q: Did they have a farewell party for you?
A: No, there wasn't time to hold a farewell party. Funny, but I was called up to serve in the Japanese Imperial Navy Air Fleet!

Q: You don't seem to like to talk much about the war.
A: Well, I think it is something that is best left in the past. I cannot describe well what we felt. It was a time of purity—great emotional strength. We believed in our minds, in our hearts and souls, that we were to lay down our lives for the nation. It was very beautiful—but very hard to explain. I had a flight accident that punctured one lung. I spent six months in two different hospitals recovering. Physical injuries heal but the devastation done to Japan looked as if it could never be healed. Japan was a sea of rubble. In Tokyo, most of the people had no housing, not even huts or tents. Everything lay in ruin. Food, clothes, essentials—all were scarce.

Q: What was your personal situation those days?
A: My karate colleagues, the practitioners of the first great age of Japanese karate, had been scattered to the wind.

Q: Where was Funakoshi sensei at that time?

A: He had gone to Kyushu in 1945, after the fall of Okinawa. He discovered that his wife was ill and dying. These were days of dark discovery. He did not return to Tokyo until about 1947. He looked very old when he returned from Kyushu. He had lost his wife, and many fine, wonderful karate students. I remember one, a much senior practitioner from Takushoku University. He had been the captain of the team and he was a very great student of Sensei's. We used to fear him because he was really powerful. In those days there was no tournament but after exchanging training, we would free spar. Sensei Funakoshi was very sad when he heard of this death.

Q: How were those sparring sessions?

A: It was not like a tournament. No rules, no protection. Just two men and a senior who called *"Hajime!"* And you fought until you couldn't fight anymore.

Q: How often did Sensei Funakoshi teach at the dojo?

A: He looked old but he remained healthy. Whenever we needed him, we went to pick him up. It was interesting because even if he looked old, when he changed into his uniform he was full of energy! Of course, he was not as active as before the war, but it was a truly honor to have him two or three times a month. There is no value that can be placed on having known him.

"I remember that the training in the second year was not so unbearable as the first."

"Just two men and a senior who called 'Hajime!' And you fought until you couldn't fight anymore."

"There were some differences but not between the masters such as Yamaguchi, Funakoshi, Mabuni, et cetera."

Q: When did the senior practitioners decide to organize the art?

A: It was around 1949. Seniors Obata, Tagaki, Nakayama, Fukui and Ito got together. They decided to invite Sensei to be Instructor Emeritus. Senior Nakayama was given the duty of being the active Chief Instructor; the others assisting. A tiny office was set up in Ginza. The original dojo—the Shotokan—had been bombed during the war. There was no place to train and some wanted to rebuild the old Shotokan building. This is how the Japan Karate Association (JKA) was created. Later on, in 1949, we decided to create a national organization and Sensei Hidetaka Nishiyama was assigned the responsibilities of technical advisor.

Q: When was the reunification of Shotokan karate completed?

A: I guess it was in 1952. But Master Funakoshi never wanted his karate to be called "Shotokan"—the "Hall of Shoto." He always called his art "Japanese karate," because it was of and for Japan. That is why there was a JKA and not a group called "Shotokan."

Q: At that time what was your opinion about the possibility of unifying all karate styles on a national basis?

A: There were some differences but not between the masters such as Yamaguchi, Funakoshi, Mabuni, et cetera. All those differences lay between the young students and not the masters. I remember we managed to give a dinner for all the masters. Unfortunately, it was a dream that for whatever reasons, and there were many, failed to come about. O

"There was no place to train and some wanted to rebuild the old Shotokan building. This is how the Japan Karate Association (JKA) was created."

"Master Funakoshi never wanted his karate to be called 'Shotokan'—the 'Hall of Shoto.' He always called his art 'Japanese karate.'"

Henri Plée

The Gichin Funakoshi of Europe

HE IS A LIVING LEGEND—THE SENIOR EUROPEAN KARATE EXPERT AND THE CENTRAL FIG-URE IN JAPANESE KARATE DEVELOPMENT ON THE OLD CONTINENT. HOWEVER, ALTHOUGH HE HAS BEEN CALLED "THE FUNAKOSHI OF EUROPE" HIS PLACE IN THE EVOLUTION AND DEVELOPMENT OF EUROPEAN MARTIAL ARTS SEEMS TO BE LESS WELL-KNOWN. HE HAS MORE THAN 50 YEARS OF EXPERIENCE AND STILL TEACHES IN HIS DOJO IN PARIS, THE CITY OF LIGHT. HIS CURRICULUM AS A MARTIAL ARTIST IS SECOND TO NONE AND HIS UNDERSTANDING OF THE REAL APPLICATIONS OF THE ARTS HE STUD-IED SHOWS THAT MASTER PLÉE COULD HAVE TAUGHT ANYWHERE IN THE WORLD. MASTER PLÉE PULLS NO PUNCHES WHEN HE TALKS ABOUT THE MARTIAL ART CALLED "KARATE," AND ITS PRACTICAL APPLICATION IN LIFE.

Q: When did you begin training?
A: When I was the pioneer of European karate in 1948, no one had ever even heard the word "karate." Some even thought that it was an invention of mine and called it "Karaplée." For ten years, without a genuine expert to guide me, I trained with the intention of combat because that was my temperament in judo. My form was very imperfect compared to photographs and films of the Japanese masters. However, I remained indifferent to belt levels—all that interested me was the mental and physical enrichment that karate brought.

Then, at my own expense. I brought five successive master karateka from Japan and corrected my style very quickly because I had always practiced with sincerity of feeling. Then when I went to China and then to Japan to study and perfect my abilities, I was surprised by being promoted to 5th dan. The Japanese masters considered, to my embarrassment, that I had mastered the true spirit of karate to a level where no one could honestly judge me, based on my intuitive and mental focus, because there were no longer any limits to what I felt I could achieve. I believe that this demonstrates the importance of practicing honestly and deeply without dreaming of quick successes or fast belt grades. Like anything in life, karate rewards come when you least expect them. Honestly, sincerity, and dedication are,

"Although the training in karate-do is the most sporting and most complete, karate refuses to be a sport, but remains a martial art."

in fact, the only true shortcuts to anything.

Q: It is true that you met the great martial arts expert and historian Donn F. Draeger?

A: Yes, it is. It was around 1952 and he was the foremost world authority on the subject. Draeger visited my school at night and observed the training. He said, "Very interesting. What is it exactly, savate?" I said, "No, karate." He was somewhat surprised because he had seen karate practiced in Japan and this was rather different. In an effort to help, he later sent me a 10-minute film of Japanese masters training. I used to run it through time after time, trying to copy the movements exactly. However, in doing this, I also succeeded in copying every minor fault, all of which had to be corrected years later. The trials and errors I went through actually enriched me more than if I had been simply "given" the techniques.

Q: Is karate a sport or a martial art?

A: Although the training in karate-do is mostly sport, karate refuses to be a sport, but remains a martial art. In a street fight, or to use the image dear to karateka, on the field of the battle, you must expect attacks of any and every kind from your opponents. Kicks will be more or less certain, fists, head-butts and knees also, and it is probable that armed attacks will occur if your resistance is serious. In such situations, the necessary state of mind is to hold oneself at the right distance from your adversaries, evade their strikes (and not to be seized), and yet be close enough to strike effectively. In fact, the most dangerous opponents are not those in front of you, but those on whom you turn your back, for they can injure you more seriously. To escape from such perilous situations, each of our attacks, "under pain of death," must be decisive. We need to turn constantly in order to survey the attackers who surround us and eventually group them according to our attacks and movements. This explains the variety of techniques and turning movements which are the basis of karate training. Each of our attacks must be decisive.

Q: What exactly does the term "be decisive" mean?
A: Mortally threatened, we cannot allow ourselves to exchange blows till a knockout results, as is the case in boxing where several rounds are often necessary, or to take the risk of clinching as in wrestling or judo, since we have only our bare hands and the opponent might be armed. In karate, the first stage is to parry or evade each attack, even if preceded by feints, and finally to strike "as to knock down a wall." If this strike does not give the anticipated result (such as fracture, unconsciousness, or momentary paralysis), then in contrast to European combat sports, we do not once more take up our fighting distance, but follow up

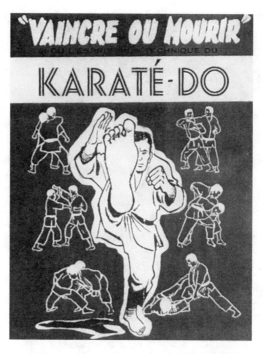

"Judokas joked about this and affirmed that it was an invention of mine, publishing in the Judo Revue of the French Judo Federation, an article where my technique was announced as 'Karaplée.' After these articles appeared I had to face challenges."

"In a serious situation a karateka will always execute this series of attacks, even if the first has every chance of being effective."

on our advance, and our risk, (because each attack is a risk), so as to strike with one of our short natural weapons, such as the elbow, knee or head.

If this follow-up is insufficient, we will overturn or throw the opponent with one of the karate throws (a little different from judo, since one does not concentrate on seizing) and finish him off immediately on the ground, whether by a strike, lock or other means. In a serious situation a karateka will always execute this series of attacks, even if the first has every chance of being effective, and its speed is so great than an onlooker will often see only one attack. Of course, one strikes in every possible way; with the hand, elbow, foot, knee and head. This is a glimpse of the weapons and idea of karate.

Q: What do you think of the growing number of challenge matches in the martial arts?

A: This is not something new. It was part of martial arts circles since the beginning. During the first few years that I was establishing karate, I was imprudent enough to tell reporters that karate was "invincible," the most terrible of combat sports and so on. But it became necessary to prove this, because at that time none had ever heard of karate. Judokas joked about this and affirmed that it was an invention of mine, publishing in the *Judo Revue* of the French Judo Federation, an article where my technique was announced as "Karaplée." After these articles appeared I had to face challenges.

At that time I was a good contestant in judo, and I still participated in all the championships. My karate was quite rudimentary. Obliged to give frequent demonstrations of breaking, I had big calluses on my knuckles, of which I was very proud. After the publication of the first article, we were presented with the sight of a huge professional wrestler who had come quite simply to storm the dojo. I tried to evade a fight by saying that I risked killing him and so on, but he didn't wish to hear any of this and it became necessary to go through with it. I no longer remember exactly how it turned out, but I succeeded in knocking him out with an elbow strike during a close-quarters exchange—by a miracle, or perhaps by instinct, since this same attack repeated itself in the course of another duel. This elbow struck full in the liver and I had to resuscitate my opponent. His abdomen had gone as hard as stone and for a while I was worried that I might not be able to revive him. My prestige rose considerably after this, but although I prayed that no one else would have similar ideas, my prayers were not answered.

I don't know how long it was afterwards that a boxer came to challenge me. He had the appearance of someone who was completely mad. This time, having more experience, I made him fight my best pupil, who was 6 feet tall and very fast. Thus I had a chance to see the boxer's favorite blows, and perhaps my pupil would succeed in eliminating him. This is how one proceeds in Japan. However, my pupil did not seem to dare to strike in earnest and fought as if it was a training session. It did not last long, (the boxer won), and therefore I had to go through with the match—and again, I no longer remember exactly what happened. I do remember that I did *fumikomi* (stamping kick) to his knee as soon as he came too close. This seemed to worry

"My prestige rose considerably after this, but although I prayed that no one else would have similar ideas, my prayers were not answered."

"I also gave them a series of strong slaps to make them realize that I could really hurt them if I wished."

307

"I remember also kicking him in the stomach with what I thought was a terrible mae geri *(front kick), which hadn't the least effect."*

him. I also remember kicking him in the stomach with what I thought was a terrible *mae geri* (front kick), which hadn't the least effect. Then seeing an opening I succeeded with a back-fist strike to his left eye, followed by a throw (my specialty) and a heel kick to his ribs, breaking them.

Following this, I had to face a French boxer, and then another professional wrestler, but they were not of a high level. Then I had a visit from two judo friends, excellent champions, who said to me; "You have sown doubt in our minds, and we have come to challenge you. We want to know if karate really is superior to judo." These were really good friends of mine, one of them had even been my student during the time I helped Master Kawaishi in judo, and I did not wish to harm them. They were forcing a fight and I was not quite sure what to do. I stopped their attacks with kicks to the shin, or used stop-kicks against their kicks, which were really telegraphed. I also gave them a series of strong slaps to make them realize that I could really hurt them if I wished.

In that era the spear hand to the eyes was considered a classic technique. Finally, the first one found an opening to seize me by the collar in the classic judo style. But I was a better judoka and, taking him by the collar also, I delivered a light head-butt to his chin. The second, a little shaken, was put out of action easily by a front kick to the stomach.

Several months after this, a weekly magazine did a long report on karate and numerous members of the public came to watch our training. It was then, during a lesson, that one of my best black belts bowed to me for a contest. This type of thing was frequent, but after several moments I realized that he wanted a real combat. Everyone stopped their practice to watch us. I am not sure how this combat unfolded but I do know that I knocked him out with a right elbow strike to the liver just as in my first challenge.

Then I received a challenge from a street fighter who gave me quite a lot of trouble. But I succeeded in hitting him in the groin with a sort of *ushiro geri* (back kick), delivered with the idea of judo´s *uchimata* throw, which was my special last-chance technique. During a demonstration in a large theatre, I had to meet a challenge from a very fast wrestler. He also I was able to put out of action. I don't know how since I myself was on the ground with a broken rib. These challenge matches gave an invaluable experience of real combat and brought, I am sure, something that can not be acquired otherwise.

"Karate without test is not real karate. One great Japanese expert said, 'What use is a magnificent, well balanced sword if one is incapable of using it? Better to possess a wooden sword and be skilful with it.'"

Q: Do you mean that without challenges martial arts are not real?
A: Karate without test is not real karate. One great Japanese expert said, "What use is a magnificent, well-balanced sword if one is incapable of using it? Better to possess a wooden sword and be skilful with it." It is evident that a great number of karateka and martial artists believe that they are seriously practicing martial arts and karate because they execute good kihons, well-done katas and, from time to time satisfactory kumites. But this is only a preparation; a sort of preliminary workout that is still a far cry from real karate.

Q: How important is the style when looking for efficiency in combat?
A: Style is preliminary conditioning to the particular ideas of the past or present master—a method of preparation or training and a mental and physical education. So much so that the different styles are shaped in the same mold, as it were, towards the finals of championship, when the finalist belong to different styles. That which could be called "karate" is a standard where karateka begin to catch their opponent from long and short distances without the latter being able to dodge, block, or avoid the attack. At this stage, ortho-

"In karate, there is the basic style or ideal, static or in coded movement as in the kata, and there is also a dynamic application in combat, where timing is of fundamental importance."

dox styles and faults are no longer of the utmost importance, and only the concentration of force and stability at the end of the attack count.

In karate, there is the basic style or ideal, static or in coded movement as in the kata, and there is also a dynamic application in combat, where timing is of fundamental importance. It is incontestably more difficult to place an attack against a worthy opponent in his moment of weakness than to be in apparent good form against an imaginary opponent or beginner. And when you are better acquainted with karate, you will know that the basis recommended in kihon should only be applied during this timing, and that at a high level the postures before and after are of no importance.

"A great master's quality can not be judged from a photographic perspective—it can't be understood in such narrow ways."

The important thing is to be constantly prepared to bound forward, backwards, or to the side; to attack with the upper limbs as well as the lower, and to block powerfully. Narrow mindedness or a strict observance of orthodox static positions in karate can limit the practitioner to a mediocre level, which he will never surpass. A great master's quality cannot be judged from a photographic perspective—it can't be understood in such narrow ways. O

Tsuguo Sakumoto

In the Modern World, But Not of It.

Tsuguo Sakumoto was born in the Okinawan village of Onno. He became the top kata performer in the world at age 34. Eugen Herrigel, when talking about kyudo (the art of archery) said, "One arrow, one life." Tsuguo Sakumoto's motto might be, "One motion, one life." Every detail of his kata performances have been perfected and repeated thousand of times. As a 7th dan in the original Okinawan style of ryuei-ryu, Master Sakumoto is a legend in karate circles around the world. A several-time world kata champion, Tsuguo Sakumoto, is also a physical education teacher in Okinawa. He is considered by many to be the best kata performer in the history of karate.

Q: When did you begin your karate training?
A: Because I am from Okinawa, everyone thinks that I started karate as a child, but this is not so. When I was a kid there was no dojo, as such. The training used to take place on the beach. It was more of a private training and you had to be recommended by at least two people. It was pure martial arts, and the conception of fighting was about life or death, not about winning tournaments. My formal training began at age 16. I was not at all sport oriented because when I was a baby I suffered first from diphtheria and then pneumonia, so I was a very weak child. I had some friends who practiced shorinji kempo and karate, so I started to learn a little about these arts.

When I completed my studies at Nippon Taiku Daigaku, I returned to Okinawa. Once there, I heard about Kenko Nakaima and the ryuei-ryu style. I tried to become his student but he refused to teach me. I started to frequent his house and I guess he got tired of seeing me so at last he allowed me to study karate under him. My teacher, Master Kenko, used to say; "Half an inch closer and you'd be dead." Of course he was talking about real karate, not sport karate. His whole philosophy was to attack the opponent without allowing him to react. He stressed striking combinations and said karateka should never let the opponent perceive our breathing pattern—otherwise, they are dead.

313

"My formal training began at age 16. I was not at all sport oriented because when I was a baby I suffered first from diphtheria and then pneumonia, so I was a very weak child. I had some friends who practiced shorinji kempo and karate, so I started to learn a little about these arts."

Q: What was Master Kenko's training history?

A: Master Nakaima Kenko was born December 23, 1911. He was a teacher in the ryuey ryu style of karate and was the fourth generation representative for this Okinawa style founded in 1832 by Ryuryuko Nakaima. Master Kenko was 6th dan in iaido, 7th dan in kendo, and he also enjoyed training in kyudo. He was a real samurai and passed away in 1990 at age 78. He started his training under his father Nakaima Kanchu, who also learned from his father Nakaima Kenri. Kenri was living in China, in Fukien, and became a student of master Wo Lou-Kin. He studied kendo under Sensei Seibu Tomegawa and Sensei Hiroshi Ishihara when he was a student at the Okinawa Prefecture School for Teachers. In fact, it is very interesting to notice that Kanryo Higaonna also was a student of Wo Lou-Kin. Nakaima Kenko also studied under Yabu Kensho and Oshiro Chojo. He taught many people not only karate but kobudo as well. Many different karatekas went to train under Nakaima Keno. For instance, the great master, Teruo Hayashi, leader of hayashi-ha shito-ryu was one of his students. Hayashi sensei later on created his own kobudo style named kenshin-ryu, which is a different pronunciation of the same *kanji* of ryuei-ryu.

Q: How did Master Kenko choose his students?

A: He was very selective. He started to teach me when he found out that I was a teacher and so could trust me not to use karate for evil purposes. For two years he taught me nothing about his style of karate—he kept me sweeping the dojo, practicing the *dachi*, *uke*, and *tsuki* kata. To be honest, I felt like giving up, but I am quite stubborn so I stayed. I didn't understand then but now I know he was testing me. After five years he seemed to begin to really trust me and he taught me the *neiseishi-no* kata. This method of testing the determination of a prospective pupil, and the refusal to teach anything other than basics, is based on similar methods used by traditional Chinese systems. In fact, Okinawa karate has a great Chinese influence but you have to look closely to discover it. The fact that he never permitted any of his students to enter a kumite contest reflects his orthodox attitude.

Q: What are the main characteristics of your karate style?

A: It was developed in Okinawa and is therefore not Japanese. It is based on both useful technical movements and mental development. The combative aspect is based on the fighting distance precept of staying no more than five-feet apart. The footwork is based on a zig-zag concept with the goal keeping the body aligned sideways to protect the vital organs. In karate you have to be very humble and always leave room for more knowledge. The techniques of the style consist of Chinese kempo techniques called *mutensho* combined with *heiho* (tactics) and *yojoho* (healing techniques). Some of the kata practiced in ryuei-ryu are the basic kata of Naha-te but there are others that are unique to our style. We use eleven kata: *sanchin, niseishi, seisan, sanseiru, seienchin, annan, pachu, wohan, paiku, heiku,* and *paiho*. We also train and study kobudo which include several weapons such as *kama, renquan, sai, yari, nunchaku, tendei, kon, bisento, gekiquan, tan-son, kusan,* and *tonfa*. In short, the style tries to keep the orthodox traditions of *ryu ryu ko* alive.

"To be honest, I felt like giving up, but I am quite stubborn so I stayed. I didn't understand then but now I know he was testing me."

Q: You are one of the best kata performers ever. Why is kata so important?

A: The art of karate begins and finishes with kata training. There are many valuable principles and teachings within kata but no "final answer" to every situation. Kata only teaches three corners of the room. When the original masters structured kata, they were trying to teach something. It's up to the student to find the fourth corner. Using kata, we can train and teach karate until the

"There are many valuable principles and teachings within kata but is no 'final answer' to every situation. Kata only teaches three corners of the room."

last days of life. Kata is the essence of karate but it depends a lot on the individual. A person's understanding is a very important aspect of the whole picture. The performer's spirit brings every kata to life. An understanding of what they are doing makes the difference.

Q: You've competed in sport tournaments but your conception of the art seems to be very traditional.

A: Sport karate has a part in the whole development of karate. Karate is popular around the world because of the sport competitions—but we shouldn't mistake the art with the sport because they are two very different things. I made a lot of great friends by competing internationally. On the other hand, karate has never been a spectator sport. These days there are too many weight divisions and too many champions. It is important to remember that in karate quick gains and grading advancement do not create the kind of karateka who can contribute to the art in the long run. They usually burn-out in a very short time. But the student who has been guided properly and worked hard, and steadily adhered to the philosophy of the art will bring karate to the state of an art form.

Q: You are very good in kumite. Why did you compete in kata?

A: I was 34 years old and I was the coach of the junior team—the students were not very interested in sport. So to set an example I decided to enter a major karate event. I thought that it wouldn't be too hard so I decided to compete in kata and, to my surprise, I won. The rest is history. I was too old for kumite competition. In modern tournaments I see important Budo aspects such as *zanchin* (continued vigilance-awareness), *kokyu* (breathing), *tenshin* (body shifting), and *ma* (distance), disappearing. If we don't control this, karate will end up being just a simple sport with nothing else attached. It's okay for young people to focus on competition as long as they do it with discipline. If there is no discipline, then they should not compete. Real karate is about spirit. Without the right discipline there is no right spirit and without the right spirit there is no true karate.

Q: Many people have changed traditional kata and proclaim that it's due to a "personal interpretation" of the traditional version. Is this right?
A: It depends on the practitioner's level. If they don't have a high level of understanding they will feel a need to change things. Some people like to change the kata rhythm. The more understanding you have about what you are doing, the less you need to change or modify. I do traditional kata, not personal kata. On the other hand, I have recently seen a certain tendency to over emphasize the "magnificence" or "exter-

"We must try to not lose the true essence behind everything used in the sportive aspects of karate."

nal" aspect of kata. We have to keep in mind that these kata were created and polished by generations and are the result of blood, sweat, and the exploration of the ultimate limits of human endurance. A kata should demonstrate this. We shouldn't be changing kata to make it look more attractive in order to win points in a competition.

Q: Many young karateka seem to like fighting and don't feel attracted to kata.
A: Well, it's human nature! But karate is not like boxing. Kata, kihon and kumite are all related and have a deep connection. Kumite, or sparring, is an important part of karate but it is not the only part. The practitioner must train the basics and use them properly for sparring. Only then they can grow in the right direction. Kata requires a form which our bodies must enter. You must adapt to this because if you don't your own body will limit your style. We must train our bodies to enter into the form. It is important for the student to take instruction and try hard to make their body suit the technique. They have to try to make the technique fit. In order to achieve this you must copy

"There is no reason why modern methods for strengthening the body and traditional karate cannot work together. I emphasize karate for health."

somebody else who is a master until you can do it to the best of your ability. Sometimes you won't be successful copying one teacher, so you have to try someone else and go another way. But you should always try to improve the technique.

It has to be understood that the body can change. Many practitioners around the world believe their bodies can't change to fit into the perfect mold and this is wrong. You must teach your body to change and perform the technique under the perfect form principles based on physiology and body dynamics. You should learn to control your body movements and create the right technique for it according to the fundamental principles of physics. Start slow and create the feeling of working without expending energy and not using strength. Then later add speed and power. This is the very basic foundation to grow from.

Q: Does kata allow a person to practice karate their entire life?
A: When you get older, if fighting is the only thing you know what's there to teach? Karate is more than simply fighting, it's a whole art. Don't forget that the spirit of kata and kumite are the same. Kihon, kumite and kata are all of equal importance. You have to develop a strong foundation for the real karate to come out. If you only do kumite when you're young, you just develop physical techniques but not the art. You develop your body but not your brain. As a practitioner you have to strive to be skilled at both kata and kumite because as a teacher you must be able to understand and transmit the complete set of principles of these two elements of training.

Q: Do you like modern training methods?
A: I'm a physical education teacher so I understand this. My master only practiced traditional methods, but weight training, for example, can be very helpful to karate students. The important thing is to understand what kind of muscles you need to make your art work. A karate practitioner needs differ-

ent kinds of muscles than a judo player. Today's sport karateka are very good, strong, fast, and very fit. They have received the benefits of scientific knowledge—what we know about anatomy, physiology, et cetera. There is no reason why modern methods for strengthening the body and traditional karate cannot work together. I emphasize karate for health and tense muscles are not good for your body. But tense muscles do not come from weight training but from incorrect use of the body during training. To be able to perform good karate you must try to use soft and hard correctly, not always rushing and tensing your body.

We have advanced far above the physical technique knowledge of say 20 or 30 years ago. We have better conditioning methods, better training methods, et cetera—so there is no real reason why these aspects can not be used with the correct karate attitude and spirit. On the other hand, I consider traditional training of great importance. For instance, I use the makiwara. Practicing on the makiwara is very important for developing kime. The pain factor during training is something to consider. One must be careful, of course, but if you know how to train correctly, the makiwara will not only improve your overall technique but also teach you a lot about yourself.

Q: Karate is going to be accepted into the Olympics. Do you think this is positive?
A: Sure it is. But it may bring some bad aspects into karate development around the world as well. Sport karate is OK, but it is not the only aspect of the art. We must try to not lose the true essence behind everything used in the sportive aspects of karate. Karate is education. It is about spirit and not only about trophies and street fighting.

Q: What's your advice for karate practitioners who wish to improve their kata?
A: There are three basic steps that a student must completely understand: 1) learn the physical techniques and the very essence of the form—its idea, and its inner concepts; 2) polish and perfect each single and small detail; 3) dedicate yourself to endless repetition of each movement and sequence, keeping in mind that using the hips brings quality and power to your physical movement.

These are the best methods to successfully perform kata. When I won the first world championships I returned to Okinawa to train under my master and he said to me, "Now you have a good base. You can begin your real training." O

Stan Schmidt

Karate's Guiding Light

SENSEI STAN SCHMIDT HAS DEVOTED HIS LIFE TO AN EXTENSIVE STUDY OF THE HISTORY, TECHNIQUES AND PHILOSOPHY OF THE ART OF KARATE-DO. HE CURRENTLY RUNS HIS OWN DOJO IN SOUTH AFRICA AND REGULARLY VISITS JAPAN TO FURTHER HIS STUDIES IN THE ART. HE COME INTO CONTACT WITH THE JAPANESE KARATE ASSOCIATION (JKA) IN 1963, BECOMING ONE OF THE PIONEERS IN THE WESTERN WORLD, STAYING IN THE *HONBU* DOJO AND GOING THROUGH THE "APPROPRIATE INITIATION PROCEDURES" FOR *GAIJIN* (NON-JAPANESE). WHEN A TRAGIC CAR ACCIDENT FORCED HIM TO HAVE A DOUBLE HIP REPLACEMENT, HE WAS FORCED TO RE-LEARN THE ART FROM A DIFFERENT PERSPECTIVE. THIS TRAINING GAVE HIM A SOFTER AND MORE RELAXED APPROACH TO EVERYTHING HE HAD LEARNED BEFORE. AMONG HIS MANY AWARDS AND ACCOMPLISHMENTS, HE IS RESPONSIBLE FOR THE BIGGEST KARATE-DO DEMONSTRATION EVER HELD IN SOUTH AFRICA. STAN SCHMIDT IS TRULY AN ICON OF THE ART OF KARATE AND KNOWN AROUND THE WORLD FOR BEING HUMBLE, RESPECTFUL, AND HUMANE. HE REPRESENTS THE BEST OF KARATE'S SPIRITUAL SIDE AND IS TRULY THE GENTLEMAN OF KARATE.

Q: What got you interested in karate-do and when did you decide to train in Japan?
A: I was a judo black belt at 19 and I broke a bone in my ankle. It was in a plaster cast and I was waiting for it to heal. While I was sitting and moping, my judo instructor threw a book into my lap and said, "Read this." The title was *Karate—The Art of Empty Hand Fighting*. I started training immediately, sitting in a chair, and graduated to standing-up as my ankle healed. After my judo class I would train with a small group using the karate book to teach. Finally, that group became bigger than the judo group. It was then that I left for Japan in 1963 with my new wife Judy. After looking around, I chose the JKA organization.

Q: Were you a professional judo teacher at that time?
A: No, not at all. In the late '50s I was working at a bank and I was training in body-building and playing trumpet. I remember I was fooling around with the drummer of the band and I couldn't hold him down for a

"All Japanese teachers were very tough. Interestingly enough they were very kind outside the dojo and took a lot of time educating me in the traditional aspects and principles of Budo."

second. This was kind of disappointing to me because I was much bigger than him! Anyway, this was my first introduction to martial arts. Because of that I joined a judo club and started training. Eventually I got my black belt.

Q: Why do you think the JKA masters took such an interest in your training?
A: I think they were all impressed that my young wife sat and watched me train every day. Then one day I went up to a black belt—I was just 7th kyu—and asked him if I could free fight him. I released a back kick and without realizing it, knocked the wind out of him—I had been practicing this back kick on the outside of my house. The next day some students came up to me and told me that I had just knocked down an All-Japan champion. The whole dojo got to hear about this and I was very lucky that Enoeda sensei and Shirai sensei then started giving me free private lessons after classes every day. In 1965 I invited Enoeda, Shirai, Kanazawa and Kase senseis to South Africa. They went to teach in different areas and later on we had the first South African Championship. What was really interesting to me is that right after winning both the kata and kumite divisions they told me I should retire and concentrate on judging and teaching. They made me realize that I needed to support the art from a different perspective. They graded me to *nidan* (2nd dan).

Q: Who was your teacher at the JKA honbu dojo?
A: Nakayama shihan was my first teacher but several other helped me greatly during all these years. Besides Enoeda sensei, Shirai sensei, Kanazawa sensei, and Kase sensei, there were later on great teachers like Nishiyama, Tanaka, Ochi, Shoji, Sigiura, Ueki, and Okazaki. I owe them a lot. Nevertheless, the training was very hard, very intense and demanding. All Japanese teachers were

very tough. Interestingly enough they were very kind outside the dojo and took a lot of time educating me in the traditional aspects and principles of Budo. They set an excellent example for me to follow and I'm still trying today.

Q: How did you progress after achieving *nidan* rank?

A: That same year, 1965, I ended up going again to Japan for instructor training. As everybody knows this training is very demanding and difficult, not only physically but

"The testing for sandan is the most difficult of all grading; it's very dangerous. For the next six weeks all I did was train and worry!"

also spiritually. I tried to improve and polish my technique. I was quite strong due to my previous judo training. One day the late Nakayama sensei approached me and said: "In six weeks you are grading for *sandan*." I was really shocked. The testing for sandan is the most difficult of all grading; it's very dangerous. For the next six weeks all I did was train and worry! I was going to be the first *gaijin* testing for sandan. And I did pass the test.

Q: You were the first Westerner to pass 7th dan, is that right?

A: Yes, it is—and I was also the first to fail the test! After nine years of being 6th dan or *rokudan*, they told me that I should test for *nanadan*. I asked what I should practice in order to prepare the grading. The answer was, "You'll find out. Seek and you'll find out. This is all about yourself, nobody can tell you." I went back and trained as hard as I could. Then I got to Japan for the testing and I passed one section of the exam but I failed my kata. I was really disappointed because I never failed a test in my life. Interestingly enough, I guess this was the best thing that could have happened to me. They told me that my technique was "too sharp." I was not smooth enough, way too rigid. I was too tense and I didn't have the mind, or the spirit, of a 7th dan. So I went back and trained differently, focusing on softness and breathing, not being so harsh on myself. Six months later I tested again and I was lucky enough to pass. I

"You always have to be approached by your teacher. Don't forget that the rank always brings a big responsibility as well. The higher the rank you have, the higher the responsibility you accept."

was always asked to test. Following the traditional customs I never asked if I could test since this would be a very bad etiquette. You always have to be approached by your teacher, which I think is the right way. I know these days it is different, but this is the traditional way and I totally agree with it. Don't forget that the rank always brings a big responsibility as well. The higher the rank you have, the higher the responsibility you accept.

Q: Some people think going to Japan to train is highly necessary; do you share this point of view?

A: Yes! There are various options. Go to JKA *honbu* dojo in Tokyo and they will assist you. They could help you enroll at a university that practices karate (like Takudai or Komazawa), or to enroll at the honbu dojo's foreigners' class. It is very difficult to get into the instructors program. I was very lucky that they invited me to join. I attended instructors classes regularly over a period of 25 years. This is where I met and trained with scores of the best karateka in the world. I believe that this is how learning should be—not academic but practical—and in the right testing environment Japan can offer this! Alternatively, we have an instructors training class in Johannesburg, South Africa every morning at 6 AM.

Q: What do you consider to be the major changes since you began your training at the JKA?

A: The very hard training in the basics have always been the same and never changed. The most important changes I have seen on the positive side is the emphasis now on bunkai—the application of kata moves for self-defense. Another big change worldwide is the emphasis on tournament and sport karate. I believe there are too many tournaments and that training in all aspects of kihon, kata and special drills should be adhered to. This means not just becoming a kata champion or kumite champion but becoming a champion of life! Good health; good self-defense; good spirit. The problem with somebody becoming a kata champion for example, is that people who only specialize in this are unable to handle a kumite attack adequately—very sad!

Anyway, things have changed all over the world and Japan is not an exception. What is interesting is that in Japan the changes are less obvious—karate hasn't changed as much as in other places. One thing I truly believe is the top-teacher of each country should travel regularly to Japan to keep learning. Only in this way can he help to raise the level of the art in his own country. As far

"Karate is a never-ending journey of discovery. The minute I think I have mastered an idea or technique then new challenges appear."

as I know, we in South Africa send more instructors to Japan than any other country. Honestly, I think this is great for the art.

Q: What would you say to someone who is interested in learning karate-do?
A: I would tell them to first go and look at a number of well-run dojos and watch the training—and if the atmosphere and spirit is right then join that dojo for at least 3 months. Be careful of cult teachers who put themselves before you, the student. True karate trains not only the body but also the spirit and soul of the practitioner.

Q: What do you mean by "soul?"
A: Well, for me "mind" is how and what we think; "will" is what we want to do or achieve, and "soul" is our emotions. Through the art of karate-do we learn to control these emotions and the physical training helps to achieve a calm state so we can be stable under pressure. In true karate, spirit is first and then comes technique.

"It is imperative to improving one's judgement and effectiveness and will condition you against someone trying to rob or injure you. The hard approach should be taken out on the makiwara or sandbag."

Q: What keeps you motivated after all these years?
A: Karate is a never-ending journey of discovery. The minute I think I have mastered an idea or technique then new challenges appear. It is the climbing of the mountain that not only tests me, but gives me the on-going challenge to reach out and occasionally attain that enigmatic thing called excellence! When one is empowered like this it is fortunate. I cannot wait for every new day to train, to know myself anew—and to understand, tolerate and love others if necessary on the journey. I enjoy empowering students but I say to myself, "How can I ever hope to empower others if I'm a loser in life? No way!" I love training! Thank God, I have been fortunate to train with top karateka who are alive today. If I could go back in time I would have liked to have trained under Master Funakoshi and his teachers Azato and Itosu on the island of Okinawa. I have never met Bruce Lee personally, but I would have enjoyed having him as a dinner guest! Some of his philosophies hit the martial arts' nail right on the head.

Q: Do you think it is necessary to engage in free-fighting in to achieve good fighting skills in the street?
A: Anton Geesink, the famous judo champion, once said, "If you want to be good at fighting, practice fighting." The more free-fighting one does with

different opponents, especially at a young age, the better. It is imperative to improving one's judgement and effectiveness and will condition you against someone trying to rob or injure you. The main point is that when sparring in the dojo it is not necessary to go at it hammer and tongs. A light type of free-fighting is recommended, with both parties able to try out moves without feeling they will be annihilated if they make a mistake. The hard approach should be taken out on the *makiwara* or sandbag. The build-up to free-fighting is very important indeed, that is why the JKA and other reputable organizations have developed a system of controlled five-step sparring (*go-hon kumite*); one step sparring (*kihon, ippon kumite* and *jiju ippon kumite*) and of course *bunkai* and *oyo* type studies.

"Kata without bunkai is like a bite without teeth. Kata are the theorems of self-defense, whereas bunkai is the teeth and claws of karate!"

Q: Kanazawa sensei is teaching goju and shito kata these days. What's your opinion about mixing karate styles? Does the practice of one nullify the effectiveness of the other or can it be beneficial?

A: Kanazawa sensei has always shown his vision and leadership and is willing to look beyond the confines of a single style and seek value in others. I am aware that Kanazawa sensei has introduced kata from other styles into his organization. First, I want to state clearly that this is *his* organization so he is entitled to do this. I have trained at the JKA honbu dojo with Kanazawa sensei and I respect him for his technique, creativity and character! My answer to this important question is this: In my own case, I had a severe auto accident necessitating two hip joint replacements and I had to formulate my own kata which my body could cope with. I still, of course, practice all the shotokan kata but there are certain moves that I am precluded from doing such as the jumping moves in various kata and dropping to the floor and side-snap kicks. So I had to modify my own shotokan kata. For example, in *ni-ju shiho* I don't do side-thrust kicks but instead I do *fumikomi geri*, as Sensei Funakoshi did in his older days.

"Championship karate is still important for our youth to motivate them to train hard and test themselves against other karateka."

A good analogy regarding your question is in the field of music. Should a jazz player play classics or vice versa? Wynston Marsailis, the famous American trumpeter, is a virtuoso in both disciplines; jazz and classics. The answer is the student must practice and know his own styles' kata; then at approximately 3rd dan, if you could train three-hours a day, six-days a week, then devoting a half-hour three times a week to another style's kata can prove beneficial—but you know your own style first. Kanazawa sensei is a shotokan master with the talent and volition to study and master other disciplines. This too is my aim. By the way do you know C.W. Nicol, author of *Moving Zen?* I developed a kata after my accident and operation that incorporated the self-defense and body-conditioning aspects that I could manage at that time. I performed it for him and a few other notables one year after my accident. They called it *"uki"*—a floating tree—push one side down and the other comes up. Nicol liked the kata. "It's for me at my age," he said. I replied, "This is only for me, I don't want to add any more kata to the curriculum. There are enough kata already to keep you busy for a lifetime."

Q: Modern sport karate is moving away from the *bunkai* (applications) in kata practice. How important do you think bunkai is in the understanding of kata and karate do in general?
A: Kata without bunkai is like a bite without teeth. Kata are the theorems of self-defense, whereas bunkai is the teeth and claws of karate! Sport karate is just one slice of the whole cake of karate-do, because what does one do after the sport side is finished? I know of a sport karate champion who was beaten, in a semi-serious fight at a party, by a wrestler who quickly tackled him to the ground and controlled him. That sport karate guy was me! Claude Chanu did it. It made me change my thinking and my way of training to what real karate is all about. In other words, the Budo way, which is the martial way instead of the sport way. But championship karate is still important

for our youth to motivate them to train hard and test themselves against other karateka.

Q: Do you have a particularly memorable karate experience that has remained with you as an inspiration for your training?

A: Yes. My *shodan* grading and initiation with T. Kase sensei. In 1964, Kase sensei visited South Africa for the first time, I was then third kyu. About 30 of us brown and purple belts trained every day, three-times a day with him, and we slept on the dojo floor. One night when I was trying to sleep, Sensei Kase called us all in and said, "Mr. Stan try shodan grading." This was at 9 PM at night. I went through the grading

"In karate-do we have five maxims: character, sincerity, effort, etiquette, and self-control. All of them form our spirit and are different aspects of it."

quite well but when it came to doing *basai dai*, I suddenly switched to *kanku dai* in the middle of it. He gave me another chance. That night we had a big party and all got to bed at about 3 AM and we all assumed that there would be no 6 AM training next day. Kase sensei, dressed in his clean white karate suit, woke us up and shouted, "OK, kanku dai. Sixty-five times we do!" This nearly killed us in the state we were in. When we finished he said, "That was Mr. Stan's initiation for *shodan*." To this day I can't understand why everybody in the class had to do it with me, and I am sure they are also still wondering why!

Q: After all these years of training and experience, could you explain the meaning of the practice of karate-do?

A: Many people choose to run the race. Some sprint in the beginning and fall by the wayside. Others amble along and somehow never get there. Still others, such as all the great champions, complete the race irrespective of whether or not they come in first or last. This is why I chose karate and aim to see it through to the end because, despite any pitfalls, the rewards are even greater because the race is yourself, a fight against your weaker self. In karate-do we have five maxims: character, sincerity, effort, etiquette, and self-

Photo by T. Hester

"Karate does not mind who practices it, therefore whatever faith one has outside of karate should be applied non-verbally inside of karate. It is a matter deeply personal to each person."

control. All of them form our spirit and are different aspects of it. They are different kind of spirits and learning how to use the right one at the proper time is an art in itself.

Q: How do you think a practitioner can increase their understanding of the spiritual aspect of karate?

A: I prefer not to use the word "spiritual" especially when it comes to my practice of karate, as my view of karate-do is a pragmatic, scientific and artistic approach, not a religious one. Karate came out of people having to defend themselves with their empty hands against oppressors. In order to gain strength a lot of these peasants on the island of Okinawa may have gone to a spiritual leader for guidance. In my own particular case my strength comes from my belief in God and the biblical principles in the Bible. In particular, the fruits of the spirit for the achievement of joy, peace, love, faith, patience, forgiveness, goodness and kindness. I am aiming to achieve these. Karate does not mind who practices it, therefore whatever faith one has outside of karate should be applied non-verbally inside of karate. It is a matter deeply personal to each person.

Q: How much should a senior karateka do to improve and get better at the art?

A: I can answer this only by telling you how I train. Basically I train every day, but my training might be only for 10 or 15 minutes on certain days, in a very gentle way, and there are days for one hour and other days for one or two hours. But my training is right across the board including strength and conditioning training, which is imperative for older or injured karateka, especially in the area of specificity which means focusing on and strengthening ones own unique weaknesses. For example, somebody with stiff hamstrings could cause himself back injuries because he has not stretched correctly on a regular basis. The answer to this question is simply to train regularly—but train smart.

Sometimes senior practitioners don't understand that doing things in a very relaxed way is more beneficial that using the hard approach. I remember Tanaka sensei often telling me after a training session in Japan: "Your shoulders are too strong Stan-san—more relax—if you overtense you will block the flow of power." I know it is very difficult to understand in the beginning, but it's true. Do everything slowly at first, getting all components parts—feet, legs, hips, torso, and arms—into alignment. Only when mistakes are eliminated should one turn on the steam. After all, if you keep practicing a mistake you'll only get good at the mistake!

Q: During your stay in Japan you took part in many *gashuku*. How important are these demanding and special training sessions in karate development?
A: This kind of training is very hard and puts the practitioner in a very difficult situation, both physically and mentally. The word "gashuku" implies a renewing of one's spirit through very hard training, usually taking place outdoors and against

"Doing gashuku beat every other karate function. You learn a lot about the spirit and how it carries you through the whole training. Your body cannot move but it is your spirit that makes you keep going."

the elements. It also means that the instructor not only stands there and instructs, but joins in for a great deal of the training, blasting away the internal cobwebs and clearing his mind and body of negative elements. It's a very demanding training and requires a strong spirit to successfully complete the sessions. You learn a lot about the spirit and how it carries you through the whole training. Your body cannot move but it is your spirit that makes you keep going. The physical is left behind and pretty soon you understand that the term "I can't" really doesn't exit and you can always do one more punch, one more kick, one more kata repetition. It's a very difficult thing to explain in words. You just have to do it and go through it. In the end you'll feel very tired, sore, and exhausted but ready to face the woes of the world again. For me doing gashuku beat every other karate function. After all, we all grow old and as Kanazawa sensei likes to say, "One day you'll have to rely only on spirit power."

Photo by T. Hester

"Every karateka has to think, 'The way you conceive your future sculpts your present.' Whatever you want for your future you must start working towards that goal."

Q: Is there anything lacking in the way martial arts are taught today compared with how they were taught in your day?

A: This is almost an impossible question to answer as most old timers will answer with the cliché, "In our days it was much harder." Now, of course, I would like to say the same thing but in truth, part of it may be correct but another bigger part may be incorrect. While our training during the '60s and '70s was at breakneck speed with thousands of repetitions, today we might do more sensible type training with less effort and more successful results. This is a very difficult question to answer.

Q: What are the most important qualities of a successful karateka?

A: Firstly, having passion for one's art—having a sense of purpose. Then comes the ability to persist—training hard, smart, regularly, and loving it. This means having courage and taking control of one's life, not blaming others for one's shortcomings—striving for that enigmatic quality of good character. Finally, having a sense of humor and not taking oneself too seriously. The greatest masters always remain students. You must be able to forgive oneself and others, put the past to rest and move ahead. Every karateka has to think, "The way you conceive your future sculpts your present." Whatever you want for your future you must start working towards that goal. Through experience, I've found out that if you work really hard towards something that you really want, nothing is impossible. Determination is the keyword.

Q: Do recommend supplementary training?

A: Supplementary training is very important, especially for older karateka and those who need to improve their strength and agility in any area. I personally do three days a week of supplementary training to keep my muscles well-toned and my joints protected. Supplementary training, also called strength and conditioning, encompasses a number of things including stretching, resistance drills, strengthening muscle groups, general fitness and stamina, makiwara, and bag work. While a lot of this can actually be achieved while doing karate, someone who has injured their leg would need to get that leg strong again and certain resistance exercises would get them back quickly to a balanced state of fitness.

Q: Do you think sport or competition karate is damaging to the art?
A: Competition karate has moved away from the concept of one killing blow. Today there are other factors to consider in order to bring more people to the tournaments. And yes, these might be damaging to the essence of the art. In the old times, there would be very few strikes but they were more consistent. Today's techniques are fast and flashy but would not be really effective in a self-defense situation.

"A true karateka has to never show pain or weakness, and this is only developed through hard physical training. We need strong characters for life as well for karate."

Attitude has also changed. In the old days we never went down, no matter how hard we were hit. It was a matter of honor. Now I see people going down after the slightest touch to try to get his opponent disqualified. To me, this is cowardice. These competitors have no fighting spirit. A true karateka has to never show pain or weakness, and this is only developed through hard physical training. We need strong characters for life as well for karate. Forging the body will develop the right Budo spirit. On other hand, I don't believe in going to tournaments too often for the simple reason that it is impossible to peak your fitness and sharpness every week. It's a matter of common sense. Two or three tournaments per year should be sufficient. In short, there is a sport aspect in karate and it's OK to enjoy it as long as it doesn't take over the art.

Q: Why do so many students fall away after only two or three years of training?
A: This might sound strange too, but in most gyms where people do weights or other training, their fall-away rate is quite often a matter of months. Someone who trains for three years is far above the average of someone taking up other sports. Some of the many reasons for giving up

"Karate is a form of self defense and that if we ignore close-quarter fighting, including grappling and ground work, we are poorer for it because many fights land on the ground."

are a) the classes may be predictable, boring and uncreative, b) extracurricular demands at school or university are hard, and c) increased pressure and responsibility after reaching high dan or kyu levels. Other reasons can be injury, pressure of work or just feeling that they have reached the level they aimed at, such as a first degree black belt. A lot of people aim at getting a black belt and once this is reached they give up, not realizing that the black belt is only the beginning of an exciting journey to the higher states of excellence one gets as the higher dan ranks are conquered and achieved. The highest level is when one finally forgets about their dan status and keeps training.

I found out that a lot of practitioners train in different systems at once, particularly in the beginning stages of their training. I don't think this is such a good idea. It's different when the student reaches a level of *nidan* or *sandan*. No single instructor has all the abilities to satisfy all his senior student's needs. After reaching 5th dan, they can go and train wherever they want and this has to be decided by themselves. Many times my students come back with very interesting techniques or approaches to something and I gladly learn from them. I believe that karate begins with discipline and eventually you reach a point of freedom, although total freedom is not possible without discipline first. This is the traditional principle of *shu-ha-ri.*

Q: Have there been times where you have felt fear in your karate training?
A: Yes. This happened to me over a period of three years when I ran into a Japanese instructor named Mr. Yano. He was nicknamed "The Animal." Just looking at this man not only gave me, but also my fellow South Africans and other foreigners instant diarrhea. In dojo fighting at the Tokyo training center he and I clashed many times, and I would be worrying about tomorrow and what he would do next. Once he actually bit me! He was a Tyson type of a guy. It was just prayer that pulled me through this dark period and I finally stood up to

him and my self-respect and confidence improved. I have learned that "I have no enemy but my own incautiousness." I have no fear if I walk in truth, keeping my eyes on my goal. Fear is normal and human, it's how we deal with it that makes the difference, and Budo helps you deal with it in a very positive way.

Q: What is your philosophical basis for your karate training?

A: My original philosophy was, "Do unto others as they do unto you" and "An eye for an eye." Then I learned via the business world to "Do unto others as they would have you do unto them,"—but I didn't like that! This is for politicians—not karateka. The philosophy that I try to live by now is, "Do unto others as you would have them do unto

"Having both my hip joints replaced after a severe auto accident changed my life entirely. The operations definitely affected my approach to karate."

you." That is not easy but I am working on it. As the great Miyamoto Mushashi once said, "I never bypass a master of any art without trying to learn something from him." I try to apply this to myself; learning from other people is paramount.

Q: You have added grappling and groundwork in your classes. Why?

A: I believe that karate is a form of self defense and that if we ignore close-quarter fighting, including grappling and ground work, we are poorer for it because many fights land on the ground. Thus in our South Africa JKA Karate Association, we adhere strictly to the basics but we have added certain grappling techniques which I am beginning to discover are in many cases subtly inherent in our kata. In old Okinawa, grappling techniques were part of their Okinawa-te. Executing certain jiu-jitsu techniques has gotten me out of trouble several times. In other words, I did not have to kick, strike or punch these particular assailants—one I stopped short with a powerful block to a nerve center. Another I applied a standing wrist and elbow joint twist, coupled with a neck lock. No blood, but they were subdued and meek as lambs afterwards. In short, we don't teach a lot of groundwork, but we do a little because is necessary. We

Photo by T. Hester

"I still train every day wherever I can, and just enjoy interacting on the floor with students and other experts."

see it as an extension of kumite, since karate movements can be applied on the floor. I believe the two are inter-twined. On the other hand, a lot of kata techniques can be applied on the ground. It is always positive to see things from a different perspective.

Q: You had both your hips replaced. Describe your personal struggle to recover and train again, and what difference it made to your karate?

A: Having both my hip joints replaced after a severe auto accident changed my life entirely. I was hit from behind and then I hit the car in front, so I received a double impact. I was frightened at first. They did one hip at a time so when the time came for the second I was almost an expert in rehabilitation! For the second operation I kind of knew what was important to a proper recovery so I began to train with weights and to eat a very healthy diet before going into surgery. The doctors told me that my bones were strong. The operations definitely affected my approach to karate. Before that time I practiced a severe and harsh type of karate training: thousands of repetitions and taking things to extremes. I was told by others that I should be more relaxed and have soft feet and soft shoulders.

Two days after the operation while lying flat on my back I started my new regime of training. It happened automatically. Small sit-ups in bed coupled with punching and striking at a flat stone held in my one hand. The hospital staff thought I was crazy but striking the flat stone was more satisfying than taking painkillers. A few days later sitting on the edge of the bed I started doing arm movements like a beginner, and then a week later I stood and did *tekki-shodan* on one spot. *Hangetsu* and *tekki* got me back into shape but I did them lightly with good form. This light training made all the difference because I find now that I can move more quickly in certain areas without too much effort. But I always have to take care to do techniques that are within a sensible range of movement in accordance with my handicap and my age of 65. Generally, I have never felt better in my life. I still train every day wherever I can, and just enjoy interacting on the floor with students and other experts. Any karateka who might feel depressed by injury or age should be encouraged by this. I believe that every person can adapt to their own physique and can recover from anything as long as they don't do dangerous things in their training.

Q: You definitely went through a lot of struggles with these operations.

A: But I would say that going through it taught me a lot of important things. As I said before, I threw out the painkillers because I didn't want to be dizzy. I cried a lot when nobody could see me but one night a nurse came in and asked me why I looked so sad. I told her, "I didn't want to live." She answered, "And you are a karate man. Where is your spirit?" I said: "Ouss!" Then she reminded me that I told her once that a good karate man never stops training and advised me that since I couldn't move I should start training my breathing. Pretty soon I was walking and feeling better. Then I did some upper body weight training—a general workout routine.

"The key is to not force things. If you're using your muscles in karate, you are not using the correct technique."

It was about that time that I met Tomiyama sensei, and I explained to him that I couldn't do the correct deep stances anymore. I showed him my new higher *kiba dachi* and he just shrugged and said, "What is the problem? This is the proper stance of the old school of karate." As you can imagine, this gave me a lot of motivation and encouragement to keep training. I made every stance shorter and began using my hip naturally, letting the movement come out without forcing it. The key is to not force things, because in the end that's what technique is all about. So if you're using your muscles in karate, you are not using the correct technique. If you use a lever, that's a technical thing; and the same happens with the art of karate. I may say that this new form of training helped me enormously in order to fully understand how karate should be executed—without unnecessarily stressing your body. The idea is to channel the moves as softly as

"I like to believe that I give them energy—good energy to pursue their own path in life, not only in karate-do."

possible in order to build power. I don't know if this kind of training fully applies to young people, but it sure does to a more mature practitioner.

Q: What are your thoughts on the future of karate-do and your personal plans for the future?

A: The true karate exponent never stops training—this is my credo. As to the future of karate-do, I see more and more top exponents getting together and sharing their ideas, skills, and expertise. I believe the future of what I call "practical karate" is excellent. This is because I am truly impressed by the attitude and skills of the next generation of true karate instructors now beginning to emerge—and practical karate is sorely needed by young and old in our high-tech society. Television has the effect on youth of making them passive onlookers; karate makes young people dynamic participants. I would like to see people going back to the old karate, where they are not so worried about egos and winning tournaments. I'd like to see a more real way of karate people communicating with each other.

As far as myself, I work hard to be a guiding light to those who train with me. I like to believe that I give them energy—good energy to pursue their own path in life, not only in karate-do. There is a line in a poem that says, "Your hardest fight from life's beginning to end, is the fight against yourself, my friend." Of course, there is pressure in the dojo in every training session, but there is more pressure outside, in society. It's there where we have to behave like true warriors, like samurai. Most of the time the big enemy is not in the outside world, but inside ourselves. One day in life each of us will have to make a decision, a very important one, and if we are indecisive we could become cowards. Weather we live or die doesn't matter. Even if there is no way out, at least we'll go out of life as a warrior and a gentleman—"bowing" as the great master said. This is what I'm trying to do—be the gentleman of karate-do. O

Karate Masters